NO LIFETIME GUARANTEE

Dealing with the Details of Death

KATIE MAXWELL

BETTERWAY PUBLICATIONS, INC.
WHITE HALL, VIRGINIA

Published by Betterway Publications, Inc.
Box 219
Crozet, VA 22932

Cover design by Deborah B. Chappell

Library of Congress Cataloging in Publication Data

Maxwell, Katie
    No lifetime guarantee : dealing with the details of death / Katie
Maxwell.
        p.   cm.
    Bibliography: p.
    Includes index.
    ISBN 0-932620-92-2 (pbk.) : $9.95
        1. Death--Handbooks, manuals, etc.   2. Estate planning--Handbooks,
manuals, etc.   I. Title.
GT3150.M29 1988
306.9--dc19   88-2909
                                                                  CIP

Printed in the United States of America
9 8 7 6 5 4 3 2

To Justin, Holly and Noah
and the loving memory of their father
Roland Eugene Maxwell

Acknowledgments

While writing a book is a lonely job, it is seldom accomplished alone. Rather, it requires the expertise of many people and the moral support of a few. To my experts, thank you for all of your time: Cathey Bertot, Certified Financial Planner; Vern Lind, funeral director; Paul Hook, insurance broker; Dr. Robert Anthony, pathologist; Mark Drobny, attorney at law; Connie Castleberry, real estate broker; Don Sloan, banker; Doris Sloan, information and referral coordinator for senior citizens; and Marta Grenfell, president of Widowed Persons Association of California. Thank yous to Fri Spivek and Jerry Mountjoy whose comments and suggestions were invaluable.

To my moral supporters, I owe a debt that can only be repaid with the love I share for them: to Michael John Nielsen, my husband, who believes in me and always sends me roses; to Sharon Rice-Grant, my friend, who prays for me; to Roy and Melba Gibbons, my parents, who love me; to Harlen and Jeanette Maxwell, my in-laws, who stand by me; to Faye Landham, my sister, who encourages me; to Bud Gardner and Duane Newcomb, my teachers, who guide me; and to God, who sustains me.

Preface

On January 29, 1982, a plane fell to earth. With its shattered parts lay my dreams and hopes for a future. Its twisted metal held the man I loved and adored. A part of me died with him that day.

The recovery process was difficult. I often thought I was going insane. Acknowledging that things would never be the same came slowly. There were few books on grief at that time. Support groups were few and far between. Information on the business aspects of death were non-existent.

Once the pain had subsided and I was able to help others who were suffering loss, it became apparent that someone should write a book so that widowed persons and others who have lost someone close to them could make an easier transition. While several wonderful books about bereavement have been written in the meantime, there is still very little to guide a person through the practical tasks of a death. It is very frustrating to make decisions when you don't know your options. It's like giving an answer when you don't know the question.

No Lifetime Guarantee is my way of helping all of those who lose the person they love and adore. It supplies you with the questions as well as the answers.

Contents

1.

Why a Book on Death?

Beginnings follow endings. Every year, men, women, and children must pick up the pieces of their lives and start over without a husband or father, without a wife or mother. The process is difficult and too often lonely and confusing. People prefer not to speak of Death. As if not to tempt fate they allow, and even choose, to be ignorant about subjects relating to biological endings. They hope by ignoring Death, their names will somehow be overlooked when their time is up. But it doesn't work, never has and never will.

Whether we like to admit it or not, Death is a part of our lives. Those who are fortunate may not have to face a death other than their own, but most of us will need to deal with losing someone we love, long before our senility or our own deaths protect us from the pain.

I was not one of the fortunate. After ten years of marriage, my husband died suddenly. Roland was one of those people who carried volumes of information around in his head. His notes were scribbled in little notebooks decipherable only by him. His papers and documents were scattered, their whereabouts known only to him. He didn't have a Will. He was only 33.

I was not ignorant of the daily affairs of running a house and business, but I was totally unprepared for the decisions I was called upon to make. The time for grieving had to be postponed long enough to make funeral arrangements. Then, feeling I had accomplished enough for a while, I was bombarded by the realization that the decision making had hardly begun. I was being asked questions that I didn't understand. Well meaning friends offering advice often knew less than I. No longer having the husband who always knew what to do, I had to learn quickly in order to protect not only myself, but also our three small children. Unaware of my options, I made some costly mistakes.

This is not a book to tell you how to stop the hurting that gnaws at your innards day and night. It does not contain any secret formulas for making things the way they used to be. There are no sets of rules to live by, so that you won't ever have to suffer again. If I held these secrets, I would give them to you without charge. If I knew where you could find them, I would lead the way. There are many good books on the market today that deal with grief. They offer insight into the process of death, emotions of death, and recovery from the trauma associated with death. At the end of this book, I've listed a few of the ones that were most helpful to me.

This is a book of practical information that will help you deal with the nuts and bolts of death. Dying has gotten so complicated. No longer does one simply stop breathing, get buried, and soon become one with the earth. Now, we have elaborate funerals, government agencies with forms and rules, estate distribution and related taxes, headstones, financial planning, Wills, attorneys, and insurance policies. Advice givers seem to come from everywhere. They tell us how we should do it, where we should put it, when we should get it done, and what we should know, so we can choose who should do it.

Instead of clarity, we get confusion. Most of us could make our own decisions, if we knew the options and had the necessary information. After all, who knows our needs better than ourselves?

Endings

According to the Census Bureau, there are over 13.5 million widowed persons in the United States. Eighty-four per cent of these are women. While the average age of a widow is 56, more than 4.5 million persons were widowed before the age of 45.

The leading cause of death for people under 44 years of age is accidents, usually involving a motor vehicle. This is followed by cancer, heart disease, suicide, and murder. Those who die after the age of 44 most often succumb to heart disease or cancer.

PLANNING AHEAD

Few of us take the time or have the discipline to plan for the last passage of our lives. The advantages of pre-planning are obvious: decisions are made when they can be weighed and investigated; emotional trauma does not hinder our thinking; there is time to ask questions and to find answers.

There are some excellent workbooks on the market today that can help you organize your family's affairs. They contain pages and pages of fill-in-the-blank forms to help your survivor locate all of the information needed upon your death. If properly filled out with complete and current information, these are valuable. Please see Chapter Fourteen, "Financial Planning," for the names of some of these workbooks.

Unfortunately, it has been estimated that 93% of us die with little or no preparation. For you survivors of that 93%, it will be more difficult, but with some facts at hand, you will survive and even feel a great sense of accomplishment as you progress in building your new beginning.

Beginnings

Like many projects, getting started is perhaps the most difficult task of all. Without guidelines, one just muddles through the process, hoping that most of the decisions made are sound ones, and won't come back to haunt. The best thing you can do is familiarize yourself with all your options before making a decision.

Use this book as a reference guide. It is a compilation of research put under one cover so that you don't have to search through many sources to find answers. It is not meant to be a book of advice, but rather a book of information, explanation, how-to, and options so that you can make your own decisions. If your circumstances are more complicated, recommendations are made for getting help to solve your problems.

Your journey into new beginnings will be like going into any unfamiliar situation. It can not only be frightening and overwhelming, but also exciting as you gain knowledge and confidence. You are growing.

2.

Alternatives for the Dying

Some of you reading this book have already lost someone you love and are in the midst of making decisions that come after death. Others are reading to gain information about preparing for your own inevitable outcome, so that the burden will be lessened for your survivors. Then, there are those of you who are having to make decisions for and with your loved ones who are dying. While dealing with death in any form is stressful, those who must watch the people they love give up life to disease or injury over an extended time suffer most.

Yet, even in dying, we have choices. This chapter explores some areas where decisions can be made before and immediately after death.

HOSPICE

According to Funk and Wagnall's Dictionary, a hospice is "a place of rest or shelter, usually maintained by a religious order for pilgrims, travelers, etc." The first hospice established for the care and shelter of terminally ill patients was begun by Dame Cicely Saunders in 1967 in London, England.

The first hospice in the United States was founded in New Haven, Connecticut. Since that first establishment in 1974, the American hospice program has grown to over 1,568 local care units. More than 120,000 people are served each year.

Unlike the original hospice, today they are centered in the home. Families and friends of the terminal patient are supported by a team of professionals and volunteers who evaluate the personal needs of the patient, as well as the family, and provide help accordingly.

The emphasis of hospice is care, not cure. It is a program for dying people who wish to live as long as possible in the familiar environment of their homes. Hospice encourages the terminally ill person to live out the last months or weeks of life to the fullest. In order to accomplish this, hospice professionals prescribe and administer pain killing drugs that enable the patient to function in an alert state.

Emotional, social, and spiritual needs of the patient as well as the family are ministered to. Care is even extended through the bereavement period when families are offered counseling.

Because everyone works together as a team, hospice enables patients to have a say in the decision making, thereby giving them control over their lives. Focusing on the quality of life, patients are encouraged to remain active as long as they are able.

The structure and organization of individual hospices vary. Some are coalitions with leadership from either a hospital, nursing home, independent organization, or a home health agency.

Others are owned by the federal or state governments. Hospices might be community, hospital, nursing home or other based programs. Different hospices offer different services. Some employ professionals full or part time, or both, while others rely mainly on volunteers.

Hospice organizations operate 24 hours a day, seven days a week, so that there is always someone to help when there is need.

Who qualifies for hospice care?

Patients must be terminally ill with a life expectancy of only weeks or months and no longer under treatment for cure of the disease.

How does one get hospice care?

Referrals are usually made by the primary physician, but can also be made by family, friends, clergy, or a health professional.

Who pays for the hospice program?

1. As of April 1986, hospice became a permanent covered benefit under Medicare and an optional benefit under Medicaid. The hospice must be a Medicare Certified program in order to qualify for their coverage. To be certified, the program must provide nursing care, medical social services, physician services, counseling, and volunteer services. Eighty percent of the hospice care should be provided in the home. The aggregate cap per patient is $7,391.

2. A majority of national insurance companies are offering hospice benefits.

3. Local fund raisers, memorial gifts, and contributions are important sources.

4. Fees are charged for services to the patient by the hospice. While these charges are usually less than those charged for hospital care, you should be certain that your insurance carrier covers hospice when making a decision.

How do you find a hospice?

1. Ask your doctor.

2. Get in touch with the nearest hospital. Often, hospitals support and operate hospices themselves.

3. Ask your health insurer.

4. Call the local health department.

5. Phone your local Visiting Nurses' Association.

6. Look in the phone book for the local or state hospice organization.

7. Write or call the:

>National Hospice Organization
>1901 North Fort Myer Drive, Suite 307
>Arlington, VA 22209
>(703) 243-5900

The national headquarters can give you complete information concerning the hospice program. Send for their publication list.

LIVING WILLS

With modern technology and medical advances, it is now possible to sustain life almost indefinitely. With the proper machines, the heart can be made to pump and the lungs to breathe even after the brain has stopped functioning. For some people, this is unpalatable. They feel that people should be allowed to "die with dignity," rather than go out in a mass of tubing and machines days, weeks, or even months after they are no longer truly alive.

The Society for the Right to Die is a not-for-profit organization that was formed to educate, support legislation, and publish and distribute literature that supports their philosophy. The Society is responsible for the production and distribution of the "Living Will," a document which informs your doctor and family that you do not want medical procedures performed that will prolong your death, if there is no chance of a reasonable recovery. Common law provides an individual the right to refuse treatment, but a dying or comatose patient may be unable to exercise that right. When this happens, someone else must make that decision. To place this burden on a loved one adds to their stress and emotional upset. A Living Will, on the other hand, gives the patient control and responsibility for himself.

PLEASE NOTE: Having a Living Will does not mean that you will be denied "comfort measures" such as pain killers or any other treatment that will make you comfortable. You may specify which, if any, life-sustaining treatment you do or do not want, such as cardiac resuscitation, mechanical respiration, artificial feeding, surgery, or antibiotics. If you fail to specify on your Living Will document, then your physician will administer only comfort measures.

Thirty-eight states and the District of Columbia now have Living Will statutes: Alabama, Alaska, Arizona, Arkansas, California, Colorado, Connecticut, Delaware, Florida, Georgia, Hawaii, Idaho, Illinois, Indiana, Iowa, Kansas, Louisiana, Maine, Maryland, Mississippi, Missouri, Montana, Nevada, New Hampshire, New Mexico, North Carolina, Oklahoma, Oregon, South Carolina, Tennessee, Texas, Utah, Vermont, Virginia, Washington, West Virginia, Wisconsin, and Wyoming.

The remaining twelve states have all had Living Will legislation introduced. Many feel that it is just a matter of time before every state in the nation will have a bill that addresses the issue.

Living Wills, also known as Declarations or Directives, have two main purposes. First, they enable a person to state his wishes in a legal document, giving explicit directions for terminal care. Secondly, they protect physicians from liability when they carry out those wishes.

While individual states have their own wordings and legal documents, most of them have the following basic provisions.

1. Recognition of an adult's right to control personal medical treatment and to do so with an advance written directive to the physician instructing that life-sustaining procedures are to be withheld or withdrawn should the person's condition be terminal.

2. Physicians and other health care professionals are exempt from civil or criminal liability if they follow the patient's directive as long as that directive is in compliance with the statute.

3. Qualification for the implementation of the directive typically means that the attending physician and one other physician must certify that the patient is terminal.

4. Life-sustaining procedures are defined.

5. A form is usually provided that must be either precisely or "substantially" followed.

6. Procedures for executing a declaration usually include the signature being witnessed by two adults who are not related and have no interest in the patient's estate.

7. A person can revoke the declaration at any time.

8. The declaration is in effect until it is revoked. (An exception to this is the state of California which states that a Living Will is effective for only 5 years.)

9. If the attending physician is unwilling to carry out the wishes of the patient, then the patient must be transferred to a physician who is willing.

10. Twenty-seven states hold the declaration invalid if the patient is pregnant.

11. A patient's current wishes supersede the wishes of the written declaration.

12. The execution of a declaration shall in no way affect life or health care insurance policies.

13. The implementation of a declaration by a terminal

patient in no way constitutes suicide or aided suicide and does not condone "mercy killing."

14. There are penalties for forging or destroying a patient's declaration.

To find out the specific differences in each state or to obtain a copy of your state's legal declaration form, write to:

Society for the Right to Die
250 West 57th Street
New York, NY 10107
(212) 246-6973

The Society has worked diligently for years to see that legislation is passed and that people are informed and educated about Living Wills. Membership dues are only $10 annually and entitle you to newsletters that keep you current of the issues. The Society is extremely helpful and quick to respond to inquiries, so if you have any questions or concerns contact them.

Only in the states of California, Idaho, and Oklahoma must terminal illness be ascertained by a physician before a Living Will is executed. In the cases of California and Oklahoma, the document will still be given consideration in the decision making process even if not executed or reexecuted after a terminal diagnosis.

California, Rhode Island, and Arizona have what is called a Durable Power of Attorney for Health Care. This is separate from the Living Will document and permits you to appoint a person to make medical treatment decisions on your behalf in the event you are incapable of communicating your wishes. Should you live in one of these states, it is highly recommended that you complete this additional form to assure that your wishes are carried out. The Durable Power of Attorney for Health Care form may be obtained from the Society upon request.

Arizona, New Jersey, Nevada, Pennsylvania, and New York have indicated through legal processes that Durable Power of Attorney can be used to terminate treatment.

The provision for a proxy is contained within the Living Will in the states of Delaware, Florida, Louisiana, Texas, Utah, Virginia, and Wyoming. Proxies are indirectly authorized in the states of Hawaii, Idaho, Indiana, and Iowa.

Should you or a loved one decide that prolonged death is unacceptable, contact the Society and request a declaration form. You must specify the state in which you live, as each is a little different. They will send to you a declaration as well as a sheet of directions, explanations, and current laws for your state. Right to Die Laws are constantly being revised. Every year additional states are passing legislation. Those which already have Living Will legislation are amending and improving their existing laws. Because of the fast developments in this area, you will need to keep abreast of the changes. The best and easiest way to do this is to become a member of the Society for the Right to Die.

What if you live in a state that does not have Living Will legislation?

The Society will send to you a "Living Will Declaration." This is a generic declaration that simply states your wishes. You fill in your wants and don't wants, along with the names of your proxies should you be unable to communicate your instructions. As in the legal declarations prescribed by those states which have Living Wills, two witnesses must sign. Although not provided for in your state's laws, these declarations carry great weight and have been upheld in the courts.

Should you decide to obtain a Living Will, fill it out accurately and make copies for your physician, yourself, and your next of kin. Do not send a copy to the Society for the Right to Die. Advise your friends and relatives of your wishes and solicit their support and commitment to follow out those instructions. Although your wishes are paramount over theirs, it is very difficult for a doctor to carry out directives when the family opposes.

Review your document occasionally. Each time you read your Living Will, initial and date it to show that it still reflects your wishes. Should you want to make any additions or changes, do so, then initial and date those changes. Don't forget that you may revoke the declaration at any time.

Should you move to another state, be sure to get a new declaration. Only Alaska, Arkansas, and Maine recognize declarations from other states. Hawaii, Maryland, and Montana will recognize out-of-state declarations only if they conform substantially with the laws of their respective states.

The American Association of Retired Persons, the National Council of Senior Citizens, the Gray Panthers, and the Older Women's League have all supported patient's rights and/or Living Will legislation.

ORGAN AND TISSUE DONATIONS

The first organ transplant took place in Boston, Massachusetts in 1954. The surgery involved identical twins. The transplanted kidney functioned normally for eight years. Eight years later, a kidney was transplanted from a cadaver. This kidney functioned normally for 21 months. Since that time, 25 different types of organs and tissues including livers, hearts, pancreas, and lungs have been successfully transplanted.

Over 50,000 people benefited from all types of organ and tissue transplants in 1986.

The Uniform Anatomical Gift Act, in effect in all 50 states, allows anyone 18 years or older and of sound mind to will their organs and tissues for transplantation or research purposes. A deceased's next of kin may also donate the organs. Minors may become donors at the request of the parent or guardian.

The need for organ and tissue donors is tremendous. According to the United Network for Organ Sharing in Richmond, Virginia permanent kidney failure affects over 80,000 Americans. That number increases by 1,000 each year. There are over 10,000 people in the United States waiting for kidney transplants. In 1986, 8,495 post-mortem kidney transplants were performed in the United States alone. Over 70,000 kidney transplants have been performed worldwide, with 70% of those coming from post-mortem donors.

Over 3,000 heart transplants have been performed worldwide. 1,073 hearts were transplanted in the United States in 1986. Approximately 320 Americans are waiting for donor hearts today.

Worldwide, there have been over 2,000 liver transplants. Six hundred seventy-five livers were transplanted in the United States in 1986. Over 300 Americans are on waiting lists for new livers.

Corneal transplants have been performed since 1905. The first was in Austria. Again, there is a long waiting list. All corneas are acceptable for donation, regardless of any abnormality in vision.

The list of organs and tissue goes on, as does the list of those awaiting transplants. Even though 22,000 potential organ donors die each year, only 10% of those become donors.

In the United States, all donors are tested for AIDS, hepatitis, venereal diseases, and infection before organs are procured. Organs are then matched according to blood type and weight. For some organs, height and age of the donor are also a consideration.

Although organ donors must be under the age of 60 and be free of cancer, infection, organ disease or organ injury, all tissue donors are considered. Tissues include eyes, bone, cartilage, and skin.

The American Medical Association guidelines provide that the patient who needs the organ the most and has the best chance of survival be first in line to receive organ/tissue donations.

A LIFESAVING DECISION

Making a decision to donate vital organs and tissues should be a family decision. The patient's request to be a donor will be negated if there is family opposition. That is why it is vital to discuss donation with your next of kin if you are considering it. Another reason to have family members informed is that time for discussion and decision making is limited.

No organs can be removed until all efforts to save a life have been exhausted. The potential donor must be neurologically brain dead and being maintained on life support systems. In most states, the doctor who certifies the death can not remove the organs.

Should you want to be a donor, most states have a donor card that you attach to your driver's license stating your wishes. You may donate all or any particular organs of your choosing. It is a simple card that merely asks you to check your desires and sign. Usually, two witnesses need to sign also. Unlike the Living Will, it is best to have your next of kin as your witness.

If your state does not have donor cards through your local Department of Motor Vehicles, then contact your local organ procurement agency by looking in the phone book, calling your local hospital, asking your physician, or inquiring of your librarian for a state or national address.

Should you change your mind about being an organ donator, simply destroy your donor card and inform your relatives of the change in your wishes.

You may want to consult a member of the clergy to make sure there are no conflicts with your religious beliefs. Most of the major religions view the desire for organ donation as a meaningful gift to mankind.

As of July 1, 1987 there is a federal "required request law" that makes it mandatory for hospital staff to assess the dying patient for donor suitability. If the patient passes the criteria, then someone on the hospital staff must approach the family of the patient at or near the time of death and ask if they are willing to donate the patient's organs. This may sound rather cold and insensitive, but really, it is a matter of necessity. Organs are very vulnerable, and the time that they can remain outside of the body is very limited. For example, kidneys can be preserved 48-72 hours; hearts, 8-12 hours; pancreas, 12-24 hours; heart-lung, 2-4 hours; livers, 8 hours. If a recipient lives in another state, travel time makes a quicker decision more critical.

The United Network for Organ Sharing in Richmond, Virginia maintains a national computer system that matches donor to recipient. It is maintained 24 hours a day 365 days a year just as your local procurement office, so that any time day or night, organs can be placed.

FUNERAL ARRANGEMENTS
AND ORGAN DONATIONS

Donating organs does not delay any funeral arrangements that you want to make. You can have an opened casket, if you choose. Your loved one will appear no different for the funeral. If this is a concern for you, talk to your funeral director. He will be able to reassure you.

NOTE: There is no charge to the family or estate of the organ donor. It is illegal to buy or sell human organs. From the time the patient is certified dead, until the body is released for disposition, the costs are incurred by the organ procurement agency.

While many procurement agencies will write the donor family informing them of the tissues and organs that were used for transplantation, very seldom will names be given identifying the recipients. You may be informed of the age, sex, and condition of the recipient.

There is a framed poster at the Golden State Regional Organ Procurement Agency in Sacramento, California. It was lovingly made by a young child and says,

Let a life begin again,
by giving from yourself within.

AUTOPSIES

Autopsies may not always be optional, but a discussion is included in this chapter because you could be approached by your physician or other professional care person and asked for permission to have an autopsy performed when it is felt something could be learned to benefit others. These autopsies are performed for research purposes and can be conducted only with the permission of the next of kin. Granting permission is entirely at your discretion. The next of kin may grant permission for an autopsy, but limit it to certain organs, e.g., the physician may examine the heart, but not the brain.

There are circumstances that make the reporting of a death to the Coroner or Medical Examiner mandatory. Reporting must be made by anyone having knowledge of a death that falls into one of the mandatory reporting categories. This includes, but is not limited to, physicians, hospital staff, morticians, embalmers, ambulance attendants, police officers, and lay persons.

Upon receiving the report, the Coroner makes a determination whether a full investigation, including an autopsy, is necessary. Reporting to the Coroner occurs before the body is removed from the place of death. This is necessary for an accurate investigation. The ultimate decision of whether or not an autopsy is performed rests with the Coroner who is regulated by law.

Mandatory reporting is required for various reasons, and may vary slightly from state-to-state. Generally, the causes for required reporting are deaths which occur unattended by a physician, where foul play is suspected (this includes euthanasia), where cause of death is undeterminable by a physician, when the person has not seen a doctor for a period of time (this can vary from 24 hours to a few weeks, depending on the state), following an injury or accident, where suicide is suspected, where poisoning is suspected, where injury (old or recent) is a contributing factor, where rape or crimes against nature are involved, where occupational diseases or hazards are suspected, and where contagious diseases that are a threat to the public are involved. Also reportable are deaths due to drowning, fire, hanging, gunshot, stabbing, cutting, exposure, starvation, alcoholism, drug addiction, strangulation, or aspiration.

Autopsies may be performed at a central facility, or in the case of smaller communities, in a hospital or mortuary.

If, after the autopsy, there is reason to suspect a crime has been committed, an inquest is held. This is a formal hearing before a jury and the Coroner who acts as judge. They determine if there is enough evidence for a grand jury hearing. Because of the time and expense involved in these procedures, many counties are replacing inquests with formal investigations.

What goes on in an autopsy?

Autopsies are performed by physicians who specialize in pathology and have advanced training in forensic medicine. Pathologists study the effects of the disease process on the body. They do tissue studies and other laboratory studies to determine norms for the body. Forensic pathologists go one step further, they must distinguish natural disease processes from unnatural. This requires one to two years additional training. Forensic pathologists are bound by laws that require them to fully investigate the bodies that are brought to them. They have feelings and are sensitive to the desires of the families, but they must do their jobs.

Should your family member be autopsied, your best link with the pathologist is through your funeral director, who can relay any requests that you might have. This does not mean that the pathologist will do any less of an investigation, but he may be able to make a different type incision that will be less noticeable to accommodate certain clothing that you want the deceased to wear.

An autopsy basically consists of three parts. First, there is an external examination of the body. If known, the name, time of death, place of death, and age is recorded. Information such as sex, race, height, and weight is next. Then, the overall appearance of the deceased is examined and described — coloration, apparent trauma such as bruises, cuts, old injuries, swelling, lumps. The pathologist is looking for anything that might render clues to the cause of death.

The second phase of the autopsy involves removing the organs in the head, abdomen, and chest. These are weighed and examined for disease or injury. Unless it is suspected that the cause of death exists in an extremity, arms and legs are left alone.

The third aspect of the autopsy is a chemical and microscopic study of tissues and body fluids.

After all tests have been concluded, the body is released to the next of kin for funeral preparations. Autopsy surgeons are careful to make incisions that can be hidden by a skillful embalmer. You should still be able to have an opened casket. The pathologist will inform your funeral director of the viewing condition of the body beforehand, so that you can be prepared. Usually, if the body is not viewable, it is not the fault of the pathologist, but rather the circumstances of the death that make viewing impractical.

In the case of autopsied bodies, death certificates will be signed by the Coroner.

Autopsy reports are generally public information and can be obtained upon request from the Coroner's or Medical Examiner's Office. There usually is a charge for copies of the report.

Autopsies are not only used to collect evidences of violent crimes, but are also used for the benefit of the public health. If several people die for an unknown reason and they have the same symptoms, autopsies may identify the cause and save many more lives. In Paulette Cooper's book *The Medical Detectives* she recounts several instances where autopsies have saved countless lives. One case involves acute allergic reactions to penicillin. At one time, penicillin was a "cure all" and was prescribed indiscriminately to patients with all sorts of ailments. Dr. Abraham Rosenthal began to realize that some of the people he autopsied could not be dying from the diseases for which penicillin was prescribed and made the connection that the penicillin itself was the culprit. Hence, greater care and control of the drug's use.

In another instance, Cooper describes the case of the redesign of the Boeing 727 after autopsies revealed that people died, not because of injuries sustained in the plane crash, but because they were trapped in a burning plane.

Dr. Alexander Wiener made the Rh-factor in blood connection after numerous autopsies on babies who had Rh-negative mothers.

Forensic medicine is important to all of us. Its earliest beginnings can be traced to the year 3000 B.C., with its real development evolving between the 13th and 15th centuries. The latter part of the 16th century saw the science develop as an aid to police investigations. The American colonists brought the coroner system with them from England. There are records of a coroner's inquest as early as 1635 in the colony of New Plymouth.

Since those early beginnings, the field has become specialized to the point of engaging experts in fields such as immunology, ballistics, polygraphy, geology, fingerprinting, serology, analytical chemistry, and toxicology.

Rather than viewing autopsy as a ghastly procedure, think of all the positives that have come out of it; all of the lives that have been saved, and the vital legislation that has been enacted to protect lives because of this science.

3.

Funeral and Burial Arrangements

Unless the deceased had a prepaid funeral or left specific instructions concerning burial, it is likely that the next of kin will need to make these arrangements. At a time when you are most vulnerable and least emotionally able to cope, you must make this important financial and emotional decision. Taking an active part in the burial and funeral planning is considered to be an important step in the acceptance of a loved one's death.

Before you go to the mortuary, it is helpful to know your options, how much you can afford to spend, and what your personal and/or religious beliefs dictate.

While there is no limit to the amount of money you can spend on a funeral, it is important to know that simple yet dignified burials can be obtained for a few hundred dollars. Almost any arrangement you want can be obtained by your funeral director. If you have a clear idea of what you want before you approach the mortician, it will be beneficial to both of you.

FUNERAL COSTS

Funeral costs are basically divided into three areas.

1. The services performed and the products supplied by the funeral director. These can include embalming, preparation of the body, use of facilities for viewing or services, the hearse, limousines, register book, memorial cards, tents and chairs, and transfer of remains to the funeral home.

2. Costs dealing with the actual disposition of the remains. This would be the cemetery lot, columbarium niche, the urn, the opening and closing of the grave.

3. The plaque or headstone to mark the burial place.

What are your choices?

Lisa Carlson has written a marvelous book entitled *Caring For Your Own Dead* (Upper Access Publishers, Hinesburg, Vermont, 1987). The premise of this book is that families can arrange for the disposition of their loved ones without (or with minimal) use of a funeral director. Carlson feels that while saving a great deal of money, caring for your own dead is the "most meaningful way to say goodbye to someone you love." The book contains state-by-state laws and regulations, as well as names and addresses of crematories. It is packed with useful information for those who are interested in taking a intimate role in the disposition arrangements of their families.

If you prefer to take a lesser role, you will need the assistance of a funeral director. After the body has been released by the attending physician or Coroner, you will be asked where you want the body sent for disposition. They will call the funeral home you select, which in turn will take the body to the mortuary and arrange for final disposition.

Although there are some differences, the terms funeral director, mortician, embalmer, and undertaker are generally used interchangeably. The differences occur in training and licensing. If the funeral home is licensed by your state, they should have the qualifications to assist you. The terms mortuary and funeral home are also interchangeable and will be used so in the discussion on such establishments.

CHOOSING A FUNERAL DIRECTOR

A good funeral director can make a difficult time much easier. He can be a wealth of information and assistance even after the funeral services are over. You may rely on him to help you make some very important decisions. Depending on his level of professionalism, he can ease much of the stress and pain or create more. Therefore, it is important to choose a funeral service professional with whom you can relate.

How do you choose a funeral director?

1. Ask for recommendations. Friends and clergymen can be very helpful. Someone who has gone through the procedure will be able to give you some information on the attitude of the staff, the facilities, and the types of services they offer.

2. Geographical location may be important if you plan to visit the deceased before burial or to conduct the services in the funeral home chapel.

3. Physical appearance of the establishment might be important for the same reasons. Sometimes in visiting a mortuary, one might be more satisfying or comforting to you than another.

4. Services offered can be a determining factor. Be sure that the type of burial you have in mind can be accomplished through the mortuary you choose. Big does not necessarily mean better. Whereas a larger establishment might have more choices, the smaller ones can usually accommodate your needs and offer a more personal service.

5. Charges for services should be a very important consideration. There is no standard markup on goods and services in the funeral industry. Prices can vary enormously from one part of town to another and especially one city to another. Funeral homes are required to give you a list of their prices. Ask for these and compare the total service charges with the same or a very similar casket.

6. How helpful and accommodating is the funeral director? This is of utmost importance. You must have confidence in his ability to carry out your wishes. You must be able to relate freely any concerns or questions that you have. He should be willing to do whatever he can to help you make decisions that you feel comfortable with. You want someone who is warm, caring, sincere, honest, and professional. If you cannot communicate your needs and wishes to him, then find someone with whom you can.

It will be necessary for you to go to the mortuary to give instructions to your funeral director. He will show you the options available. The more you participate in these choices, the more likely you will be satisfied with the results.

There are two main types of disposition, TRADITIONAL and CREMATION. Many variables exist within these two types. Below is a discussion of each and some of the choices that are yours.

TRADITIONAL SERVICE

In the United States, the traditional service is still the most popular. It can, but does not have to, include choosing a mortuary, embalming the body, selecting a casket, preparing the body for viewing, visitation at the funeral home, funeral services, and burial in a cemetery.

Embalming

The process of removing most of the body fluids and replacing them with a temporary preservative and disinfectant solution is called embalming. This is accomplished by opening a main artery and injecting chemicals under controlled pressure. The body fluids are forced out through a vein.

Embalming did not become popular in the United States until the Civil War when bodies of soldiers needed to be preserved until they could be returned to their homes for burial.

It is important to understand that this procedure only temporarily preserves the body, usually until the final disposition is complete. It does not mummify the body.

Embalming is seldom required by law. If the remains must be transported by common carrier (plane/train), the company transporting the body may require this or if the body is to be kept several days without refrigeration, it could become a practical necessity.

A form giving permission to embalm, must be signed by the person responsible for the disposition of the body.

Casket Selection

Most funeral homes have a variety of caskets to choose from. They can vary in price from a few hundred to thousands of dollars. Often, the least expensive caskets will not be displayed, but are available upon request. You can see everything from fabric covered wooden boxes to solid bronze. Linings can vary from thin satin to plush velvet, and come in several colors. If you do not see a pleasing color, ask what other colors are available. The shapes of the caskets can also vary. There is the elliptic (round) end, scroll end, square end, and even octagonal end.

Basically, your choices in material will be threefold: Wood (soft woods such as pine and redwood or hardwoods such as oak, mahogany, walnut, and maple), Metal (steel that comes in various gauges from sixteen to twenty, stainless steel, bronze, and copper), and fiberglass.

The cloth-covered soft wood casket and some lower gauge steel and metals will be the least expensive. Next come hardwoods, fiberglass, higher gauge steel, and some metals. The most expensive will be the solid copper and bronze. Keep in mind that the plushness and features of the lining will also affect the price.

Sometimes it will be necessary to take into consideration the size and weight of the person if considerably above the norm.

Because they do not rust, the fiberglass, copper, and bronze caskets offer the most protection.

One feature available on the metal casket is a seal. This is intended to keep moisture out of the casket.

Whatever your choice, remember the purpose of the casket is to display the deceased during the funeral ceremony and to act as a protection for the body when it is buried. *It will not preserve a body.*

Be sure to read the manufacturers warranties. The funeral home does not guarantee its caskets. Should you have any problems, you would need to contact the company which made the casket, through the funeral home which sold it.

Preparing the body for viewing

Do you want the body "made suitable for viewing"? This can be done whether or not it will be viewed by anyone. This usually includes makeup, hair dressing, and reconstruction when necessary. It is helpful to the funeral director if you give him some indication (especially in the case of a woman) as to the amount and colors of makeup she wore. Makeup is also used to hide discolorations due to sickness or injury. False teeth should be given to the funeral director as quickly as possible so that the mouth will look more normal. Give the director some indication of the hairstyle the deceased preferred. Do you want glasses on or off? Do you want the person buried with jewelry, or jewelry removed before burial? Decide what clothes you want the deceased to wear. This can range from a lovely gown or dress for a lady, to a suit or casual attire for a man. Anything or even nothing can be worn if the body is not to be viewed. You might want to purchase something new or simply choose something from the deceased's existing wardrobe.

Services

There are two types of services: the funeral where the body is present and the memorial where the body is not present. In most TRADITIONAL funerals, the body is present. You will need to decide whether you want an opened casket or closed casket, i.e. do you want people to see the body or would you rather they didn't? The viewing can be prior to, after, or during the service.

Where will the service be held? Funeral homes have facilities available for services. These can be ornate and elaborate or simple and casual. You will need to know how many people it can accommodate so you will know whether the facility is adequate for the expected turnout. A place of worship is a traditional setting for a funeral or memorial. Graveside services are popular for smaller funerals during the more pleasant seasons of the year.

Who will conduct the service? Anyone can conduct the funeral or memorial service. Fraternal organizations, friends, clergy, military, family, or any combination of these. If you would like a minister, but neither you nor the deceased are members of any particular church, the funeral director can suggest one from any religion you choose. They keep lists of those ministers willing to perform funeral services for people who are not members of their congregations. In this case, the funeral director pays the minister an honorarium and charges you for the service, based on the amount you direct him to be paid.

Music can be handled much the same way. If you want music but do not know a musician, your funeral director will be able to assist you in finding one. For graveside services, you might find someone who can play a portable instrument such as a guitar.

Final disposition of remains

The two most common means of final disposition in the traditional funeral are INTERMENT and ENTOMBMENT. Interment is the more common and simply means to bury or inter the body in the earth. Entombment means to place or entomb the body in an above or below ground enclosure known as a mausoleum.

CREMATION

An alternative to the Traditional Funeral Service is Cremation. This form of disposition is gaining in popularity, but still represents only a small percentage of burial options at this time. In Japan and England, it is the preferred and most common disposition method.

Cremation is the reduction of the body to its component elements by intense heat (approximately 2,200 degrees Fahrenheit). Because the cremains, commonly referred in laymen's terms as "ashes," are actually bone fragments weighing approximately five pounds, they are gravelly and need to be pulverized if the intent is to "scatter" them.

It is not necessary to buy a casket if cremation is your choice. Funeral homes will sell you what they call a wooden "tray," or a plain wooden or cardboard container. Should you want a funeral with the body present and then have it cremated, a rental casket may be obtained for the visitation and/or services. Compare the price of renting a casket with buying one. In some cases, it may be less expensive to purchase.

Should you decide to have the body cremated before the services, a memorial service may be at a place of your choosing.

Final disposition of the cremains

There are three common ways to dispose of cremated remains, or cremains, as the funeral industry refers to them.

1. Bury. Cremains may be put into a container and buried. As in conventional burial of caskets, the cemetery will charge an opening and closing fee. Often it is less because the size of the opening is neither as deep nor as large. Usually, it will be placed under the marker.

2. Scatter. Cremains may be scattered. Often crematories are in proximity to lovely gardens where either you or they will scatter the cremated remains. Some people like to scatter them in the ocean. There are businesses whose purpose is to deal solely with cremated remains. Some states have laws governing the scattering of ashes. Check with your crematory or funeral director on the laws of your state.

3. Inurn in a columbarium. Columbarium comes from the Latin word *columba* meaning dove. Doves make their nests in a dovecote which contains many niches. Columbaria, which may be simple or elaborate, are filled with niches where the urn containing the cremains are kept. Urns, like caskets, can range from modest amounts to thousands of dollars. Most often, they are made of bronze or marble.

Often there are rules and restrictions relating to plaques and adornment. Sometimes, a niche has a glass front and any engraving is written on the urn itself. In other columbaria, an engraved plaque may appear on the outside of the niche.

Immediate disposition of cremains

It is possible to remand a body directly to a crematory for immediate disposition. If the crematory is in conjunction with a cemetery or funeral home establishment, they can assist you with the necessary paper work and final disposition of the cremains. You can then choose to hold a memorial service or dispense with any kind of service at all. Obviously, this is the most inexpensive. If the establishment is strictly a crematory, it may not provide the service of final disposition of the cremains and may not help with any paper work.

Generally, cremation is less expensive than the traditional form of funeral because fewer products and services are rendered. However, as stated earlier, funeral arrangements involve emotional decisions as well as financial considerations. Decide what you want and what you think your next of kin would have liked.

There are Cremation Societies organized to help you. Look in your phone book to see if your area has one or write:

Cremation Association of North America
111 E. Wacker Drive
Chicago, IL 60601
(312) 644-6610

MEDICAL SCIENCE

Another option to consider is donating the body to medical science. The Uniform Anatomical Gift Act gives you or your next of kin the right to donate your body to medical science. You should contact the medical school in advance to learn of its requirements. Most schools will not accept a body that has been embalmed, had organs removed, died of certain diseases, is emaciated, or extremely overweight. There may also be a surplus of bodies causing it to be rejected.

Therefore it is important that you have alternative arrangements in case the body should not be accepted.

Should you want the residue of the body for interment after studies are completed, this can be handled through your funeral director. If you do not, some schools will handle this for you with or without charge. Some will not, regardless. It is important for you to ask these questions in advance.

Cost comparisons of the various methods of disposition are difficult because there are so many variables. Generally, cremation is less expensive than interment of a casket. But if you choose the traditional funeral, rent or buy a casket for viewing, have the body prepared for viewing, purchase an expensive urn and place it in a columbarium, then you may be looking at a price comparable to the full service funeral. On the other hand, if you have the body sent to the crematory from a hospital, scatter the ashes, and have a memorial service at your church, then the cost will be minimal.

Most funeral directors will give you whatever you want and charge accordingly. Some examples might be:

1. Graveside service with or without visitation.
2. Memorial services — immediate cremation or burial.
3. Memorial services — no care of remains.
4. Visitation only — no services.
5. Immediate burial — no services.

Any combination of these services should be available if you have chosen the funeral director who is willing to work with your desires and needs. Since services are listed and priced individually, it is simply a matter of stating what you want and adding the totals.

MEMORIAL SOCIETIES

Recognizing the high cost of dying and endeavoring to do something about it, the first Memorial Society was formed in 1939. They did not gain much recognition until 1963 when the Continental Associations of Funeral and Memorial Societies was organized. In 1971, The Memorial Society Association of Canada formed a separate yet closely connected organization. These associations are democratic, non-profit organizations run mostly by volunteers whose purpose is to provide simple, economical, and dignified funeral services for their members. Membership is open to peoples of all nationalities, colors, and creeds. There are over 200 such societies in the U.S. and Canada.

According to their literature, memorial societies are the only consumer organizations dedicated primarily to protecting the interests of the consumer in the field of funeral practices.

Typically, there is a nominal one-time membership fee to cover organizational costs. Memorial societies generally do not perform funerals or supply any services or products. What they do is contract out to a mortician who provides simple services at low costs. This does not mean that you are bound to one particular service if you are a member. Should you prefer some "extras," these can be added to the basic plan for additional fees.

Should you move to another area of the country, your

membership can be transferred.

Memorial societies provide a lot of educational materials. It is in your interest to investigate your local organization as an option in planning a funeral. The society will provide you with a worksheet that contains questions to help you make plans.

To find a memorial society in your area, look in your phone book or write:

Continental Association of Funeral and
Memorial Societies, Inc.
2001 S Street NW, Suite 630
Washington, DC 20009
(202) 462-8888

If there is not a memorial society in your area, the Continental Association will provide you with information on how to obtain a low cost funeral and/or organize your own society in your community.

CAUTION: The Continental Association claims that it screens all of the applicants to ensure they are a legitimate society formed to aid its membership. There are some memorial societies that are simply "fronts" for profit-making businesses. Do some investigative work to assure you are working with a bona fide non-profit society, if that is your intention.

CHOOSING A CEMETERY

There are religious, fraternal, public, and privately owned cemeteries. Provided the proper permits are secured, cities, counties, and private individuals may purchase land and develop a cemetery. There are also 103 national cemeteries that the federal government maintains for veterans. As discussed in the chapter on Survivor Benefits, you and your spouse may be entitled to plots in a national cemetery or area designated as such in a public cemetery if you or your spouse was a veteran.

There are many considerations in choosing a cemetery for a burial plot.

1. Look at the cemetery. Is it well maintained? Are the grounds cared for carefully? Are the markers in good condition?

2. Are there provisions that accommodate the type of burial you prefer? (inurnment, entombment, or interment of cremated remains)

3. Is the type of memorial marker you want allowed in the cemetery?

4. Should you move away is it possible for you to sell your lot?

5. Will the cemetery be open whenever you want to visit?

6. Are flowers or other decoration allowed on the grave-sites?

7. Is the price of a plot within an affordable range?

8. Is there a perpetual care or endowment fund that pays for the maintenance of the cemetery? If so, how much of the cost of the plot is devoted to this?

9. How are the care funds administered and by whom?

10. Does the cemetery require a grave liner or vault? A liner is usually a concrete, metal, or wooden box with loose-fitting lid. A vault is sturdier and has a lid that seals. Whereas state and federal laws may not require a liner or vault, some cemeteries do in order to prevent the ground from sinking with the deterioration of the casket. Vaults and liners may be sold by the funeral director or the cemetery.

CHOOSING A MEMORIAL MARKER

Markers have come a long way from the old tombstones that once adorned graves. Colorful and even humorous epitaphs have become more dignified and solemn. Materials such as marble, sandstone, and slate have been replaced with granite because of its durability.

Your choices of markers are almost as varied as those of caskets. You may want the bronze or granite veteran marker supplied without cost by the government. You might want to plan ahead for your own death and buy a double headstone (provided of course that you have purchased a burial plot next to your spouse). You might even want to purchase several lots for a family burial area and build a family mausoleum. These are examples of the least expensive to the most expensive. There is a wide choice between.

First, you must check with the cemetery to see what their restrictions and requirements concerning markers entail. Many times, your monument dealer will have this knowledge, but it is wise to double check. Often, cemeteries sell markers, and may charge more for setting the stone bought from an independent dealer.

Next, visit several monument dealers. These are often located near the cemetery. Looking in your phone book, asking the cemetery for recommendations, or asking friends who have needed these services are all ways to get leads.

When you visit the dealer, there are several things you need to know:

1. Who manufactures the stone, and what guarantee does the manufacturer supply? You want to be sure that there is an unlimited guarantee on the product and workmanship. This guarantee should have no time limit and be enforced by either the purchaser or the cemetery where the marker is erected. The more reputable manufacturers offer these warranties. The manufacturers Guild Seal will be sandblasted somewhere on the stone. This enables you to always show proof of your warranty.

2. Markers are not warranted against vandalism, acts of God, or acts of war.

3. There are many grades of granite. Look for fine, even grain. There should not be any pattern to the grain. The color should be even as should the texture. Colors range in shades of gray, pink, and white.

4. Granite may either be polished or left with its natural matte finish. This is a matter of taste on the purchaser's part.

5. Some dealers engrave their own stones while others have it done by the manufacturer. Ask which is the procedure and look at samples. The letters should have sharp, even edges. Their depth should be uniform. Engraving will sometimes show flaws that were undetectable before, so check carefully after the stone is delivered.

6. There is a cost for "setting" the marker. Be prepared for this expenditure.

7. There are many styles and shapes. Be certain that what you choose is within the cemetery's rules.

8. The more ornate and/or wordy the engraving, the more costly your monument.

Flowers or?

The giving of flowers either in the form of fresh cut, live plants, artificial arrangements, or dried flowers has been traditional for funerals. Many people see this as an expensive extravagance and would rather see donations to a favorite organization, church, or charity. If your preference is the latter, you can request that it be put in the obituary.

Often, after the funeral service, family members take the fresh-cut arrangements to hospitals or nursing homes so that the joy of a beautiful bouquet is shared with others.

Funeral Directors, a source of help and information

As mentioned already in this chapter, the funeral director will help you with the actual planning of the funeral service and disposition of the body. He will also help you with other items.

1. Obituaries: He will notify the local newspaper or any other that you choose. Obituaries, especially in large metropolitan areas, are not free. You will be charged by the length. Your funeral director will help you with the wording when provided with the basic information such as age, place of birth, occupation, military service, college degrees, fraternal memberships, outstanding recognition, survivors, time and place of services.

2. Death Certificates: The director will file the necessary documents to secure certified death certificates. The number you need will depend on how much property you own, how many insurance companies you will file claim with, whether you qualify for Social Security and veteran benefits, etc. Take an inventory of your financial affairs to determine how many copies you need. Generally, financial institutions and companies where you are seeking financial compensation require certified copies. All others will accept a copy of the certified copy. There is a charge for each certified copy that you order.

Information needed for a death certificate includes: date of birth and death, hour of death, sex, race, birthplace, name and birthplace of father and mother of decedent, country of citizenship, dates of military service if any, Social Security number, marital status, name of surviving spouse, occupation, number of years at that occupation, employer, kind of industry or business, usual residence, place of death, immediate and underlying cause of death, whether body was autopsied or biopsied, whether surgery was performed. In addition, there is a section for the physician's certification and coroner's information. The funeral director will supply the remaining information about his licensing numbers, etc.

3. Veteran's flag: Necessary forms will be completed. The director obtains the flag for you and presents it at your request.

4. Insurance notification: If you so choose, the director can notify and help make claim for your life insurance policies. To do this, they need only to know the insurance companies and policy numbers. There is no need for them to know the value of the policy.

5. Flowers: The staff will arrange and transport flowers that are sent to the funeral home. Often, they will collect the cards and make notations describing the arrangement so that acknowledgment is made easier.

6. Notification of lodges, clubs, and churches: The funeral director can do this for you if you provide a list.

LAWS GOVERNING FUNERAL PRACTICES

In May of 1984, the Federal Trade Commission mandated that Funeral Directors itemize charges and that consumers pay for only those goods and services that they select. In instances where items are required by law, the specific law must be stated in writing.

Prices MUST be given over the phone, or prior to entering into price discussions.

Embalming is not required by law except in special cases (transportation of body in common carrier, death by certain communicable diseases). Customers may not be charged for unauthorized embalming.

A casket is not required for direct cremation.

A casket other than a wooden box or alternative container is not required for direct disposition of a body.

No claim can be made that embalming will do more than *temporarily* preserve a body.

Funeral directors must disclose, in writing, the goods and services (obituary notices, clergy honoraria, musician's honoraria, etc.) that are paid for by the funeral establishment in advance.

State Laws

Your state may have some additional laws pertaining to funeral practices. Most of these concern the mortuary and health codes in handling bodies. Contact the Board of Health or go to a law library in your state to get more information on specific laws.

The funeral industry has created its own watchdog called ThanaCap. This is the National Funeral Directors Association's complaint resolution agency. It is staffed by consumer advocates and will help you if you have a grievance. You can contact them at:

> ThanaCAP
> 11121 West Oklahoma Avenue
> Milwaukee, WI 53227
> (414) 541-2500

Outside of the industry, take your complaint to your state licensing board. Send a copy of your letter to your state Attorney General's office, your state legislator, and any local consumer agencies.

PRE-NEED OR BEFORE-NEED PLANS

There is a recent move within the funeral industry to sell price guaranteed funeral arrangements before there is an actual need or death. This pre-planning is supposed to alleviate stress, overspending, and funerals inappropriate to the decedent's wishes.

Most commonly, the purchaser of a pre-need plan pays in full or in installments for the type of funeral he/she wishes for himself. The interest that accrues goes to offset inflation so that your choices will still be covered at the time of death, even if it occurs years later.

Questions to ask before you sign a Pre-Need Contract

1. What if you change your mind, can you get your money back? Are there penalty fees?

2. Is the money given to the funeral director, placed with an insurance company, or held in trust until the death?

3. Is the interest used to offset inflation or does the funeral establishment get it?

4. What specific goods and services does the pre-need contract cover? These should be detailed so that inferior products can not be substituted at the time of death.

5. What laws in your state, if any, control pre-need arrangements? (In California, the Funeral Directors and Embalmers Laws provide that the consumer give no money to the funeral director but open a state-supervised trust account at a bank or savings association. The consumer retains control of the money and can withdraw it and revoke the contract with the funeral director at any time. If a service is price guaranteed, the interest on these monies can be withdrawn by the funeral establishment to use as they see fit. Therefore, should the mortuary cease to exist or you change your mind, you would regain your principal, but not your interest.)

6. What happens to principal and interest if the mortuary closes?

7. What happens if you die before final payments are made?

Advantages to the Pre-Need Contract

1. The buyer can leisurely plan and compare prices.

2. It relieves the survivors of any undue financial pressure.

3. It diminishes the emotional distress.

The American Association of Retired Persons suggests a lawyer be consulted before signing any pre-paid documents.

Alternatives to the Pre-Need Contract

1. Take out an additional life insurance policy to cover funeral costs.

2. Open a trust with a friend or relative who knows your wishes and can be depended upon to carry them out.

Should you choose to do either of the alternatives, be sure that you leave specific written instructions for those responsible for the disposition of your body. Do not put these instructions in a safe deposit box as it might be sealed upon your death. Give a copy to a friend or relative or let them know where such instructions can be found when you die.

There is a definite distinction between pre-need planning and pre-pay planning. It is a good idea for everyone to do some pre-planning, but whether or not you want to pay for these plans in advance will take some gathering of information on your part.

DEATH IN A FOREIGN COUNTRY

The United States Consulate is responsible for giving assistance in the case of death in a foreign country. Everyone traveling abroad should carry with his passport, instructions to be followed in case of death. This enables the Consul to carry out your wishes. It is very costly to return a body to the United States. For this reason, some Americans who die overseas choose to be buried in the country in which they die. If this is the case, burial is usually with regards to local customs. Or, you may choose cremation, where available, and have the cremains mailed to you for disposition at home.

In foreign countries, cremation does not necessarily mean cheaper. If you prefer the most economical disposition, so state in your instructions. It is also helpful if you list an alternative to your wishes in case your first choice is impractical or unavailable.

A "report of death" will be furnished to the next of kin by the consulate. This is the equivalent of a death certificate in the U.S. If the deceased has personal property, the consul, for a nominal fee, can serve as a "provisional conservator."

No matter when, how, or where you make funeral plans it can be emotionally and financially draining. Keep your expenditures in mind realizing that you will have to live with the outlay of the funeral for years to come. As one funeral director said, "I tell my clients that you can't make up for something you said or didn't say, did or didn't do, by overspending."

Be practical and realistic, while keeping in mind your emotional needs.

WARNING: There are unscrupulous people who read funeral notices for the purpose of robbing the family's home while they are gone. Please arrange for someone to house-sit while you are attending the funeral.

4.

Team up with Professional Advisors

People's lives have become complicated in today's world. We must keep track of vast amounts of paperwork, documents, and figures, each operating around a set of different rules or laws. It is no wonder that we put off dealing with the matters of our estates, or that frustration sets in so quickly when we do try to decipher the material and make good decisions.

Many job areas have been created because of the system we live in and must work through. There are highly trained professionals to help us through each hurdle of the bureaucracy. The size and complexity of your estate will determine the number and skill of the professionals you need. Your willingness to learn and take part will also determine how much professional help you need.

The more you know about your affairs, the easier it will be to select your advisory team. Not only will you save money, but you will gain confidence in your ability to make decisions.

DO YOUR HOMEWORK

Doing your homework takes a lot of time, but it is time well spent. Now that you're widowed, you have more time to spend on yourself. You will feel much better about yourself as you learn how to become more independent. With each mistake you make, you will learn a lesson. With each good decision you make, you will gain confidence in your abilities. This is a time for you to grow in areas that might have been previously unfamiliar to you. Even if you aren't particularly interested in the court system or finances, it is in your interest to learn as much as you can to protect your resources, which may be limited now that you are on your own.

Consider taking some classes through your community college, college extension, or parks and recreation departments. There are seminars and workshops offered by women's organizations, senior citizen groups, and government agencies.

Don't discount classes because of time or financial commitments. Most are very inexpensive and are of short duration. The subjects can be very general or very specific. A few examples of actual class titles found in a middle-sized metropolitan city include the following: Financial Planning, Personal Financial Planning, Financial Planning for the Not So Rich and Famous, Successful Budgeting, How to Get A Job, Write Your Own Will, Understanding the Financial Pages, Dealing Constructively with a Contractor, How to Buy a Car at the Best Price, and The New Tax Laws and How They Affect You.

Most seminar and workshop leaders are professionals who are either promoting their books, adding to their incomes, or soliciting new clients. Their credentials are usually listed along with the description of the class in the catalog or flyer. If you have any questions about the instructor, call the group or institution that is sponsoring the speaker and ask, before you register.

READ! There are books and articles on every subject you can imagine and more on subjects that you can't imagine. Visit your local library. If you haven't been to the library lately, you will discover some new things. Computers locate and print out magazine references, magazine articles are read on electronic screens, card catalogs have been replaced with automated viewers.

One thing that hasn't changed is the willingness of the librarian to help you locate the information you need. As you enter the library, look for the sign or ask directions to the reference section. Here, there are specially trained people who know how to locate anything and everything. The more specific your question or topic, the easier it will be for them to help you. Most will not give up until you are satisfied that you have the answer. If the branch you are using does not have the particular reference you need, they can direct you to another library. They may even have the library send the reference to them so that you don't have to go across town.

Don't be intimidated by any machines that you may need to use. The instructions are printed on the equipment in very simple language. If you need help, the librarian is always ready to give you a quick lesson. Soon, you will feel comfortable and know your way around the stacks. The library will become a warm place for you to do your homework.

NOTE: Some reference materials can be checked out, while others can not. Magazines usually can not be loaned. So, take paper and pencil with you for note-taking, or a lot of change so that you can use the copy machine.

Because laws and financial matters change so quickly, be sure that you read current material. Whereas older books may give you a good foundation for understanding the basics, you need to read up-to-date material to keep abreast of the ever-changing information.

Consider subscribing to magazines that offer information in the areas you are interested. Today, there are magazines on thousands of topics — business and finance, career and college, consumer service, retirement, self-improvement, accounting, business management, real estate, and many, many more. There are books that list all of the magazines published and a description of each. Ask your librarian to help you locate these.

There are government publications on thousands of subjects that you may write for. Many of these are free, while for others there is a nominal fee. Send for the list of publications catalog to see if it contains any pertinent information. There are two free catalogs, "U.S. Government Books" which lists the 1000 best selling titles, and "New Books", a bimonthly list of all government publications placed on sale in preceding months. Both of these may be obtained by writing:

Superintendent of Documents
Government Printing Office
Washington, DC 20402
(202) 783-3238

The Monthly Catalog of U.S. Government Publications is available through subscription or at a depository library.

The Consumer Information Center publishes a catalog four times a year. It selects the best consumer booklets that the federal government publishes and lists the title, along with a brief description of each. Many are free, the rest are of nominal cost. This is an excellent resource. Write for your free Consumer Information Catalog:

> Consumer Information Center — C
> P.O. Box 100
> Pueblo, CO 81002

The homework you do will accomplish several things for you. First, it will help you to evaluate the professional advisors you choose. If they can not answer some of your questions, or give poor answers, then you know to look elsewhere. If advisors see that you have a knowledge of the subject, they are less likely to give you a "snow job." Second, by doing your homework, you will know what information is required of you and what you want to accomplish with the advisor. Since most professionals charge by the hour, you will be saving yourself a lot of money. Third, you will be able to maintain control over your own affairs. Don't ever turn yourself or your financial matters entirely over to another person. No matter how much you trust that person or persons, no one can make the best decisions for you, but you.

An advisor is just that, an advice giver. They give advice based on the current rules and regulations and on the information given them by you. You pay well for that advice, but it may not be infallible. Use your advisor to accomplish your wants and needs.

On important matters, don't hesitate to get a second opinion, just as you would with a physician if you were facing major surgery.

PROFESSIONAL ADVISORS

As you are doing your homework, you are getting a clearer picture of who you need to help you. No one can be an expert in all areas. Professionals are becoming specialists. There are probate experts, tax experts, estate planners, insurance experts, corporate and business experts.

The size and complexity of your holdings will determine who and how many advisors you will need. There are overlapping services among professional advisors. One may be able to take care of several matters for you, instead of your having to have one for each task. That is part of the evaluating you will be doing as you interview your advisors. Here are some basic questions to ask everyone you are considering.

1. What are your qualifications? What licenses, credentials, and/or certifications do you hold? What is your educational background?

2. What are your areas of expertise?

3. How long have you been practicing your profession?

4. Of what professional organizations are you a member?

5. Do you offer a free initial consultation or get-acquainted interview? Many do as long as you are not asking for advice about your problem, but instead are seeking information about the advisor's training, knowledge, and business practices.

6. What is your fee structure? Is it possible to make monthly payments that fit my budget?

7. Will you be readily available to answer any questions or solve any problems that might arise?

8. Can I get in touch with you at odd hours in case of an emergency?

9. Are there any conflicts of interest that would prevent you from advising me objectively?

10. In the event you are unavailable, who will help me?

11. Are you willing to put your fees and estimates in writing?

12. Do you itemize your billings?

13. May I have a list of current clients?

What other things should you look for in the advisors you choose?

1. The location of their offices are geographically desirable.

2. The appearance of their offices reflect organization.

3. The secretary/receptionist is friendly and helpful.

4. The advisor is able to communicate effectively.

The most important test for an advisor is their ability to communicate with you. An advisor may be knowledgeable but have a manner that is abrupt or intimidating, condescending or negative. In which case, you would do better to find someone else. You must be able to relate matters to this person that perhaps no one else in the world knows. This has to be a person you trust with your money, your secrets, your wishes and goals. Make sure it is someone you feel good about. Some people call it a "gut" feeling. Listen to your instincts.

A Rule to think about

Don't select close friends or relatives. A problem arises if you are not happy with their performance. It is very hard to replace them without hurt feelings if they can not meet your needs. You may be more reluctant to speak freely about your concerns than you would be with a stranger.

Putting your team Together

Now that you have some general information on the selection of your team, let's get more specific. Of the six listed below, you may find that you need all or only one or two. Evaluate your situation along with your willingness to contribute your new knowledge to create your advisors.

ATTORNEYS

The discussion on advisors logically begins with attorneys. Unless the estate you are dealing with is very small, and the laws of your state provide simple means of dealing with said estates, you will need a lawyer. The sooner you make contact with an attorney, the sooner the matters dealing with the estate can be settled.

If you already have an attorney that you feel comfortable with, be sure that he has the knowledge to effectively deal with your new situation. He might be wonderful at criminal law, but know very little about estate law. If your attorney is in a large law firm, there is probably someone in the firm that deals with wills, probate, and estates. If so, that would be a good place to start your interview. If your present attorney is not in a diversified office, he should be able to recommend someone who is a specialist in that field.

Be wary of using your spouse's business attorney, especially if there is another partner involved. This amounts to a conflict of interest and you would do much better to have someone looking out solely for your interests.

If you have never had occasion to hire a lawyer, then you must begin your search from scratch. There are several places to look.

■ Ask friends, co-workers, small business owners, and relatives for recommendations. Find someone who is going through or has just gone through what you are experiencing and ask if they are pleased with their attorney.

■ Check with your local National Organization for Women group. They can recommend a lawyer to you.

■ The local bar association can give you a list of attorneys who specialize in the field you need.

■ The trust officer at your bank can tell you who they use.

■ There are lawyer referral services. Lawyers pay a fee to be placed on these referral lists.

■ A local law school can recommend someone.

■ The Yellow Pages list attorneys according to their areas of practice.

■ The Martindale-Hubbell Law Directory is an extensive state by state listing of attorneys. You will find a short biography along with the lawyer's field of specialization. Most libraries have the directory in their reference sections.

What will a lawyer do for you?

A lawyer will do as much or as little as you want. You can turn everything over to your attorney and say, "Take care of me," or you can delegate only the matters that you feel unqualified to handle. Obviously, the more you do, the less the whole process is going to cost you and/or the estate. Probate fees are set by statute. If the estate is not probated, then fees are on an hourly basis.

Attorneys can contact all possible sources of survivor benefits. They can write letters to your creditors, file the necessary papers with the courts, petition the court for disbursement of funds, and transfer deeds and titles to your name. They may be able to complete your tax forms.

Or, you can do a lot of it yourself, thereby saving the attorney's time and your money. Have all important documents with you when you see your attorney. Make a list of the family's names, birth dates, and social security numbers. Using the chapter on survivor benefits, contact possible benefit sources yourself. Your attorney can give you or tell you where to get the proper forms to do a lot of the work yourself. Use your lawyer to look over the work that you do, to insure that you are legally correct.

Be sure to select a lawyer that can speak your language. If legal terms are used that are unfamiliar, ask for an explanation in words that you can understand.

Wrongful death suits

If you feel that the death of your loved one was due to someone's negligence, you may want to file a wrongful death suit against the person or persons responsible. There are time limits on filing such suits. In most states, the statute of limitations for starting civil action is two years. In five states (California, Kentucky, Louisiana, Tennessee, and Washington, DC), it is one year. Others range from three to six years. In the case of a suit against a municipality or other government agency, the time may be less. An attorney who specializes in this field should be contacted immediately. Evidence needs to be collected before it gets lost or destroyed. Liability lawyers usually work on a contingency basis, which means they get a percentage of the money you receive should you win. Expenses will usually be added to that percentage. Should you lose, the attorney would collect nothing. Make sure that he also absorbs the cost of the expenses. You may still be liable for court costs. Contingency fees range from twenty-five to fifty percent with the average being thirty-three percent. Remember, you are dealing with a lawyer, so make sure you understand what you are signing, even if you must take it to another lawyer for clarification.

If you collected a sizeable life insurance benefit, the attorney will in many cases solicit the paying insurance company to provide for or divide the costs of the trial and investigation against the defendant. It is in the interest of the insurance company to do this, for in winning they recoup the amount of insurance paid to you from the court settlement.

ACCOUNTANTS

The next person on your advisory team should be an accountant. If you had one before the death of your spouse, the accountant's office would be one of your first stops. It is here that you should be able to get copies of forms that contain the information your lawyer will need to process the estate in the courts.

If you don't already have a list of your stock and bond securities, real estate holdings, retirement funds, etc., then the accountant should have these available to you.

In some instances, you may not want to continue using the same accountant you had with your spouse. As with other professions, the area of accounting is highly specialized. Some deal mainly with businesses, others with tax implications, and others with financial investing. Your needs may be entirely different and require a different expertise for handling estate matters.

If you are changing accountants or never used one before, the same general rules apply that were mentioned above. In addition, you need to know the different types of licensing and certification of accountants and what each can do for you. The following is a list to provide some guidance.

CPA — Certified Public Accountant. A CPA must pass a national test given by the American Institute of Certified Public Accountants and work for a public accounting firm for two years.

PA — Public Accountant. A PA is not certified. They do much the same type of work as a CPA, but are not able to represent you during tax audits or in tax court.

Tax Accountant. A tax accountant specializes in preparing tax returns and may represent you during an audit.

LLM — An attorney who specializes in tax law.

If you need an accountant, there are several good places to find one.

■ Recommendations from satisfied customers. Ask your friends and acquaintances.

■ Recommendations from your banker.

■ Recommendations from your attorney.

■ Call your state licensing board. While they can not guarantee competence, they can give you a list of currently licensed accountants.

What an accountant should do for you

Accountants should do more than just keep track of figures. They should keep you abreast of the latest tax laws and the ramifications of those laws on your money.

Typically, they make no recommendations with regards to investment, but they should be able to make projections in terms of tax liability or savings given the information concerning the investment you wish to make. Making projections is one of the most important aspects of accounting. If next April you are going to owe IRS $5000, you need to know well in advance. It is the job of your accountant to save you from paying penalties due to ignorance or neglect.

Will there be potential estate taxes? Do you need to file quarterly returns? How much is it going to cost you in taxes should you sell your stocks for ready cash? How will selling your spouse's motorhome and boat affect you? These are questions that an accountant will be able to answer.

If the estate is small, you may only need a tax preparer. Be certain that whom you choose is familiar with filing estate returns. Ask if they have ever done Federal Tax Form 706. If you live in a state that has "inheritance" or "death taxes," additional state returns must be filed. The following are sources for help with tax returns:

1. Enrolled Agents must pass a two day test administered by the U.S. Department of the Treasury. They may represent you before the IRS during an audit. Fees vary, but generally are less than those of a CPA. You can get a list of Enrolled Agents from the national organization by writing to:

National Association of Enrolled Agents
6000 Executive Blvd., Suite 205
Rockville, MD 20850
(301) 984-6232

2. **Volunteer Income Tax Association Program** is a volunteer group trained by the IRS and state tax agencies to assist people in filling out their returns. Contact your local IRS information center for location.

3. The IRS itself has information lines. The information is generally accurate, but not always. More complex questions can be difficult to answer over the telephone without knowing all the surrounding circumstances. If you need a detailed answer you would be well advised to seek a tax professional. The IRS is not bound by the information they give you over the phone.

4. **Commercial tax services** spring up everywhere during tax season. Fines for improper tax preparation have gotten stiff and this has helped weed out a few of the incompetents, but generally, if you have anything more than a simple tax return, go to someone who does taxes year round. Seasonal tax preparers are usually unfamiliar with the preparation of estate tax forms.

5. **Tax Counseling for the Elderly** is an IRS-funded program. Trained volunteers provide free service to older citizens. Ask your local senior citizen group for information about location of a Tax Counseling Center.

FINANCIAL ADVISORS

Before you make any decisions about how to spend or invest your survivor benefits, it would be wise to visit a financial advisor. Financial planners typically don't prepare tax returns. They are trained to analyze your assets, weigh them against your liabilities, and come up with recommendations. They might, after looking at your financial data sheets, tell you that you need to cut back on spending. They might show you where you have some extra money to invest. Investment recommendations are based on your financial goals and your personal investment philosophy.

You should talk with them before you make a major purchase such as buying a house, to see what type of financing is best, or how much you should put down on a down payment, or the maximum you can afford in monthly payments.

They will warn you if you are too heavy into credit, or

need to obtain lower house payments, etc. This is called assessing your financial history.

Typically, a financial advisor will look at what you have and what you expect to have in the future and balances it against current and future debt. This is accomplished by establishing a workable plan that fits your needs and your present situation, and then by giving you suggestions to implement your personal financial plan. This is followed up occasionally with current advice as your situation changes.

Good financial planners will pay for themselves many times over. Some charge a flat hourly fee. Others charge a commission on sales. Still others charge both. Be sure that you understand your financial advisor's fee structure.

Where do you find a financial planner?

■ Recommendations from happy clients.

■ Recommendations from bankers.

■ Recommendations from attorneys.

■ Recommendations from accountants.

■ By contacting the International Association of Financial Planners or the Institute of Certified Financial Planners (addresses below).

Financial Planners

The financial planning industry is a relatively new profession and is not yet regulated by the state or federal government. But, there are persons who have specialized training in this field and hold certifications.

CFP — Certified Financial Planners have passed a six part exam with the College for Financial Planning in Denver, Colorado. ChFC — Chartered Financial Consultants have passed a ten part exam through the American College and do financial planning.

CFA — Chartered Financial Analysts have taken a three part exam over a period of three years and specialize in portfolio management and analysis of stocks and bonds.

RIA — Registered Investment Advisors have filled out a form and paid a fee to the Security and Exchange Commission and are registered by them to give investment advice.

Stockbroker — Stockbrokers buy and sell securities. They work on a commission which amounts to a set fee or a percentage every time you buy or sell stocks or bonds.

Investment Advisor, Counselor, or Broker — Investment advisors may also sell stocks and bonds, as well as build your portfolio through other types of investments such as real estate partnerships. They typically charge a percentage of the holdings they manage, limiting their services to substantial accounts.

JD — Financial planners who hold a degree in law.

Estate Planner — Estate planners analyze your situation from your heirs' point of view. Their goal is to minimize the state and federal taxes of the estate.

Trust Officers — Some banks have trust officers that will manage your estate. They can either invest your assets or simply hold them for safekeeping. Banking institutions tend to be very conservative. There are often minimums on the size of the estate they will manage, and the fees are rather steep.

Security Analyst — Security Analysts study individual stocks and bonds to decide whether they should be bought or sold. They look at the company's record, their financial reports, their management and so on, to make a determination.

After studying the above list, you can get an idea of who would best meet your needs. Some overlap into other areas, so be sure to ask where their experience is focused.

The Securities and Exchange Commission and the National Association of Security Dealers are the watchdogs for the securities industry. While they can not certify competence, they do assure you of the broker's ethical conduct and trustworthiness. If you have any questions or a complaint about a particular broker, contact the SEC by writing:

> Securities and Exchange Commission
> 450 Fifth Street, N.W.
> Washington, DC 20549
> (202) 272-7450

Consumer complaints concerning financial planners who are members of IAFP or ICFP may be lodged by contacting:

> International Association of Financial Planning
> 2 Concourse Parkway, Suite 800
> Atlanta, GA 30328
> (800) 241-2148

Institute of Certified Financial Planners
Two Denver Highland
10065 East Harvard Avenue
Suite 320
Denver, CO 80231
(303) 751-7600

BANKERS

The banking industry is changing rapidly. It is no longer simply a place where you have a checking and/or a savings account. With the changing of government regulations, banks are able to offer more services and to be more competitive. There are all kinds of special accounts and incentives for opening those accounts. Finding a geographically convenient bank is no longer a problem as one can be found on almost every corner. Safety is no longer the concern it was during the Great Depression, as deposits up to $100,000 are insured by the Federal Deposit Insurance Corporation or the Federal Savings and Loan Insurance Corporation.

Before you choose a bank, do some homework.

■ Make a list of the banks that are geographically convenient.

■ Make a list of all of the services you might be interested in. That list might include: checking account, savings account, loans, safe deposit box, trust department, bank credit cards, and notary services.

Now you are ready to start visiting the banks on your list. You can begin by sitting down with the new accounts person. Tell this person that you are shopping for a bank and you have some questions. First, you want to know if your deposits are insured with either FDIC or FSLIC. Ask for an explanation of how this system works and how long it would take to get your money if the bank actually did fail. Second, ask the new accounts person what services their bank offers. Banks always have lots of brochures explaining the different services and departments. Check your list of needed services that you made earlier to see if each is addressed. Third, ask when the bank is open for business. Some banks are now open on Saturday and have extended hours. Fourth, make sure there is a twenty-four hour automated teller machine if you want access to your account at all times. Ask what the maximum automated teller withdrawal limit is per day. You may also be interested in banking by mail if it is difficult for you to get to the bank, so ask if this is provided. Fifth, what are the interest rates on checking and savings accounts? If you are thinking of buying certificates of deposit, compare their interest rates to others.

By now, you should have a pretty good idea of what this bank has to offer. Take your notes and brochures home and look over them. Repeat this process with the other banks on your list.

Eliminate any bank that did not meet your needs. Exclude any that did not feel comfortable or accommodating. Now, call the bank or banks that you liked and ask for an appointment with an officer of the bank. This might be a loan officer or a manager. You want someone with authority. At your appointment, evaluate the officer according to his ability to answer your questions, his willingness to take time for you, and his attitude and sensitivity toward your situation.

Why do you need a banker?

It is important for you to establish a personal contact at the bank where you do business. A good banker can make your life a lot easier. When you have a problem, you can go directly to "your banker" who will use his clout to intercede or expedite a solution and can assist you in identifying the proper people to contact in non-local departments. A banker can give you telephone numbers that will speed answers. They can guarantee signatures so that stock certificates can be transferred. Bankers can give you advice and moral support. They can help you with financial statement forms. If, later down the road, you want to borrow money, you have someone to go to who already knows you. You want someone who will take a personal interest in you, and a good banker will do this.

A TIP FROM A BANKER: Do not spread your funds out too thinly. It is better not to deal with more than two banking institutions. First of all, it gets too complicated keeping everything straight. Second, the more money you have deposited in a bank, the more clout you have. Many banks circulate lists to the bank officers of those people who have $5000 or more in their banks. If you are one of these people, a good officer will make a point of knowing who you are and catering to your needs.

INSURANCE AGENTS

Soon after the death of a spouse, you will need to reevaluate your insurance. There are many reasons for this. You may no longer be covered by your spouse's health insurance, you may never have had a life insurance policy of your own, your housing situation may be changing, thereby needing different types or amounts of insurance, or you may be deleting automobiles, boats, recreational vehicles, etc.

A good insurance agent will be happy to take the time to do this evaluation with you.

When looking for an insurance company, begin with *Best's Insurance Reports*. One volume contains Property and Casualty, the other contains Life and Health. These volumes can be found at your library and at most insurance offices. They contain a wealth of information. According to Best's, "The objective of Best's Rating System is to evaluate the various factors affecting the overall performance of an insurance company in order to provide our opinion as to the company's relative financial strength and ability to meet its contractual obligations."

Best's contains complete reports and ratings of nearly 1,650 life and health insurance companies. It uses a rating system using A+ (superior) to C (Fair), to rate each firm. These ratings are based on the annual financial statements of the insurance companies. You may or may not understand all of the facts and figures listed, but you can definitely learn a lot about your insurance company.

In 1905 there were only 95 legal reserve life insurance companies operating in the U.S. Today, that number has grown to over 2,400. Best's makes it easier for you to choose a good company.

Another excellent feature of *Best's* is its list of state

officials having charge of insurance affairs for all fifty states and the District of Columbia. The address, name, official title, and telephone number is given, simplifying any complaints or questions.

Best's Directory of Recommended Insurance Attorneys and Best's Directory of Insurance Adjusters are two other publications that you may have occasion to use.

Now that you've chosen the company that you want, it's time for the serious business of selecting an agent. The owner of an insurance company said, "Insurance companies are legitimate. They are not going to beat you out of a nickel. They pay what the contract says. What's not always legitimate is the agent."

Good insurance agents sell service as well as a policy. They should be on top of any changes in your needs and keep you advised as well as posted on changes within the company, laws, etc.

A reputable agent takes into consideration the amount of money you can afford to spend and will work within that to provide the best coverage possible. A good agent doesn't want you to be "insurance poor." If an agent gets pushy or encourages you to spend more than your budget allows, then find someone who respects your current situation.

A conscientious agent will quickly catch and correct mistakes, will list a home phone number on a business card, so that you can get in touch with him in an emergency, and will return your calls promptly. Ask for a list of clients so you can check this out.

While you want an established insurance company, don't discount agents who have been in the business for only a year. Typically, they are eager and work harder for your business. Also, their training is more recent and they may be more current on the new regulations and policies.

It is also important to have an agent who has an office staff. This frees the agent to take care of your insurance needs and not the mundane paperwork.

The highest designation for life and health agents is Certified Life Underwriter. For automobile and homeowner agents, it is Chartered Property and Casualty Underwriter.

REAL ESTATE AGENTS

A competent real estate salesperson can be an important member of your advisory team. After the death of a spouse, you may want to sell vacation property or rentals, or buy a smaller home or condominium. The entire process can be made easier or more difficult depending on the knowledge, ability, and enthusiasm of your broker or agent.

There are independent brokers who work out of their homes and there are agents who work in large firms. Some specialize in commercial property, others in residential. Depending on what you want to buy or sell, choose someone whose specialty fits your needs.

The field of real estate sales is highly competitive. The seller commonly pays the agent's fees which are usually based on a percentage of the selling price. Because the seller is paying the bill, the agent is working for the seller. This sounds rather obvious until you get in the midst of negotiations and then sometimes wonder just whose side the agent is on. After all, the salesperson only gets paid if the sale goes through.

How do you find a good realtor?

■ Referrals from friends, relatives, business people, advisors such as lawyers, accountants, bankers, and financial advisors. As with other advisors, this is the best way.

■ If referrals are not available to you, then select the largest real estate firm in the town or city in which you wish to buy or sell. Ask to speak to the broker. Tell the broker that you want the name of the top salesperson. There is a difference between the top lister (one who goes out and gets listings) and the top seller (one who actually closes the deal). It is hard to go wrong with this combination.

■ Some real estate schools will give you referrals. Agents must return to school for periodic training that updates their knowledge of laws, regulations, and procedures.

After you have a referral, check out the agent's background. You want someone who has experience in the area and is a member of the local multiple listing service. If they are a member of the Board of Realtors, you can check with the Board to see if there have been any complaints, censures, or reprimands involving the agent.

Conversely, should you have any complaints, contact the:

National Association of Realtors
777 14th St., N.W.
Washington, DC 20005
(202) 383-1000

for the address and phone number of your local Board. Only sales agents who are members of the NAR have the right to use the term "Realtor." Every Realtor is subject to NAR rules and regulations, and subject to their standards of conduct.

There is a difference between salespersons and brokers. Sales agents work under the supervision of a broker. Brokers must sign every contract a sales agent negotiates. They are also responsible for maintaining records for a specified time. They must maintain a trust fund for deposits on sales. They must have been a sales agent for a specified number of years. After meeting the qualifications for brokers in the state in which they live, brokers are then licensed by that state.

What should you expect from your real estate agent?

1. Your agent should take the time to explain things, not assume that you are already aware or informed.

2. They should keep in close touch by contacting you periodically to let you know what they are doing.

3. Their fee structure should be in keeping with other agents in your area.

4. They should be willing to tell you in writing if, when, and how many times they plan to advertise your property in the newspaper, through open house, a multiple tour (where other agents tour your home), and office tours (where the other salespeople within the firm tour your property).

5. Your agent should be a member of multiple listing. In this way, a description of your property will be seen by many other agents, thus giving you more exposure.

6. You should be informed every time the agent wishes to show your property. They should clear all appointments with you.

7. They should send you copies of the ads they place.

8. They should give you help and suggestions in making your home its most appealing. This might include cleaning out closets, removing furniture, arranging flowers, baking cookies, painting, etc.

9. The agent should do a comparative analysis to help you reach a fair market price. This compares your home to others in your neighborhood. It shows what other homes sold for and how they compare to yours in size and condition. Using this information, a good agent will be able to advise you of a fair asking price.

10. Your agent should always keep appointments and be very prompt. Likewise, so should you. Time is valuable to both of you.

When you find an agent you like, make sure that there are no plans to make a move to another firm while holding your listing. A listing stays with the firm, not with the agent.

Try to get everything the agent promises in *writing!*

THE TEAM: Attorneys, accountants, financial planners, bankers, insurance agents, and real estate agents can all be vital players on your team. The goal is to guide you as painlessly as possible through the process of dealing with the details of death. You are the captain of the team. After listening to the professional advice of your hand-picked players, you make the calls. Your willingness to learn, through continuing education classes and reading current material, will serve you well. You are ready to tackle all problems that might arise.

5.

Understanding Wills and Probate

Wills conjure up all sorts of movie scenes in our minds.We picture the mourning sons and daughters gathered around Father's huge desk in the study. The family attorney sits in ol' Dad's leather chair, a foreboding look in his eye. He has called everyone together for the reading of the Will. The lawyer realizes there will be an outcry of protest from the wayward daughter, when she realizes she has been disinherited. The playboy son will be shocked at the pittance of an allowance he will receive. Yes, only the nurse who cared for him all of these years will leave this meeting pleased at its outcome. Father has gotten the last laugh.

Whereas, this scenario is a frequent one in the old movies and on television screens from time to time, it is far from the reality of the real world. Many of us associate Wills with wealth. We see no reason to Will away our small estates, trusting that our spouses or children will end up with it in any event. Why go through the hassle and expense of making a Will?

The purpose of this chapter is threefold:
■ To help you understand the basics of a Will,
■ To explain the probate process, and
■ To outline your responsibilities as an executor or administrator of an estate.

The following was written to take away much of the mystery concerning Wills and probate. It will enable you to comprehend more of what your attorney is saying as he reads the Will. If your spouse did not leave a Will, you will know the procedure for dealing with intestacy (the distribution of an estate when there is no Will). Although all of the information is accurate at the time of writing, laws and statutes are forever evolving to meet the needs of a changing society. Check with an attorney on the current laws of your state before taking any action.

If, after completing this chapter, you decide that leaving a Will is part of wise estate planning, then you will be interested in the discussion of trusts in Chapter Fourteen, "Financial Planning," and in Chapter Thirteen, "Taxes and Death."

According to a study done by the American Bar Association, only fifty percent of the population have Wills, and half of those are outdated. Perhaps one reason for this is that people are uninformed as to what a Will is and what it can do.

Simply stated, a Will expresses your desires for what happens to your worldly goods after your death. It provides for an efficient transferral of your property to those you want to have it.

THE IMPORTANCE OF A WILL

There are many reasons for having a Will, and very few for not having one. A properly planned and executed Will can save your heirs many, many of your hard earned dollars. A good financial planner or attorney with estate planning background can show you the various ways of minimizing taxes before and after your death, through your estate plan and Will.

A Will gives you, rather than a government agency, the opportunity of choosing those you want to inherit your property. It also gives you the choice of guardians for your minor children as well as for the estate they inherit.

A Will helps to establish a domicile (place of residence). This is especially important if you own property in more than one state or move frequently from state to state. Without having domicile established, you risk overlapping claims to state death or inheritance taxes. For property owned in states other than domicile, ancillary probate proceedings must be initiated in those states.

In many many states, a Will can be a perfect vehicle for avoiding probate or for filing a Summary Administration in small estates. (Typically, small refers to no real estate and less than $60,000 total assets). Check with your attorney for your state's requirements. Summary Administration is a sort of "mini" probate.

Although Wills should be periodically reviewed and updated, provisions can be made in your Will to cover contingencies that may occur between the time you write your Will and the time of your death. For example, Aunt Mary dies the week after you have your Will drawn. She bequeaths $200,000 worth of stocks to you. A good Will makes provisions for these types of situations so that if you should die soon after, the distribution of the property inherited from Aunt Mary will still be covered in the language of your Will.

In a Will, you name a person (executor(trix)) to be responsible for the handling of the matters of your estate. Without a Will, the court may appoint someone you would not have chosen.

The reasons for not having a Will are time and money. Yes, it will take a little time for you to write down what you have and to decide who you want to have it. It will take a little time to discuss your desires with a professional advisor to see if your ideas are financially sound. You will have to make a couple of trips to the lawyer's office. It will cost you some money, though not as much as you might think, to have a Will written. Most attorneys have set fees for drawing up simple wills, so shop around. Now, you need to decide whether a few hours of your time and the amount of money you would spend on a night-on-the-town is worth the great amount of time and the great amount of money it is going to save your heirs.

If you're still not convinced, let's talk a little more about what happens to your estate if you die intestate (without a Will). Laws vary greatly from state to state in regards to the decedent's property. Each state has a "Statute of Descent and Distribution." An excellent resource for Inheritance Rights as well as laws pertaining to Marriage, Dissolution of Marriage, Domestic Violence, Reproductive Rights, Unmarried Couples, Fair Employment, and much more is *The State-By-State*

Guide to Women's Legal Rights by the National Organization for Women/Legal Defense and Education Fund and Dr. Renee Cherow-O'Leary (McGraw-Hill Paperbacks, 1987). Check at your bookstore or the local NOW office for a copy.

If you were to use the NOW guide to compare each state, you would see that there are few common provisions. Initially, it was my intent to chart the state-by-state provisions for you, but as research indicated, it would be impractical if not impossible. Here are a few examples to illustrate the wide differences of provisions for surviving spouses when no Will has been left.

In Arkansas, the surviving spouse is entitled to the entire estate only if he/she has been married for three years or more and the decedent left no children or grandchildren. If they were married less than three years and there are no children or grandchildren, surviving spouse gets one-half. If the deceased left children or grandchildren and he and his wife were married less than three years, the surviving spouse gets nothing.

In New York, the surviving spouse is entitled to the entire estate if there are no other heirs. One child; spouse gets $4000 in money or personal property plus one-half of the estate, child gets the rest. More than one child; spouse get $4000 and one-third of the estate. If there are no children, but the decedent's parent(s) are alive, the spouse get $25,000 in money or property and one-half of the estate, while the parent(s) get the remainder.

In California (a community property state) the surviving spouse gets all of the community property. Spouse will also get all of the separate property (see explanation of terms in Chapter Eight) if decedent left no children, parents, siblings, or issue of siblings deceased or alive. Spouse gets one-half of the separate property if decedent left one child or issue of a deceased child or if no issue, a parent(s), or their issue. If the decedent had more than one child or one child and the issue of one or more deceased children or left issue of two or more deceased children, the spouse is entitled to one-third.

These examples are meant to give you an idea of how courts are required to deal with estates that are not provided for through a Will.

Distributing and settling the assets of an estate without the protection of a Will can increase the time and expense of probate proceedings. Petitions and notices must be filed, bonds must be posted (can be very costly), and court approval on many matters must be sought.

Venita Van Caspel, in her book, *Money Dynamics for the New Economy* (Simon and Schuster, 1986), states that, "In reality, everyone has a will — either the one that you have written to accomplish your own wishes or the one the state will write for you after your death."

With few limitations, you are given the legal right to dispose of your property as you see fit. Generally, you must provide for a spouse and for minor children. Other than that, if the Will is executed properly, according to laws of the state wherein it is subscribed, it is difficult to dispute.

Right of election

Most states give the surviving spouse the right to "elect" or "take" against the Will. This means that if you do not like the terms of your deceased spouse's Will as it applies to your share, you may choose to receive what the state laws would provide for you as if there had been no Will. State laws generally provided a minimum of one-third. Those states which do not make the right of election provision are Arizona, California, Georgia, Louisiana, Nevada, New Mexico, Texas, and Washington. The states of Alabama and South Carolina provide for wives only.

Rights of curtesy and dower

Some states make special provisions for the surviving spouse called Rights of Curtesy (husband) and Rights of Dower (wife). These laws state that the surviving spouse is entitled to the use of a minimum of one-third of the deceased spouse's property (real estate only, except in the states of Kentucky and Arkansas where personal property is included) for as long as the surviving spouse lives. Arkansas, Hawaii, Kentucky, Massachusetts, Michigan, Ohio, Vermont, Virginia, Washington, DC, and the state of West Virginia have provisions for curtesy and dower.

TYPES OF WILLS

There are four types of Wills.

1. Nuncupative Wills are oral Wills whose restrictions and limitations are so great that this should not be considered by anyone who really cares what happens to their estates. They are recognized in about one-half of the states, but limited to personal property of limited amounts. Restrictions on who may make nuncupative wills vary among states, but fall into one of three categories — soldiers in actual service or mariners at sea, those in imminent peril of death who die from that peril, or persons during their last illness. Two witnesses are required and the provisions of the Will must be written within a few days of the oral declaration.

2. Holographic Wills are Wills in which the material provisions are written entirely in testator's (person writing the Will) handwriting. There are specific bits of information that must be included such as the month, day, and year and a sentence that says that the document you are writing is intended to be your Will. Although it is not necessary that it be witnessed, it must be signed by the testator. The problem with holographic Wills is that they are subject to long litigation. It is much easier to contest a holographic Will than a formal Will. If you decide to go this route, it is strongly suggested they you pay an attorney for fifteen or twenty minutes of time and have the finished document read. In this way, the proper structure of the Will is assured.

Holographic Wills are valid in the following twenty-six states: Alaska, Arizona, Arkansas, California, Colorado, Idaho, Kentucky, Louisiana, Maine, Michigan, Mississippi, Montana, Nebraska, Nevada, New Jersey, North Carolina, North Dakota, Oklahoma, Pennsylvania, South Dakota, Tennessee, Texas, Utah, Virginia, Washington, DC, West Virginia, and Wyoming.

Because laws are constantly changing, verify the validity of holographic Wills in your state before you consider this option. A phone call to any attorney who writes Wills should be able to tell you.

3. Statutory Wills are pre-printed forms where the testator merely fills in the blanks. California developed two types of forms for its residents. One is called the "California Statutory Will" and the other the "California Statutory Will With Trust." These are valid legal documents in the state of California. Because no variations are allowed, their use is rather limited to those with uncomplicated holdings who wish to include very few heirs. It does provide for an executor, guardian, and the waiving of bond for the executor and guardian. Two witnesses must sign. The rules and limitations are printed on the back of the form and should be read very carefully. Again it is suggested that you should choose this type of Will, have a lawyer look it over.

Other states may eventually follow suit and produce statutory Wills. It took California years to produce an acceptable legal document, so your wait may be long. Check with an attorney to see if your state has this type of Will in the making.

4. Formal (sometimes called Witnessed) Wills are by far the "safest" way to distribute your assets. Safest meaning least chance of having the Will "set aside" (legalese term meaning invalidated or thrown out). Formal Wills must adhere to certain legal requirements including the following:

■ The document must be in writing. Computer disks and video tapes may accompany or be a reading of the Will, but can not replace the written document.

■ It must be signed by the testator at the end of the document. The judge looks at everything above the signature and nothing below. A "P.S." after the signature will be disregarded.

■ The signing by the testator must be in the presence of at least two witnesses (New Hampshire, South Carolina, and Vermont require three).

■ Thirty states plus the District of Columbia, state that the witnesses must be disinterested. By disinterested it is meant that they will not inherit either outright or through marriage any portion of the estate. Neither may they have been entitled to inherit under intestate provisions.

■ There must be a statement of intent, i.e., "I declare this to be my Will."

■ The document must be dated.

■ The county and state where the Will is executed must be stated.

■ The testator must meet minimum age requirements. Generally, this is 18. Exceptions are found in the states of Georgia (14 years) and Wyoming (19 years). Some states have lower ages if the person is in the military service, married, or widowed.

■ Testator must have mental capacity. The capacity requirements are less than contractual requirements and include the testator being able to state his name, being able to name and recognize "the natural objects of his bounty" (his heirs), know what he is doing, and understand the nature and extent of the property that he holds. The witnesses who sign the Will are stating not only that they witnessed the signing of the testator's name, but also the testator's mental capacity to do so and the fact that he was under no influence or duress at the time.

■ Surviving spouse and in almost every state, children, and sometimes grandchildren, must be mentioned in the Will. This does not mean that you must leave them something. What it does mean is that you list their names, e.g., "I am married to John Smith and I have two children Mary Smith and Robert Smith. I have one grandchild Louise Brown, born to my deceased daughter Alice Brown."

■ An executor of the will must be nominated. Whom do you want responsible for carrying out the provisions of your Will?

OPTIONAL PROVISIONS IN A WILL

The above list specifies the mandatory provisions of a Will; what the law requires. There are optional provisions which, while not being legally required, can be very significant. These include the following:

1. Naming an alternate executor and guardian. This is very important, if for some reason, the first choice can not or will not accept appointment.

2. A stipulation for the waiving of the bond requirement. Executors and guardians must be bonded. Perfor-

mance bonds insure that the person responsible handles the estate prudently and honestly. The amount of the bond is determined by a percentage of the estate and can be very costly to those chosen. Unless you waive the need for the bond in your Will, then it automatically will be enforced.

3. Granting someone the power to buy, sell, or operate your business.

4. Inserting a "No Contest" clause. This basically says that any heirs who contest your Will get nothing.

5. Disinheritance of any heir should be spelled out. Simply omitting the name of someone you don't want to receive your property can be risky. Make a statement that you are intentionally making no provision for the person.

6. You may wish to give specific gifts to certain people. Examples might be, "My gold pocket watch to my brother George. My antique dining room table to my friend Molly."

7. Designating "Class Gifts." After you list the specific gifts, you can lump everything that is left and say, "I give the residue of my estate to my children."

8. Making provisions for predeceased heirs. This would become important if your child should die before you and you want his/her share to go to his/her issue (child, grandchild).

9. Providing for the residue of the estate. The residue is anything left over after all specific bequeaths, debts, expenses, and taxes have been paid. It can be very sizable and is often the largest part of the estate.

10. Establishing trusts and appointing trustees giving them general powers and instructions.

11. Allocating funds to pay taxes.

12. Although not required, numbering and initialing each page can prevent admission or deletion of pages.

REVOCATION OF A WILL

A Will can be revoked by burning it, shredding it, or writing on the face of it (interlineation invalidates provisions in the Will which are crossed out).

The best way to revoke a Will is with another Will. In the new Will you would state, "I revoke all Wills and Codicils previously made by me," or something to this effect.

What if you only want to make one change in your Will?

If the change is not complicated, thereby affecting other provisions of the Will, you can have a codicil drawn. It is simply an amendment to your original Will. Most attorneys recommend that you don't overdo the codicils or they can make the Will ambiguous. It is better to start all over with a new Will if the changes become numerous or complicated.

Codicils must be witnessed just as Wills. The testator would say to his/her witnesses, "This is a codicil to my Will." They would each witness the testator's signature and then sign themselves.

NOTE: Joint Tenancy with Right of Survivorship supercedes a Will. The person with whom you hold these types of ownership will inherit these assets regardless of what is stated in your Will. See Chapter Eight, "Transferring Assets," for further explanation of Joint Tenancy.

PROBATING A WILL

You now have a basic understanding of what a Will does and what is required to have a valid one. To insure that the Will being enforced is indeed your Will and that the provisions of your Will are carried out, lawmakers instituted a process called Probate.

Probate Court is a designated court which has the power to administer an estate. In most states, there is a time limit within which a Will must be filed with the court. This will vary state-to-state but generally will be about ten to thirty days. Your attorney can advise you on the time limit or you can contact the probate court yourself and ask.

If there is no Will, you must report this fact to the probate court. Time limits are usually commensurate with those of filing a Will.

The purpose of probate

There are several reasons for probating an estate:

1. To insure the authenticity of the Will. Signature of testator is verified. Codicils are examined. Pages are examined for any unusual markings or placement that might indicate additions or omissions to original document.

2. To satisfy creditors. Notice is given in newspapers that the estate is being probated and if there are any claims against the estate, these must be filed within a certain amount of time (time limits vary state-to-state, but typically run three to six months). Any claim filed after the designated limit is not subject to payment. All timely claims are scrutinized for validity and paid, provided enough money exists within the estate to do so. Legal fees and probate costs are included in the debts that must be paid by the estate.

3. To provide for the collection of all taxes due the state and federal governments. This is accomplished with the inventory of assets of the decedent at time of death. A report is filed in the court for the state tax commissioner's office. This report, along with a list of separate property, is forwarded to the tax commissioner. Similar procedures are followed for federal taxes.

4. To appoint an executor(trix) (when there is a Will), or an administrator(trix) (when no Will exists). The duties of an executor are discussed in detail later in this chapter. It can save the estate money if the spouse is given this appointment.

5. To clear titles to property. Any property that was held solely by the decedent must be transferred to the rightful heirs.

6. To oversee the distribution of all assets of the estate to the rightful heirs under the provisions of the Will or in the case of intestacy, under the provisions of the state laws.

7. To protect the interests of minors and incompetents.

The Probate Estate

That portion of the estate which must pass through probate is called the probate estate. Not all property is subject to probate. Assets that pass directly to the heirs without benefit of probate proceedings include the following:

■ Assets held in joint tenancy. By definition, any property held as such passes to the surviving tenant(s) upon the death of one of the owners. This includes bank accounts.

■ Assets held in Living or "Intervivos" Trust.

■ Community property held in joint tenancy.

■ Life insurance policies, provided the beneficiary is

alive and the beneficiary is not the estate.

■ Some small estates. Many states have provisions for the settling of small estates through the use of an affidavit to transfer property. In California, for example, personal property amounting to no more than $60,000 can be handled with an affidavit as long as the value of the real property does not exceed $10,000.

■ Annuity contracts.

■ Totten Trusts. Sometimes called Informal Trusts, Pay On Death Accounts, or Savings Bank trusts, these types of accounts are controlled entirely by the owner of the account during his lifetime. The named beneficiary has no rights to the account until the death of the trustee, at which time the proceeds pass to the beneficiary without going through probate.

■ Any other assets listed in beneficiary form. These would include IRA's and Keogh's and U.S. Savings Bonds.

What is subject to probate?

Generally, all assets distributed through a Will, including assets held as separate or owned only by the decedent, and any property held as tenants in common, are subject to probate proceedings.

The disadvantages of probating an estate

Depending on the size of the estate and the claims against it, probate proceedings can be costly and time consuming. Many states have set fees that are based on a percentage of the fair market value of the probate estate. This is the gross value, not the value after all liabilities have been satisfied. Other states allow "reasonable compensation" for fees pertaining to probate. In these states, it would be wise to shop around for the most reasonable fee. If you feel that you have been overcharged, bring it to the attention of the probate judge and he will rule on the matter. Those persons due compensation can include the attorney, executor, accountant, and various appraisers, depending on the types of property involved.

Besides the expense involved, there is the element of time. The average probate for a simple estate is about one year. If there are complications such as law suits or the estate is quite large, it may take years to settle.

The third disadvantage involves privacy. Probate proceedings are public record. Creditors are invited through newspapers to make claims. Anyone can find out the provisions of the court. This may or may not be important to you.

The advantages of probating an estate

All of the advantages center around settlement of claims and disputes against the estate in the future. Through probate, indisputable title is transferred to the heirs, the assets of the estate are precisely distributed within the laws of the state, thus minimizing future conflicts, and creditors are dispensed with once and for all (maximum time limits are set for them to make claims). This would be especially important if the decedent owned a business.

DUTIES OF THE EXECUTOR/ADMINISTRATOR

As stated earlier, one of the obligations of the probate court is to appoint an executor of the Will or an administrator of the estate, if there is no Will. If one has not been nominated in a Will, the probate judge usually appoints the surviving spouse or next of kin. If the spouse was named in the Will as executrix (female executor), the executor fees can be waived.

Unless provided for in the Will, the executor will need to be bonded. This bond is based on a percentage of the probate estate and can be substantial. The performance bond guarantees that the executor does not mishandle the funds entrusted to him. Duties of the executor and administrator are similar, except the administrator does not have the benefit of a Will to guide his decisions. Disbursements to heirs will be guided by state laws rather than decedent's wishes. Otherwise, the procedures are much the same for executors and administrators. The following list of duties can help you understand the requirements of the job. Don't be intimidated by the length of the list. Some points may not apply to your spouse's estate, while others will be accomplished with the help of your attorney.

1. Within a few days of the death (this varies with each state) the Will must be filed with the probate court. If there is no Will, the court must be notified.

2. Petition the court for appointment as executor/administrator.

3. After appointment as executor/administrator, open a bank account to facilitate the collection of monies due the estate and to pay the valid debts of the estate.

4. Inventory all assets. This includes personal property, bank accounts, collectibles, artwork, jewelry, real estate, securities, and anything else that the decedent owned. You may need to hire appraisers or they may be appointed to place an accurate value on some items. Banks have "blue books" to help you determine the value of vehicles.

List all of the decedent's separate property together; then, list property held in joint tenancy or community property with spouse; finally, list the property held as tenants in common with other individuals. Property held in trust should also be listed. Property in the decedent's safe deposit box is inventoried.

5. List all costs of administration (appraisers, attorneys, accountants, court fees, executor's fee if any, etc.). One-half of the mortgage payments, one-half of the property taxes, one-half of the insurance premiums, and one-half of any other expenses incurred on property owned jointly can also be included in these expenses.

6. List all claims against the estate (funeral expenses, hospital, doctor, lab fees, other creditors, taxes for the past year and the current year.)

7. File State Inheritance and Federal Estate Tax forms. All tax monies due must be paid before any property can be transferred to heirs.

8. Where applicable, ascertain the amount of allowance needed by the surviving spouse and children and petition the court to approve and release these funds.

9. Pay all bills of the estate. CAUTION! Funeral expenses and medical expenses may be paid before the time limit for creditor's claims is up, for they take precedence over other claims; but the remainder of the bills should not be paid until all have been received and you are certain there is

enough money in the estate to meet the payments.

10. Collect obligations to the estate. There may be monies owed to the estate, make a list of these and collect where possible.

11. Liquidate any assets in order to satisfy creditors if necessary. Federal death tax laws require that liquidated assets be placed only in government insured instruments. Be sure to consult your financial advisor on tax implications revolving around selling assets.

12. If there is a business, make decisions for continued management or sale. This area may have been provided for in the Will and have a separate administrator who is qualified to make these kinds of decisions. If not, seek advice from your professional team.

13. Provide for the safekeeping and insurance coverage where applicable for any of the estate assets (house, vehicles, equipment). If only half of the asset is the estate's you must make sure that half is fully covered.

14. Prepare an accounting for the courts. This shows everything you received and everything you paid out. If you are the sole beneficiary of the estate, the court may not require an accounting, but you will still need it for tax purposes.

15. Petition the court for disbursement of assets to the rightful heirs. This includes any specific gifts.

16. Disburse the assets. Pay the executor. Pay the attorney.

17. Advise beneficiaries of the new tax basis of inherited assets. Taxes will be discussed in detail in Chapter Thirteen.

Don't be afraid to use your attorney. He should be willing to explain and advise when asked to do so. Don't hesitate to call him with any questions that you might have. As executor of the Will, you will receive copies of all documents that come through the court. Be sure that you understand them. Keep these papers in a safe place so that you may refer to them if needed.

Make sure that your attorney files petitions in a timely manner. You want probate completed as soon as possible. By providing the needed information to your attorney, he will be able to act as quickly as the courts allow.

6.

Notifying
Those Concerned

There are numerous people and businesses that you need to contact concerning the death of your spouse. Some should be notified immediately, others within a few days, others within a few weeks. There are several points to notifying persons that are often overlooked. Keeping a few things in mind can save you time and money.

1. Writing is less costly than long distance calling. Often, when dealing with businesses, you are put on hold until the correct person can speak with you. Also, you may have to explain your business first to the receptionist, then again to the appropriate person. It is a very emotional thing to say that your spouse is dead. Don't put yourself in the position of having to explain it more than necessary over the phone to strangers.

2. Many companies have local offices that can handle your needs or they can contact the out of town or state office for you.

3. One letter with all of the information contained can be duplicated and copies sent to various businesses. If something additional is needed for a particular company, type or write a post script at the bottom of the page.

4. This is a job where others can help. People want to feel useful. Most will not only feel flattered, but also grateful that they can do something concrete to show their love and respect for you and your spouse. Don't rob people of a chance to give back to you a portion of what you have probably given to them over the term of your friendship.

5. If you must contact persons by phone who live across the country, use the time difference to your advantage, i.e., at 7 A.M. in Oregon, it is 10 A.M. in New York. Call after five o'clock P.M. if you live in the east and need to contact persons on the west coast. Your phone book has a map that shows you precisely where the time zones are located. If the state you are calling is divided between two zones, just ask the operator.

6. Many companies have toll free (800) numbers. To find out if the one you need does, call the toll free operator at 1-800-555-1212.

As you read about the different people and businesses you must notify, take notes of how you can use the points above to minimize your time and expense in each.

PEOPLE YOU NEED TO NOTIFY IMMEDIATELY

Friends and relatives

After notifying the immediate family, there will be other relatives and friends that you will want to inform. It is suggested that you wait until after funeral arrangements are made to contact them. Otherwise, they will have to be advised a second time of that information. Be sure that you have the time, date, name, and address of the funeral home or memorial site near the phone. Don't trust your memory at a time like this.

■ Make a list of every friend or relative who needs to be contacted. Making a list is more efficient than just rambling through your address book, especially if you ask someone else to make contacts for you. Leave space for a mark or note to show whether you were able to reach them.

■ Group the names together geographically and put names of mutual friends together.

■ Look at your groupings. If Aunt Mae lives in New Orleans, then she can call all of the other friends and relatives who live there. While speaking with her, give her the names and numbers on your list and ask her to do this. She will be delighted. Don't forget to give her the funeral information.

Even though people may not be able to attend, they may want to send flowers.

■ Look at your groupings. If there is one close friend who is also friends with several others on your list, ask her to contact those people for you. Your friends will also need the funeral information.

■ Keep grouping to whittle down the people you must contact directly. Unfortunately, bad news has a way of traveling faster than good news. Most all of those notified by others will be calling or writing you within minutes of hearing of your tragedy. They, in turn, will think of people you forgot and will call them. You will be surprised of the long-lost friends and relatives you hear from.

■ Make a list of everyone you were not able to contact, and those who were not close enough either socially or geographically to reach by phone. To these people, send either a copy of the memorial card, newspaper obituary, and/or a brief note. If you decide on the note, and there are very many, write your message on a blank sheet of paper the size of the stationery you have selected. Take the stationery and the note you have composed to the local printer. They can copy your message onto the stationary for a nominal fee. They will look hand written and be very appropriate for your needs.

Business associates

If your spouse worked in a large firm, notify someone in his department. A secretary whom you are familiar with is just as appropriate as the head boss whom you may have only met once or not at all. It is much easier talking to someone you know. There is no right or wrong. Word will spread rapidly. There is no fear that someone will be uninformed by the time the day is over.

If your spouse had a partner, then the partner should be notified directly and immediately. Depending on the type of business, the death could have a direct and immediate affect on the operation of the business. Within a few weeks, you will want to sit down with your attorney and the partner to discuss the future of the business. This will in large part be controlled by the terms of the partnership agreement.

If your spouse was an independent contractor and had no co-workers or bosses, it is likely that he had many contacts in the business world. Most people who have this sort of business keep a card file of some sort. Look through it for names that you recognize. Select several and call. Word will spread from there.

If your spouse was a professional who had clients who depend on him/her for regular advice or help, then it will be necessary for you to contact someone to refer them to should they call your home or office. Another person in the same field who your spouse respected and admired would be a good place to start. If you already have an attorney, he might be able to recommend someone. Whoever takes over your spouse's clients needs to inform them of the facts and offer to help them until other arrangements are made. Discuss this with your attorney first, as you may want to sell your spouse's business or keep it and run it yourself. Right now, you just want someone to handle the cases that need immediate attention.

PEOPLE YOU NEED TO NOTIFY
AFTER THE FIRST WEEK

Insurance companies

An in-depth discussion about filing insurance claims is in Chapter Seven, "Survivor Benefits." Call your local agent or office and ask that the forms be sent to you. The insurance company will not process your claim without a *certified* death certificate. Depending on where you live, obtaining the death certificate may take only a few days or it may take several weeks. It will do little good to return your claim form without the death certificate, and may even increase the chances of it being misplaced or lost if sent separately.

Many people pay their health and life insurance premiums annually. If this was your spouse's habit, you may be entitled to the portion of those premiums that will not be used now that he/she is dead. Ask your agent when you apply for the death benefits.

Banks

If your spouse had a checkbook and you are unable to locate it, there is a possibility that it could have been lost or stolen. If this is likely, *immediately* contact your bank so that payment can be stopped on any checks.

If your spouse was receiving any direct deposit checks such as Social Security that would be affected by his/her death, contact the bank before those checks are due and instruct the bank to return them to sender. You will have to repay any that you are not entitled to. By allowing them to accumulate, the sum could become substantial. Be sure to notify (in the case of Social Security, by phone) anyone sending direct deposits. See the chapter on Social Security for more details.

Open an account in your own name. Some banks will merely take the spouse's name off the account, while others require that you open a new account. Be sure that you take out enough cash to pay for your day-to-day needs, for unless a store knows you personally, they may not accept your temporary checks that do not have your name and address imprinted. It usually takes two weeks to get new checks.

Should you need a notary, banks have one.

A Federally Chartered bank (not a savings and loan) can guarantee signature cards for changing names on securities.

The sooner you contact your banker, the more he will be able to help you.

PEOPLE YOU SHOULD NOTIFY
AFTER THE FIRST MONTH

Credit card and charge card companies

As with missing checks, if there is a possibility that the deceased's credit cards or charge cards are lost or stolen, notify the appropriate companies *immediately*. Otherwise, this is not something you have to concern yourself with the first few weeks. If the cards were held in the deceased's name only, destroy all the cards and write to the companies concerned. Give the account number and name in which the account was held. Tell them the name of the person who will pay the bill. This could be you or the executor or administrator of the Will should the two be different. The creditor will then either send you the final bill or make a claim against the estate in probate court.

If credit cards were held in both of your names, or you were an authorized user of your spouse's card, contact the company using their toll free number or by mail, and ask that the deceased's name be removed. The company will either simply do that, or more likely, send you an application to apply for a card in your name alone. Be prepared for the possibility and probability of being granted a lower credit line if you are a woman and your monthly income is substantially lower because of your husband's death. This will be explored further in the chapter on establishing your own credit.

Utilities

Telephone, gas, water, sewage, electricity, etc., are easily changed to your name by simply filling in your name where it asks for changes in name or address on the payment stub. You can use this method for many types of bills that come due. You may have to do this several times or write it in big red letters before they notice the change. You may or may not want to change the telephone listing in the phone book to your name. Many women prefer to list only a first initial and no address when they are living alone. Look through your telephone directory to see how people list their names to see if any particular thing appeals to you, then contact the phone company should you want it changed.

Department of Motor Vehicles

This is not really something that needs your immediate attention, unless you want to sell a vehicle that is registered in both of your names. Because each state motor vehicle department operates differently, be sure to call first to see what documents you will need. Typically, an "or" between your names will require your filling out a simple form and paying a small fee for the transference. If there is an "and" between your names and the estate isn't being probated, then a different form will be filled out (in California this form is called a Certificate for Transfer without Probate). If the estate is being probated, then you will have to show proof that you have the authority to make these changes. Your attorney will give you certified copies of the letters testamentary or the letters of administration as proof. You will also need the pink slip (Certificate of Ownership) and the registration slip.

If a loan institution holds your pink slip, take a certified copy of the death certificate to the loan officer who can help you complete the title transfer to your name.

Health club memberships

Read the contract. It should state in the terms what will happen in case a membership can not be continued. If dues were paid in advance, you may be entitled to a refund. Any reputable club will not hold you liable for dues for a dead person. If this becomes a problem, see your attorney.

In some clubs, you actually own title to a membership slot. It may be necessary for you to sell your membership to another person. Seek the advice of the club management to determine the fair price and advertise in your local paper. Often, there is a waiting list and the manager will be able to give you names of prospective buyers.

Book clubs or other subscription memberships

If your spouse had magazine subscriptions or record or book club memberships, you will need to decide whether you want to continue them. If you decide to cancel, most clubs have provisions for doing so at any time. Write a letter (make several copies) and send to the record or book club. They are notorious for ignoring the first notice, so you may continue to get books and records. Without opening them, return them to the post office and explain the situation. Now, send one of your copies of the first letter. This may need to be repeated more than once.

With magazines, you can do the same, but since the subscription has already been paid, it is unlikely that you will be able to get any refund. It may not be worth your time and effort especially if there are only a few months left to the subscription and you are receiving only one or two magazines monthly. If it bothers you to have his or her favorite magazine arriving at your door each month, consider notifying the magazine publisher of a change of address and put in the address of a friend or institution who would appreciate receiving it.

Rentals and leases

You will need to notify any companies with which you hold rental or lease agreements. If the contracts were signed only by your husband, you may have grounds for discontinuing the arrangements. Explain your situation to someone of authority and hope that you get a sympathetic ear. Rentals are usually simple, because you do not commit yourself for extended periods of time. You simply return the item or equipment when your need for it has ended.

Leases are more difficult. There is a lot of fine print. You typically have made a sizeable down payment and are paying high interest rates. Your investment can be substantial. An actual case can give you an idea of how many leases work.

John leased a $12,000 tractor to use on his ranch and in his small business. He put $1,200 down and made payments of $437 a month. At the end of four years, he would own it. Tax-wise, this was appropriate. Seven months later, John is killed in an accident. The widow, not wanting the payments and no longer needing the tractor, decided that she would just turn the tractor back over to the leasing company. Upon calling them, she found out that it was not that simple. The company would indeed take the tractor back, but would then put it up for auction. If the tractor did not bring the $10,900 still owed, the widow would have to make up the difference. This meant that if the tractor only sold for $7,000, the widow would have to come up with another $3,900 to satisfy the leasing company.

In this case, the widow could advertise the tractor and try to sell it for what is owed the lessor or try to find someone to take over the lease payments. In the meantime, she must still make the payments, or the tractor will be repossessed and the same procedure followed as if she had turned the machine back in.

If you decide to maintain your spouse's leases, remember that the equipment must be fully insured at all times.

HOW TO HANDLE PHONE CALLS AND INQUIRIES

We've discussed who you should call and what you should say. What about when people call you?

The first few days, your phone will probably be ringing constantly. As people read the death notice in the paper or hear through the "grapevine" or from a mutual friend, they will want to call and offer their condolences.

Sometimes you will be able to talk with them; other times you won't. You may be taking a much-needed nap; you may be out for a walk; you may be at the funeral home; you may be too emotionally upset at that particular moment. If someone is staying with you (a good idea for the first few days), have them answer the phone and door for you. Keep a tablet and pen handy so that they can record each call or visit. Your callers and visitors will understand and will appreciate your knowing they contacted you.

For weeks, months, perhaps even a year after your spouse dies, you will get an occasional call asking to speak to the deceased. No matter how long afterward, it is always a shock. Don't say your husband/wife is deceased until you find out who is calling. When they ask for Mr. Jones, simply say , "This is his wife. Can I help you?" Usually, they will explain their business and you can discern the caller's legitimacy and respond accordingly. If you recognize the name or company and decide it is appropriate to tell of your spouse's demise, the party usually feels embarrassed and apologizes for bothering you.

If you feel the call is not bona fide, ask for their name, company, and phone number so that you might return the call at a more convenient time. They'll probably hang up at this request or fumble around for some invented address. If they do give you the information, and you are interested, return the call.

Or, you can ask that they put any business they want to discuss in writing and send it to your attorney whose address is . . .

Never give your address to someone you don't know or whose identity you can not verify.

Use common sense. If you should have any problems with phone calls, contact your telephone company and they will help you.

7.

Survivor Benefits

There are many places to look for survivor benefits. Some, like life insurance are more obvious, while others such as professional organizations and travel clubs may be less apparent. Keep in mind that many benefits have application time limits. If you do not complete the necessary paperwork within the allotted time, you may lose any opportunity to receive these benefits. In other cases, such as Social Security, your benefits may be unnecessarily delayed at a time when you desperately need the funds to cover unexpected expenses.

Therefore, it is vital that you investigate all possible sources of survivor benefits as soon as possible and make application. The following is a list of places to begin your search. While you may not qualify for all of these, do not discount them without some investigation. Your spouse may have signed up for some benefit that you may not be aware of or have perhaps forgotten about. Seldom will a benefit come looking for you. So, take the responsibility for making a phone call or writing a brief letter and simply ask if you, as the surviving spouse, are entitled to any benefit. Do not bother with documentation until you get a positive response, making sure then that you ask what information is required to receive said benefit.

Because of its broad scope, Social Security will be discussed in a later chapter.

LIFE INSURANCE

It is not difficult to file a claim or collect proceeds for a life insurance policy. The trick comes in knowing what kind of insurance you have and how you want your proceeds.

There are no time limits on filing a claim for life insurance. Companies have been known to process a claim several years after a death just because the heirs did not know a life policy existed.

If you think there is a life insurance policy, but you cannot locate it and do not know the name of the company, The American Council of Life Insurance may be able to help you. They have access to approximately 100 of the largest insurance companies in the United States. Contact them by writing to:

> Policy Search
> The American Council of Life Insurance
> 1001 Pennsylvania Avenue
> Washington, DC 20004

Ask them for a policy search questionnaire. You must send a self-addressed, stamped envelope. When they receive your completed form, they will send it out to the insurance companies. If a policy is found, the insurance company will notify you. This is not a quick procedure. It may take months. If you do not hear from any insurance carriers within three months, you can assume that there probably is no life insurance on the person you are inquiring about. There is no charge for this service.

There are three main types of life insurance.

Decreasing term insurance

Insurance bought for a specific amount of time, for a specific purpose, is called term insurance. Decreasing term means that the amount of your death benefit decreases as it nears its expiration. People often buy this type of insurance for home mortgages because it is inexpensive and the premiums do not increase. Let's say you have a thirty year $100,000 mortgage on your home. You could buy a $100,000 worth of insurance for thirty years. But, remember, that if you should die in fifteen years, your life policy would only be worth approximately $50,000. At the end of thirty years, your policy has no cash value and you have no insurance. If you have decreasing term insurance, consider the number of years it has been in effect to get a rough estimate of what the payoff will be should you die.

Level term insurance

Again this is insurance that is bought for a specific amount of time for a specific reason. The difference is that the death benefit remains level. Perhaps you feel that you only need life insurance until your children have finished college. You might buy a $100,000 policy for fifteen years (the date their college education should be completed). Should you die fourteen years after you bought the policy, the death benefit would still be $100,000.

That is why this policy is called Level Term. What is not level are the yearly premiums. These increase annually. The older you are, the more it costs to buy. Again, there is no cash value at the end of the term of your policy. This too, starts out relatively inexpensive.

Permanent insurance

This is insurance that lasts as long as you pay the premiums. The premiums do not increase yearly. The amount of the premium is based on the amount of coverage you want and the age at which you initiate your policy. The amount of your death benefit increases the longer you own the policy, because you earn interest on your money. The amount of this interest varies with the money market rates. With this type of insurance, you have cash value.

There are many variations and many names to these three basic types of life insurance. An agent can tailor almost any policy to your needs and pocketbook.

Knowing the kind of insurance you have helps you to understand the amount of the benefits you will receive, i.e. face value in the case of level term, less than face value on decreasing term, or face value plus interest in the case of permanent.

SUICIDE AND CONTESTABILITY CLAUSES

Most companies have a two year suicide or contestability clause. This means that should the insured commit suicide or buy life insurance knowing they have a terminal illness and die from that illness, within that two years, the insurance company does not have to pay. By the same token, if the insured dies or commits suicide after the two year period, the insurance company must pay off regardless. The insurer is granted two years to find out anything there is to know about the person they are insuring. If the company fails to discover a pre-existing condition, then it still must pay the beneficiary.

SURCHARGES OR UPCHARGES

Mention should be made here to be aware of specific occupational or recreational involvements. If the insured has what is considered a dangerous occupation or hobby, your insurance may not pay off if he/she were engaged in that activity when death occurred, unless you have paid an upscale payment known as a surcharge or upcharge. Such hobbies and occupations include aviation of all types, scuba diving, rock climbing, car racing, explosives, sky diving, and many others.

The additional amount to cover these activities may be substantial or minimal. Usually, an additional notice will be attached to the policy that informs the insured that he has obtained coverage while participating in listed activities.

HOW TO MAKE APPLICATION FOR LIFE INSURANCE BENEFITS

This is a simple process. Contact your insurance agent or company and tell them of the death. They will either send the forms to you or the agent may come to your home and help you complete them. You will need to know the following information:

> Deceased's name
> Date of death

Place of death
Cause of death
Occupation
Address
Place of birth
Duration of illness
Name(s) of attending physician(s)
Beneficiary's name
Relationship to deceased
Date of birth
Address
All life insurance policy numbers
Beneficiary's social security number

In addition to the above, the standard claim form will ask for a medical release so that they may examine the medical history, illness, and treatment of the insured.

It will also ask for some tax information which will be discussed in Chapter Thirteen, "Death and Taxes."

A *certified death certificate* must accompany the forms. It takes approximately thirty days to process your claim, depending on the delay clause chosen at original inception of the policy. A delay clause is written into your policy by the agent when the policy is purchased. It could be thirty days or even sixty. More than that is unnecessary and you should ask your agent for an explanation.

Choosing your payment option

Now comes one of your most important decisions. How do you want your money? The insurance company will give you a form that explains the different ways you may receive your payment. These will include the following:

1. Fixed amount of income — a specific amount of money is paid either monthly or annually for as long as the proceeds last. These payments include any interest accrued.

2. Fixed period — proceeds to be divided over a chosen amount of time. Proceeds are paid monthly or annually and include both principal and interest.

3. Interest only — you receive the interest on the money for the contracted time in either monthly or annual installments. Interest is set by the policy contract. It can be

more should interest rates rise, but never less than the policy contract. These rates are usually not as much as on the open market.

4. Lifetime income — based on life expectancy. Should the beneficiary not live to that expectancy, his/her estate will be paid the remainder.

5. Lump sum — You receive the entire amount in one check to dispose of as you see fit.

OUT OF THE COUNTRY DEATHS

As far as collecting benefits for deaths that occur abroad, there are no additional problems unless there is an investigation because of the two year clause. An investigation in another country could significantly increase the waiting time element.

Otherwise, proceed as you would in the United States by obtaining a certified death certificate and filling out the insurance forms.

WHERE TO KEEP INSURANCE POLICIES

Insurance policies can be replaced if destroyed. It is not necessary that they be placed in a safe deposit box. This can actually be a dire inconvenience should the box be frozen at the time of death or the key's whereabouts are unknown. Therefore, put all policies in one place. It can be in a tin box or your file cabinet, wherever you can gain easy access. Thieves have no use for insurance policies so there is really no need to put them under lock and key.

ACCIDENTAL DEATH INSURANCE

Accidental death insurance is a form of life insurance, but because it has some of its own peculiarities it is discussed separately. Accidental insurance is usually very inexpensive. Statistically, the odds of dying in an accident are greatest before the age of 25.

Some life insurance policies offer double indemnity plans for accidental deaths. Should you elect to include this option in your policy, the company would pay twice the face value if you died in any accident as opposed to an illness. Investigations are much more likely in the case of accidents. There may be a question in some cases as to which came first, the chicken or the egg. An example would be the case of the man who had a stroke while he was driving. The stroke caused him to lose control of the car and crash into a post. He and his daughter died. The question arises did the stroke kill him or did the car crash?

Another reason accidental death policies are inexpensive is that in many accidents, someone can be found at fault. This being the case, the insurance company will sue the other party and regain their losses.

Read your accidental death policy carefully to see what type of accidents they will not pay for. If you are unsure, notify and make claim anyway. This way the burden is on the insurance company and it will be up to them to explain why they will not pay out on the claim.

UNIONS

If your spouse was a member of a labor union, he may have significant benefits. Every labor union is different. Even individual locals within the same national labor organization will vary. Some locals provide death benefits, others do not. Death benefits negotiated with individual employers may be all that is provided. Should your spouse die, contact your local labor union and ask about survivor benefits. You will need a certified death certificate. The application form will require similar information to that of other life insurance policies.

VETERANS ADMINISTRATION

There are many benefits for veterans who were discharged for "reasons other than dishonorable." For the purposes of this book, only death benefits will be discussed.

Everyone who served in the military should have a copy of "A Summary of Veterans Administration Benefits." It is made available without cost by the Veterans Administration. Look in your phone book under United States Government.

Find the regional office number under Veterans Administration. Although the regional office may be in another city, the calls are generally charged as a local number, not long distance. Ask for VA Pamphlet 27-82-2. It will be mailed to you in a short period of time. These pamphlets are revised regularly, so the information will be current. Much of the following information comes from this pamphlet.

There are significantly more benefits for veterans who die of a service-connected disability. These benefits will not be covered in this book, but are explained in the pamphlet. Read it carefully to determine all benefits available to a disabled veteran.

For all veterans who were separated from service "under conditions other than dishonorable," there exist three burial benefits.

1. Burial Flag. An American flag is furnished to drape the casket of the veteran, if desired. Funeral homes often acquire these flags for you and will present them to the next of kin or friend or associate of the deceased. Should your funeral home not provide this service, you may get your flag at any VA office, VA national cemetery, or most post offices. The following information must be provided on form 90-2008 to receive your flag: Complete name of deceased, branch of service, type of service (WW I, Korean Conflict, etc.), condition under which veteran was released from service, VA file number, Social Security number, service serial number, date of enlistment, date of discharge, date of birth, date of death, date of burial, place of burial, name and address of person entitled to receive flag, and relationship to deceased. All of the above military information can be acquired from the military discharge papers.

2. Interment in National Cemeteries. Veterans, their spouses, or minor children are eligible for burial in a national cemetery where space is available. One gravesite is authorized per veteran. There is no charge for a grave in a national cemetery. You must apply at the time of death to the director of the nearest national cemetery. Check with the regional VA office to find the one closest to the city where you wish burial. Many county and state owned cemeteries have a veterans section where eligible veterans will be buried free of

charge. Ask your local cemetery district if they have such a section.

3. Headstones or Markers. The VA will supply the grave of a veteran with a headstone or crypt marker. VA form 40-1330 must be completed. You will be given the choice of an upright headstone of American white marble, or a flat marker of American white marble or light gray granite, bronze, or slate. The flat markers are 24 inches long and 12 inches wide. The upright is 42 inches long, 13 inches wide and 4 inches thick. Certain items of information are required to be printed on the marker: Name, rank, branch of service, year of birth and death. Optional items which may be inscribed at government expense may include an emblem reflective of a religious or non-religious belief, grade, rate or rank, war service, month and day in the dates of birth and death. Any additional information may be added with VA approval for a nominal fee. It takes approximately three months for a marker to arrive. The applicant must pay to have the stone set.

Form 40-1330 must be signed by a cemetery or firm official who accepts receipt of the marker or headstone. The name and location of the cemetery is required. The cemetery official must also state that a marker of the type you have chosen is acceptable and will be permitted on the unmarked grave of the deceased.

Should you choose to purchase your own marker, the VA will pay an allowance not to exceed the average actual cost of a headstone furnished by the government. This allowance can only be applied for after a veteran's death. If you have already purchased a headstone prior to the death, then the allowance may be paid for engraving an existing headstone following the death.

You will need to fill out VA form 21-8834. Include with the form proof of veteran's death and a receipted bill which shows the name of the deceased, the name of the person by whom payment was made, a description of the headstone, marker or additional engraving, the nature and costs of the purchase, and a statement as to the amount paid by the purchaser, and all credits to the account if not paid in full. If the veteran has never filed a claim with the VA, a photocopy of the discharge certificate is necessary. If he/she has filed a claim, include the VA file number in the appropriate space.

All other information that you will need can be found on the military discharge papers. If the veteran served in any war, a $150 plot or internment allowance will be paid unless he/she is buried in a national cemetery. Should the veteran be buried in a state-owned cemetery without charge for the cost of a plot or interment, in an area used solely for persons eligible for burial in a national cemetery, then the allowance may be paid to the state.

If death occurs in a VA facility or in a contract nursing home to which the deceased was properly admitted, the allowance amounts to $300.

All claim applications (VA form 21-530) must be accompanied by proof of death, unless already submitted with a previous VA claim and a statement of account from the funeral director and the cemetery. A service record is required unless already on file with the VA.

If you can't locate your spouse's service record, contact:

National Personnel Records Center
Military Personnel Records
9700 Page Boulevard
St. Louis, MO 63132

All claims for all types of burial benefits must be filed within two years after burial or cremation.

VETERANS ADMINISTRATION LIFE INSURANCE

There are five insurance programs administered by the VA. One available to WW I veterans (USGLI), one to veterans of WW II (NSLI), one to veterans of the Korean conflict (VSLI), one to service-disabled veterans (SDVI), and Veterans Reopened Insurance — reopened NSLI coverage to WW II and Korean veterans with service-connected or serious non-service-connected disabilities (VRI). Eligibility and dividend information for these plans are listed in the VA pamphlet 27-82-2.

The VA is required to pay only the person or persons named as the beneficiary on the policy. So, make sure these designations are current.

A lump sum settlement will be paid only if selected by the insured during his/her lifetime.

GI life insurance is administered at VA Regional Office and Insurance Centers in St. Paul, Minnesota, and Philadelphia, Pennsylvania. Write to the office administering your policy and give the insured's policy number. If this information is unknown, give the insured's full name, date of birth, and Social Security number.

PROFESSIONAL AND FRATERNAL ORGANIZATIONS

If your spouse was a member of any fraternal or professional organization, especially on a national level, contact the local president and ask if there were any death benefits. These can be offered as an option or may be included in the dues.

The Veterans of Foreign Wars, for example, offers an accidental death policy to its members on a national basis. Some state VFW organizations offer additional plans.

Sometimes, rather than a monetary benefit, the benefit may be a burial plot in a particular section of a cemetery or special funeral services.

MORTGAGE INSURANCE

Mortgage insurance is life insurance by a different name. It is intended to pay off the mortgage on your house in the event you die. This can be established with any one of the three types of life insurance previously discussed. Some people don't want to discuss life insurance, but they will consider mortgage coverage. Therefore, the industry gave the rose a more palatable name.

Many banks work with insurance companies who will supply mortgage insurance for their borrowers. Unless stipulated, this covers only the FIRST mortgage. You will still be liable for the second unless your policy specifically states that it is covered. These policies are often written only as accident policies, so if you die of a heart attack, there may be no coverage. Read your policy or ask your bank for details.

Send a certified copy of the death certificate to the insurer. The check will be made out to the lender. This may take a couple of months, and in the meantime you will receive payment due notices and late charge notices if you do not make the payments on the regular schedule. This will be taken into account and you will not be charged additional fees for not having made the payments after the death of the insured.

Mortgage insurers are less likely to be concerned with the insured person's occupation or hobbies, so your chances of getting mortgage insurance are often better than straight life insurance.

CREDIT CARD INSURANCE

Some companies that issue credit cards also make available insurance policies that pay off the balance of your account if you die or become disabled. This can be a real gold mine if you keep a high monthly balance; however, it is costly.

Skim the brochures that come with your monthly bill. Some companies carry accidental death insurance if you pay for your airline, bus, train, or other commercial transportation ticket with your credit card.

TRAVEL CLUB INSURANCE

Many package tours include travel accident insurance. It is very limited in scope, usually covering you only in conjunction with the commercial airline in which you are riding. The coverage costs the travel agent only pennies so is usually "free" to the ticket buyer.

AUTOMOBILE CLUB INSURANCE

If you are a member of an automobile club, the ones that offer towing service, etc., you have probably had the opportunity to purchase a life insurance policy through them. This may be a regular life policy or an accidental policy.

AUTOMOBILE INSURANCE

If death occurred in an automobile accident either as a passenger or driver, there should be automobile insurance coverage. Find out who the carrier is and make claim as you would in any other life insurance claim. An investigation may delay your proceeds.

EMPLOYER DEATH BENEFITS

Most employers have a group life insurance policy on their employees. Call the employer and ask for a copy of the policy, the amount of the benefit, and the procedure for applying. Employer benefits, if counted on to be the sole benefit, can often be disappointing because these policies are not usually substantial. Keep in mind that if you leave the company for any reason, you can't take your policy with you.

SICK LEAVE

Check with the employer to see if your spouse had accumulated any sick leave for which he should be compensated. If death occurred from a long illness, this might be unlikely. On the other hand, if death occurred in an accident or after a short illness, it may be a sizeable amount.

VACATION PAY

As with sick leave, there may be some paid vacation time that was not taken by the deceased.

COMMISSIONS

If your spouse worked on a commission basis, be sure to ask the employer if there are any outstanding commissions payable. Unless you have an intimate knowledge of your spouse's business, it may be hard to get an accurate figure, so you will just have to trust the employer to be fair. If there is a large discrepancy between the final commissions and the monthly average commissions before death, bring it to the attention of the employer and ask for an explanation.

WORKER'S COMPENSATION

Employers are required by law to provide Worker's Compensation benefits for their employees. If the death occurred as a result of employment, as in an industrial accident, then claim should be made to the insurance company providing the Worker's Compensation policy. The amount collected will be determined by several factors: number of dependents, whether the deceased was the sole provider, and what other sources of income are available.

An accident report from the company will be required along with a certified death certificate. An investigation will be made by an adjuster and benefits determined.

EMPLOYER PROFIT SHARING OR STOCK PURCHASE PROGRAMS

Some companies offer their employees an opportunity to participate in company profit sharing or stock purchase programs. Contact the personnel director of your spouse's company to see if he participated in any of these programs. You may be presented with the option of cashing in or transferring title and holding on to these assets. Discuss your options with your financial advisor, who will know the tax implications.

PENSIONS

Pensions are a type of retirement plan that an employee and/or employer contribute to during the worker's employment. There are many types of private pension plans. The type your spouse has will determine the benefits you receive upon his death.

Government gave widows a big break in 1984 with the passage of the Retirement Equity Act. It contains provisions for joint and survivor annuities. Under this law, a widow is entitled to one-half of the lifetime retirement pay when the spouse dies. Additionally, the law states that both spouses must sign to waive survivor benefit protection in pension plans. Before, the working spouse could choose to exclude survivor benefits with his signature alone.

Each year, your spouse should have received a summary of his pension benefits. This summary explains how his pension plan works, and will list the total contributions to the plan. If you cannot locate this summary document, contact the employer for a duplicate.

Ideally, you already know how the pension plan works and you know how much you are entitled to. If not, you will need to discuss survivor benefits with the employer because provisions will vary among plans.

Be aware that taxes are due on pension funds and when receiving annuity checks, you might want to have the taxes withheld from them before you receive them. Otherwise, you will have to estimate and prepay this amount or face penalties. If you decide to have taxes withheld from each check, ask your state tax board, the IRS, or the payor for pension withholding forms.

FEDERAL CIVIL SERVICE

If your spouse worked for the federal civil service for a minimum of eighteen months and you were married for a minimum of nine months, or had children born of that marriage, you are eligible for benefits. The amount of the annuity is based on the amount of time employed by the civil service agency and the amount earned. Even if you are not eligible for this annuity, you still may receive your spouse's contribution to the retirement fund. Also check to see if your spouse had Federal Employees' Life Insurance. You may find this out by contacting the personnel office of the agency for which he/she worked.

The Office of Personnel Management has an information line that gives you instructions for applying for benefits, changing an address, receiving information about the status of your retirement, withholding taxes from your annuity checks, direct depositing your checks, and so on. You may get this information by calling (202) 632-7700 or writing to:

Employees Services and Records Center
Office of Personnel Management
P.O. Box 45
Voyers, PA 16017

To report the death of a retiree or survivor, you can simply call (202) 632-2910 and leave the following information on the answering machine: name of annuitant, Social Security number, date of death, date of birth, and civil service claim number.

This office is open from 7:30-5:30. If you are calling from the west coast, take advantage of the three hour time difference by calling before 8:00 A.M. It will take six to eight weeks to process your claim, so contact O.P.M. as soon as possible.

Information about retired federal civil servants may also be obtained by writing to:

Compensation Group
Office of Retirement Programs
Office of Personnel Management
1900 E Street, N.W.
Washington, DC 20415

STATE AND LOCAL CIVIL SERVICE

State and local civil service benefits will of course vary. Your spouse will typically have had to work for a certain amount of time and/or earned a specific amount of wages to qualify. Even if it has been years since he held the civil service job, he may still have accrued benefits, provided he did not draw them out when he left the agency.

RAILROAD WORKER'S BENEFITS

Employees of the railroad who have worked ten years or more have their own retirement system and benefits. If the employee has worked less then ten years, his credits and earnings become part of the Social Security system. You may get information about the Railroad Retirement Act from your Social Security office. For information about railroad service, contact the:

Railroad Retirement Board
844 Rush Street
Chicago, IL 60611

STATE UNCLAIMED FUNDS

Although a long shot, the payoff could be worth your investigation. The controller's office of each state has an account where companies and banks must turn over any unclaimed property after a certain amount of time. Unclaimed inheritances, dormant bank accounts, uncashed checks, securities, and refunds make up a large portion of the unclaimed holdings. In the state of California, there are 750,000 rightful owners to a total of $300 million dollars, just waiting to be claimed. A phone call to your state controller's office could turn up some refund long forgotten by your spouse.

Remember, there are time limits on some of these survivor benefits, so don't delay applying. If there is no beneficiary listed on the insurance form, the proceeds will be paid to the estate.

It is the policy holder's responsibility to keep the beneficiary of the policy current. Insurance companies will pay only the name listed as beneficiary on the policy. If for some reason you wish to change beneficiaries, you must do so in writing. Contact your insurer and he will send you a form to complete and sign. It will go into effect immediately.

ONE LAST COMMENT: If you are unsure whether you are entitled to a death benefit, *ASK!*

8.
Transferring Assets

Unless a surviving spouse, son, or daughter has had experience with the financial world, settling the deceased's financial matters can be frightening. The fact that money is involved puts greater pressure on the survivor to do things properly. Extensive laws have been made with provisions to protect the property of the dead person, so don't be afraid of making mistakes or letting the wrong person get those assets. The holders of the assets will not release any funds, titles, property, etc., unless proper proof of entitlement is shown.

It is strongly advised that you do not make any decisions about selling stocks, withdrawing large sums from mutual funds, cashing in bonds, etc., without first consulting a member of your professional team, most likely your financial advisor.

What we will look at in this chapter are the requirements for getting the deceased's assets transferred into the appropriate names. The most common types of assets will be mentioned, with the exception of real estate, which will be covered in Chapter Eleven, "Real Estate."

TITLE OF OWNERSHIP

The way in which title to the asset is held will determine what has to be done to transfer title to your name. There are several ways in which property can be held.

Joint tenancy

A title which lists owners as joint tenants is specifying that each name listed on the title is an equal owner. Upon death of one of the joint tenants, the deceased's share passes to the survivor(s). Assets held as such do not pass through probate court.

NOTE: You may not will away your share of any asset held in joint tenancy. When you die, it reverts to the other partner(s) whose name(s) appear as joint tenants on the title. Most joint tenants are husband and wife. Therefore, if the husband dies, the property becomes the wife's and vice versa.

Be cautious of entering into joint tenancy with people other than a spouse, keeping in mind that while alive, each joint tenant has a right to sell or give away his share of the asset without the consent of the other joint tenants.

With this type of ownership, you also risk the possibility of inadvertently disinheriting a joint tenant. Such was the case of Agnes, a widow, who wanting to avoid probate for her two grown daughters, listed them as joint tenants on the deed to her home. Agnes died, and just as planned, the property passes to Julie and Marta. Two years later, Marta is killed in an automobile accident. Julie becomes the sole owner of Agnes' home, while Marta's children get nothing.

Tenancy in common

Tenants in common own a specified interest in the asset, but not necessarily an equal interest. One partner may own fifteen percent, another fifty percent, still another thirty-five percent.

Each owner has the right to sell, give away, lease, or use as collateral his share without the agreement of the other tenants in common.

Upon death, the deceased's share goes to his heirs, not to the surviving co-owners.

Tenancy by entirety

This form of title applies to real estate and is available only to co-owners who are married and do not live in community property states. Upon the death of one spouse, the property passes to the other. Should one of the owners want to change the agreement, he would need permission of the other.

Community property

There are eight community property states: Arizona, California, Idaho, Louisiana, Nevada, New Mexico, Texas, and Washington. In these states, anything that was acquired after marriage or is voluntarily designated as such becomes the property of both spouses. Each spouse is entitled to one-half.

While alive, one spouse must have the consent of the other to sell or to give away his share. Upon death, however, the deceased may will his entire share to whomever he pleases.

Separate property

Although married, separate property is that which is owned entirely by one spouse. This may be property that was the spouse's before marriage or may have been given to or inherited by the spouse. If there has been co-mingling of the assets, then the courts could rule that the property is no longer separate. For example, John Smith owned a duplex before he married Joyce. After the marriage, Joyce helped him make payments for the monthly mortgage, insurance premiums, maintenance, etc. They co-mingled their assets to maintain his duplex. This may entitle her to a portion of the property, which will be determined by the courts.

If not provided for by a Will, there are state laws that govern the disposal of separate property. These laws are discussed in Chapter Five, "Understanding Wills and Probate."

Separate property is subject to probate unless held in trust or exempted by statute.

Common law property

All of those states which are not community property states are common law states. In the forty-two common law states, the person who earns the wages to obtain the property is the owner of that property. If there is no Will, the non-wage-earning spouse's share of an estate is dictated by the laws of the state in which he/she lives.

You can now see the importance of planning title ownership to your property before death. There are tax and probate implications to each situation. A good financial advisor or accountant will be able to advise you on the best way to title your assets.

If the time for planning has passed, then you are stuck with what you've got. The complexity of getting titles to property transferred to your name depends on how those titles are held. Let's examine the most common types of assets and see what will need to be done.

DOCUMENTATION

No matter who holds the title, there are certain documents needed. Be sure to take these with you. To save time, call the institution first and ask what documentation is necessary to transfer title. If you do not have everything you need, ask them where to obtain the additional papers and they should be able to advise you.

1. Certified Copy of the Death Certificate. A photocopy will probably not suffice. It must have the raised seal and original markings.

2. Identification to prove who you are. This could be in the form of a driver's license or passport.

3. Marriage Certificate if you are transferring title from your spouse's name to yours.

4. Letters of Administration or Testamentary which can be obtained from the courts through your attorney.

5. Guaranteed Signature Card which can be obtained through your banker from a federally chartered bank (not a savings and loan).

BANK ACCOUNTS

There are very few people in the United States who do not have some sort of banking account. The ease and convenience of shopping with a checkbook instead of cash has been lauded by the banking institution since its inception.

Although credit and charge cards are beginning to outpace check writing, it is still the most common way to pay bills, especially when using the mail. When a spouse or next of kin dies, their banking accounts must be dealt with. How do you go about it?

Checking and savings accounts

Begin by asking the customer service representative how the accounts were held. This may or may not be done over the phone, depending on bank policy. If you are able to get the information on the phone, be sure to ask about the documentation you will need.

In addition to the documentation listed above, you will most likely need your checkbook and/or passbook, a sample of your spouse's signature to verify the account, a form provided by the bank called a Withdrawal Request and a release from death tax liens.

If the account(s) were held as *joint tenants*, the funds will usually be transferred to you as surviving joint tenant. You may request that a new account be opened in your name, or you may withdraw the funds. Be certain that all checks have cleared before closing the account or you can be held accountable for checks written against insufficient funds.

With a *Tenants in Common Account* the deceased's share goes to his/her heir(s), not to the other surviving co-owners. If the estate is in probate, the funds can be released to the administrator or executor of the estate.

Individual Accounts (separate property) must go through probate before funds can be released, unless it was held in trust.

Pay-on-Death Agreements are sometimes placed on individual or tenants in common accounts. They provide for the beneficiary to be paid the funds upon the death of the account holder. The funds go to the beneficiary named without going through probate.

Types of savings accounts

The type of savings account that you and/or your spouse have will also affect the release of your funds. Let's look at the most common ones.

Passbook accounts are so named because you usually get a small record keeping notebook to keep track of the transactions that you make as money passes into and out of the account. The bank will request that you produce your passbook to withdraw funds or transfer title.

Certificates of Deposit are timed savings accounts. There is usually a minimum deposit required. In order to avoid early withdrawal penalties, you must commit the deposit for a certain length of time. This may be from seven days to years. The amount of interest is guaranteed to you as long as the certificate is valid. Typically, the more you deposit and the longer you leave it in the bank, the higher the interest rate. This does vary according to the market and the bank, so be sure to check.

In the case of death, there is usually no penalty for withdrawal or transfer of title if funds are released before the maturity date of the CD. CD's will be reissued to the beneficiary or in the case of probate to the executor or administrator when the letters testamentary or letters of administration are presented to the bank.

Trust Accounts are accounts where you control the account when you are alive, and the account passes to your beneficiary upon your death. You are liable for the taxes on the interest each year. This is often referred to as a revocable trust, because you may change a beneficiary or close the account whenever you choose. The account passes automatically to the beneficiary upon your death, without going through probate.

Custodial Accounts differ from trust accounts in that the beneficiary is responsible for the taxes. You may not change the beneficiary or close the account. The beneficiary is fully entitled to the account upon your death.

Safe deposit boxes

Because safe deposit boxes have been known to be hiding places for large sums of money, jewelry, gold coins, etc., state governments made laws concerning the removal of items upon the death of the owner of the box.

At the time of your spouse's death, your joint safe deposit box may be sealed until a tax official accompanies you to the bank and takes an inventory of the contents of the box. This is why you will hear over and over again, not to put your burial instructions, Wills, or life insurance policies in your safe deposit box.

Usually, you can obtain permission by court order to open a box to retrieve these types of papers, but if death occurs on a weekend or holiday, you are out of luck. You will need a certified copy of the death certificate, and depending on the bank, a sample of the deceased's signature.

If the box is rented in both of your names, you may remove your separate property provided you can prove through the use of receipts or bills of sale that the property is yours alone. If the estate is being probated, the administrator or executor must accompany you to claim your possessions.

The signature card, completed when the box was initially rented, contains the names of all those authorized to have access to the box. Hopefully, you know where the key to the box is located, or there can be greater delay and expense in opening it.

SECURITIES

Stocks and bonds come under the heading of Securities. If you own corporate securities, it means that you own an interest in a corporation. Certificates are proof of that ownership.

The easiest way to transfer title on securities is to first call your broker and tell him what you want to accomplish. He can tell you exactly what you will need and how long it will take. Most brokerage firms suggest that you hold your securities in "street name" and let them retain the actual certificate. This makes it much easier and faster to sell stocks and bonds. A simple phone call can accomplish most of your business. If you do have custody of the actual certificates the same things can be accomplished, but it will take a bit longer.

To transfer titles, you will need a certified copy of the death certificate, and a guaranteed signature card (available from your banker or broker). An *assignment* will be prepared requesting the name change. If the estate is being probated, you may need letters testamentary or letters of administration. Other required documents could include Consent to

Transfer, Inheritance Tax Waiver, or Affidavit of Survivorship. For the benefit of the IRS, you will need the purchase date and purchase price of the securities. Your broker will help you obtain these.

All of this information will be sent to the transfer agent of the issuing corporation. If the transferring agent is in a state other than the one in which you live, you will need to complete an Affidavit of Domicile stating the state residency of the deceased.

The transfer agent will complete the name transfer and reissue the new certificates, mailing them to the broker or banker that helped you. They in turn, will notify you when the new certificates arrive. This takes one to two weeks to accomplish.

Government Securities include Treasury bills (life is for one year or less), notes (life is for one to five years), and bonds (life is for more than five years).

U.S. Savings Bonds may be issued in beneficiary form and will pass to the beneficiary upon death without going through probate. These are called Payable on Death bonds. You may have them reissued in your name or redeemed by presenting a certified copy of the death certificate and having your signature verified after signing the back of the bonds. The bonds will then be sent to the Federal Reserve Bank for processing. If they are held in joint tenancy, they can either be redeemed, reissued, or remain the same. Most banks can facilitate redemptions and reissues.

If you decide to have the bonds reissued in your name, or with a new co-owner or beneficiary, you will need to sign the backs of the bonds, have your signature verified, and provide a certified copy of the death certificate. The bank will send the bonds to the Federal Reserve Bank where they will be reissued.

For redemption of co-owned bonds, again you will need your signature verified on the reverse side of the bonds. You will not need a copy of the death certificate. If the bonds are Series E and EE, you can get your money immediately. If the bonds are Series H and HH you must wait for payment from the Federal Reserve Bank. Payment can be either sent to you or to your account at the financial institution helping you.

Should your U.S. Savings Bonds be lost, stolen or destroyed you can replace them by writing to the:

Bureau of Public Debt
Department of the Treasury
P.O. Box 1328
Parkersburg, WV 26106-1328
(304) 420-6112

Request form PD 1048, Application for Relief on Account of Loss, Theft or Destruction of U.S. Savings and Retirement Securities.

Give as much information as possible such as the issue date, serial numbers, your address at the time they were issued, and your present address, name, and Social Security number.

If you have inherited some stocks that are not listed on any stock exchange, you can find out their value by sending $25 for each stock, and a copy of the certificate to:

R.M. Smythe and Co.
26 Broadway
New York, NY 10004
(212) 943-1880

Mutual and Money Market Funds

When investors pool their money for the purpose of obtaining a diversified portfolio of securities, it is called a mutual fund. If this fund invests in money market instruments, it is called a money market mutual fund. This security enables a small investor to invest like large institutions. Mutual funds are managed by a firm. You can choose the fund that best suits your goals and needs.

If the deceased had mutual fund investments, the transference of title will depend on how those funds were held. You will need the same type of documentation and will follow the same procedure as with securities. For help, contact the brokerage house, bank, or insurance company who handles the account.

While the estate is being settled, the portfolio managers are free to continue buying and selling as they see fit.

Deferred retirement funds

There are two widely known and accepted deferred retirement funds. The first is an Individual Retirement Account (IRA).

In 1974, Congress provided for retirement accounts to supplement Social Security. Recognizing that Social Security may not provide people with an adequate income during their older years, Congress gave individuals a chance to take responsibility for their retirement future. In 1981, with the Economic Recovery Tax Act, the provisions were expanded and better defined.

Basically, it provided that working individuals are allowed to invest with a custodian, 100 percent of their incomes up to $2000 per year. Dividends, interest, or any gains are tax-free until the money is withdrawn after age 59 1/2 and before 70 1/2. In addition, a working spouse may deposit an additional $250 per year for a non-working spouse.

Salaries, wages, alimony, and any other incomes subject to Social Security taxes qualify for IRA's. Plans must be funded by April 15 of the year you take the tax savings deduction.

You are allowed to withdraw your IRA funds once a year, but must place them in another IRA account within sixty days or be penalized. You may make a trustee to trustee transfer of IRA funds from one account or type to another, without ever withdrawing the money, as often as you like without penalty.

This involves contacting the financial institution which holds your account and requesting that they transfer the funds to another account or to another firm. You may not take physical possession of the funds at any time. It must be handled between the two trustees.

There are many investment vehicles for IRA funds. Banks typically offer three types. One is the Fixed Rate Certificate of Deposit. With this, you commit your money for a specific amount of time and are guaranteed the interest rate for that committed term. Another type is the Variable Rate Certificate of Deposit. Again, you commit your money for a specific amount of time, but the amount of interest you receive goes up or down according to prime interest rates. A third type of bank IRA is open ended, without specific time commitments. There is no penalty to transfer your funds to another type of IRA at any time you choose.

There are other ways to invest your IRA funds besides banks. Brokerage firms and insurance companies will also invest your IRA's. Many are insured with the Securities Investor Protection Corporation which insures your brokerage account up to $500,000, including $100,000 in cash. Most companies have several mutual funds to choose from. Your choice would depend on your goals, tolerance for risk, and need for flexibility.

Individual Retirement Annuities guarantee an income for the rest of your life, once you reach retirement age and qualify to withdraw your IRA funds.

Some companies offer a plan where you can independently make your own choices about stock and bond investments. You exercise the right to trade, buy, and sell at your option.

What you may *not* invest your IRA funds in are hard assets, tangibles, and art, with the exception of U.S. gold coins.

You may *not* borrow against or use as collateral any IRA funds.

Should you withdraw money from your IRA account before age 59 1/2, you are subject to a ten percent penalty and will be taxed as ordinary income on the amount withdrawn.

The *exception* to the age rule is when the owner of the IRA account becomes *disabled or dies*. IRA's provide for a beneficiary. In case of death, the funds pass directly to the beneficiary without going through probate. Taxes on the IRA funds are paid by the estate of the decedent.

For self-employed people, Congress enacted the Self-Employed Individuals Tax Retirement Act of 1962. It became called the Keogh Act after its author Congressman Keogh. More recently, it is correctly referred to as a defined contribution, money purchase, or profit sharing account. Very much like the IRA, except that self-employed people are allowed to contribute twenty percent or up to $30,000 of their net income, whichever is less. The same rules and restrictions apply as for the IRA's. Upon death, the funds pass to the beneficiary.

To receive beneficiary funds, present to the institution where the IRA funds are deposited, a certified copy of the death certificate along with identification to prove you are the named beneficiary.

SOMETHING TO THINK ABOUT: Your spouse made the investments he/she did because they felt they were wise. You were made the beneficiary so that these investments could take care of your needs. Don't be too quick to withdraw large sums of money before you have your goal well defined and know what you need in the way of financial security. Have titles transferred to your name, then sit tight for a little while. The investments will keep earning interest while you figure out your plan. What may seem like a logical plan today, may have tremendous tax implications on April 15. Work with your professional advisors to devise the best plan for your newly acquired assets.

9.

Social Security

The Social Security Act, which established the Old Age Survivors and Disability Insurance System, was signed into law by Franklin Delano Roosevelt in 1935, toward the end of the greatest depression in United States history. Its intent was to alleviate the mass destitution indicated by the length and severity of the Great Depression.

The first recipients began collecting their retirement checks in 1940. It took them about four months (with a maximum benefit of $40 per month) to recoup their contributions to the system.

Today, there are 37 million people (one out of every six), being served in some manner by the Social Security System. It takes about two years to recoup your contributions now. The average person will receive five times the amount of those contributions throughout his/her lifetime.

Employee contributions are matched by the employer. Because the contributions of the employers and workers have not been able to keep pace with those eligible to collect benefits, the Social Security System began working with a deficit in 1981. Money to keep the system afloat was borrowed from the Medicare Fund.

Recognizing the severity of the problem, a special bipartisan National Commission on Social Security Reform was established in April of 1983 for the purpose of rewriting the laws to protect the system. While effective, the new laws and enactments fall short of solving all problems. Therefore, more changes are expected in the near future.

Provisions of the 1983 Reform Act included:

1. A regular increase in the wage base and tax rate went into effect. The maximum amount of earnings on which Social Security taxes are paid in 1987 is $43,800 at a tax rate of 7.15 percent. Based on average wage levels, the wage base will continue to increase. The tax rate will rise to 7.51 percent in 1988-89, and to 7.65 percent in 1990 and later. Rates for self-employed persons are approximately double because there is no matching contributions from an employer.

2. Federal employees and those working for nonprofit organizations are now part of the Social Security system, provided they were hired on or after January 1, 1984.

3. The retirement age has been increased. If you were born after 1937, the retirement age will rise in two month increments to a maximum age of 66 for those born between 1943 and 1954. For those born in 1960 or later, the retirement age will rise to 67 years.

4. A maximum of one-half of your Social Security benefits are subject to Federal taxation. The amount of tax will be the lesser of one-half of your benefits or one-half of the amount by which your adjusted gross income, plus tax-exempt interest, plus one-half of your Social Security benefits exceeds $25,000 if you file a single return; $32,000 for a married couple filing a joint return; $0 for a married couple, filing separately, who live together during any part of the year.

Social Security will send Form SSA-1099 each year, informing you of the total amount of benefits you received during the year. Additionally, you will receive an IRS Notice 703 worksheet to help you determine whether you owe any taxes.

5. Cost-of-living increases fluctuate with the balance in the combined Social Security trust fund. If funds are less than fifteen percent (through 1988, twenty percent beginning 1989), of the expected year's benefits, the COLA (cost-of-living adjustment) could be frozen or even reduced.

6. There are reduced benefits for those who earn wages over the annual exempt amount. Only if you are over 70 years old may you earn unlimited wages. Between 65 and 70, you may earn $8,160 annually. Those less than 60 years old,

may earn $6,000. These are the 1987 earning limits. The amounts increase nominally each year.

If you exceed the exempt amount, you will be penalized $1 in benefits for each $2 you earn above the exempt amount. Beginning in 1990, that figure will decrease to $1 for every $3 for people above 65 years of age. Adjustments for the age at which withholding rates apply will begin in 2003, when the retirement age increases.

What is *not* considered wages? Income from savings accounts, most investments, gifts or inheritances, annuities, rental income (unless you are a real estate dealer), any type of retirement pay, royalties you receive in or after the year you are 65 if obtained before that year, gains from sale of capital assets, Veterans benefits, and insurance payments do not affect your Social Security exempt amount. Check with your local Social Security office if you have a question about your income sources.

These are the major changes affected by the 1983 laws. Keep abreast of new developments through the various literature published by the Social Security Administration. A very helpful and easy to read pamphlet entitled "Your Social Security" and another called "A Woman's Guide to Social Security" are available free by calling the Social Security Administration listed under U.S. Government in your phone book.

A more complete guide to the workings of the Social Security System is *The Complete and Easy Guide to Social Security and Medicare* by Faustin F. Jehle (Fraser Publishing Company, 38 Academy Street, Box 1507, Madison, CT 06443). This manual has sample forms for filing all sorts of claims and is revised every year.

The New Social Security Guide edited by Fred W. Evicci (Capital Publications, 1780A 36th Street, Sacramento, CA 95816) is a simplified, condensed summary of many Social Security publications. It puts under one cover information found in several sources. Both of these books are excellent and highly recommended.

DETERMINING BENEFITS

Now that you know the history of the Social Security system and the direction it is taking in providing benefits for your present and future, you will want to know how credit is earned. More specifically, do you qualify for benefits under your deceased spouse's record?

Benefits are determined by the amount and the length of time one pays into the system. In 1987, you earned one credit for each $440 of your covered annual earnings, up to a maximum of four credits for the year. The amount needed to earn a credit or quarter increases each year. In 1979, one quarter was credited for each $260, up to a maximum of four quarters. In 1982, it was $340. The number of quarters needed to qualify also increases with each year, i.e., 1981, thirty quarters were needed; 1987, thirty-six quarters; 1991, forty quarters.

How can you find out how many credits or quarters you have? You may request a Statement of Earnings from the Social Security Administration. This statement shows your earnings covered by Social Security since 1937. Be advised that the last year may not appear on the statement because of the time required to process and record this information. Upon request, the number of credits or quarters of coverage along with a benefit estimate can be included in your statement.

The Statement of Earnings will reflect all wages from your employment since 1937, and any self-employment income reported on your income tax return since 1951.

To receive your statement call your local Social Security office and ask for Form SSA-7004-PC called a Request For Statement Of Earnings. The completed form goes to your regional Data Operations Center. This is the fastest and simplest way.

You may also send a letter or post card to:
Social Security Administration
P.O. Box 57
Baltimore, MD 21203

Include the following information with your request: Complete name, complete address, social security number, date of birth, all names used previously (maiden name), sex, and a request for a summary of the Work Record.

When you receive your statement, check for accuracy. Because of the volume of names and numbers dealt with, mistakes are made. Should you find an error, take your tax returns and W-2 forms to your local Social Security office. If necessary, you may obtain copies of returns for the last six years from the Internal Revenue Service by filling out Form-4506, Request for Copy of Tax Form. Each year's return costs $4.25 and will be sent in approximately six weeks.

You should request a summary of your work record every three years. Technically, you have only three years, three months, and fifteen days to make corrections.

TYPES OF SOCIAL SECURITY BENEFITS

Social Security benefits are divided into four categories: Retirement Benefits, Survivor Benefits, Disability Benefits, and Hospital Insurance (Medicare). For the purposes of this book, we will explore, in depth, only those benefits affecting survivors. There is some overlapping of the categories as they apply to survivors. If you want information on the other types of benefits, the books mentioned above will serve you well.

Survivor benefits

LUMP SUM DEATH BENEFIT — The Social Security Administration provides a lump sum death benefit to help defray the costs of burial. As of 1986, this payment amounts to $255.

The order of priority to whom this benefit is paid is first, to the spouse living in the same household as the worker at the time of his/her death; second, to an entitled widow(er) who was eligible for benefits on the deceased's work record the month of worker's death; third, to children who are eligible or entitled to benefits based on the work record of the deceased in the month of death. Lump Sum Death Payments can not be made to the funeral home or to persons who paid the funeral expenses, if different from those listed above.

WIDOW(ER)'S BENEFITS — Widows(ers) are entitled to survivor benefits if:

1. They are 60 years or older and the deceased worker is fully insured. A person 60 years of age will receive 71.5 percent of the spouse's age 65 benefit. At 61, the benefit would increase 5.7 percent, continuing until it reaches 100 percent at the age of 65. Remarriage after the age of 60 will not prevent the payment of benefits.

2. They are the surviving divorced spouse. The marriage must have lasted ten years. Divorced spouse must be at least 60 years old and may not be married at the time of application. Divorced spouse may be any age and married for less than ten years, if caring for an entitled child of which she is the natural or adoptive parent. Benefits are equivalent to those of surviving spouse.

3. They are disabled. Disabled widows(ers) are entitled to benefits between the ages of 50 and 59, if the worker was fully insured and the widow(er) becomes fully disabled within seven years of the death of the worker. There is a five month waiting period in which time the claimant must have been disabled the entire time. Disabled persons may marry after the age of 50 without consequence to their benefits. The benefit amount for the widow(er) aged 65 or older is 100 percent of the Primary Insurance Amount (PIA) of the deceased worker. If the benefactor chooses to receive benefits between the ages of 50 and 65, the amount will be reduced by 0.475 percent for each month, plus an additional 0.179 percent for each month between ages 50 and 60.

4. They are caring for entitled children up to 16 years old. The children must be unmarried and up to 18 years of age (19 years if they are attending an elementary or secondary school full time). Children who are disabled before the age of 22 can get benefits at any age as long as the disability continues.

This provision applies to dependent children, whether natural, adopted, step-child, illegitimate, or grandchild. In the case of grandchildren, the parents of the child must be dead or disabled at the time the grandparents die, become disabled, or become entitled to retirement benefits. Each child is entitled to benefits as long as they are dependents of the grandparents. The benefit amount for the surviving spouse caring for an entitled child is seventy-five percent of the dead worker's PIA. This continues until the youngest child is 16 or the widow(er) remarries. Children's benefits are also seventy-five percent but continue until the age discussed above.

In cases where the widow(er) is caring for entitled children while working and earning wages, the reduction or deletion of the parent's benefit is determined by the same rules discussed earlier in the chapter. In 1987, only $6,000 may be earned before your benefits are reduced. This reduction will only apply to the parent's benefits, not to the children's. Their checks will be unaffected by either your income or remarriage.

Benefits based on your own work record

It may be that you qualify for benefits under your spouse's work record and under your own. If this is the case, you may only collect under one or the other, whichever is higher. This option is available to you at the age of 62.

Other choices

If you have been widowed more than once, determine which deceased spouse had higher coverage. You are entitled to the higher(est) benefit.

It may also happen that you are the divorced widow of one and the surviving widow of another. Again you can choose the higher benefit.

You will always have the highest benefit, but you may only choose one.

COST OF LIVING ADJUSTMENTS (COLA's)

As mentioned earlier, one of the 1983 reforms dealt with cost-of-living increases. Instead of an automatic increase every June as was in the past, COLA's are now effective January 1 and are based on the Consumer Price Index or the increase in yearly national average wages, whichever is less.

To give you an idea of the possible fluctuation you can

expect, the cost-of-living increase in 1982 was 7.4 percent; in 1987, it was 1.3 percent. The increase for 1988 was 4.2 percent. Unfortunately, the yearly increases are usually offset by the increase in Medicare payments for those 65 and over.

HOW TO APPLY FOR SOCIAL SECURITY BENEFITS

A lot of information has been given to you so far on the history and background, benefits, and procedures within the Social Security Administration. All of this knowledge will be helpful to you as you make application for your survivor benefits. The more homework you do, the more you will be able to ask questions and understand the answers. If, when talking with an SSA counselor, you get information conflicting with what you have researched, be sure to ask for clarification. Ideally, you should take your sources of information with you so that you can show the counselor where you obtained your information. If you still are not satisfied, ask to speak with a supervisor.

Begin the process of applying for your survivor benefits with a call to your local SSA office. Many times, the funeral director will notify them for you. Be sure that if he doesn't, you do. Social Security benefits do not come automatically. You must apply for them. You can receive back payments up to twelve months, but will lose benefits for any months beyond that. It usually takes six to eight weeks to receive your first check if you are not in the system already, so apply promptly.

Documentation

To receive survivor benefits, you will need to prove your age and that of your spouse, the fact that you were married to the deceased, the age(s) of any children, and that your spouse is dead. Most all of the documentation must be certified copies of the originals (the raised seal with original markings). These will be returned to you after the information has been recorded.

The following is a list of documents you will need. There are alternatives in parenthesis if you can not produce the preferred document.

1. A certified copy of spouse's death certificate.

2. Social Security numbers for your spouse, yourself, and any children. If you do not have Social Security cards for your children, you may apply for them at the same time you make application for survivor benefits.

3. Certified birth certificates for your spouse, yourself, and any children. (certified copy of hospital records, census records, school records, passports, voter's registration cards, draft registration records, driver's licenses, notarized affidavits of witnesses to birth, baptismal records, immunization records, or family Bibles). More than one of these may be requested.

4. Certified copy of your marriage certificate.

5. Copies of deceased's most recent federal income tax return, W-2 form, Social Security eligibility form, or Schedule C for self-employed persons.

6. Proof of citizenship, if a naturalized citizen.

7. Military discharge papers. You can receive additional credits for active duty military service if you need them to qualify for benefits or if your benefit would increase because of it. The military began withholding Social Security contributions in 1957. If the deceased did not have enough quarters to qualify, but served in the military before 1957, he/she can receive credits for this service.

8. Divorce papers, if you are making claim as a divorced widow(er).

9. Medical records, if you are making application as a disabled widow. These records should include names, addresses, and phone numbers of doctors and hospitals that treated you for your disability.

10. Proof of support, if you are claiming benefits as a dependent parent. This can be a notarized affidavit.

If you can not locate all of the information above, do not delay your claim. The Social Security counselor will help you locate them, or give you alternatives. The Department of Health and Human Services publishes a twenty page booklet entitled "Where to Write for Vital Records." It tells you how to obtain certified copies of birth, death, marriage, and divorce certificates. Send $1.50 to R. Woods, Consumer Information Center-C, P.O. Box 100, Pueblo, Colorado 81002. It will take approximately three weeks to receive your copy.

Generally, the types of records you need will be found in the state department of vital statistics. These departments are usually located in the capital or largest city of the state. The names will vary, sometimes called Bureau of Vital Statistics, Division of Vital Records, and Bureau of Records and Statistics. All of them have either the word "records", "vital," or "statistics" in their department titles. Given this information, directory assistance should be able to help you.

Military records for veterans of the Army, Navy, Marine Corps, and Air Force can be located by writing to:

> National Personnel Records Center (Military
> Personnel Records, for the Army)
> 9700 Page Boulevard
> St. Louis, MO 63132

They will require that you fill out Form 180, "Request Pertaining to Military Personnel Records." This form is available from the address above.

U.S. Coast Guard Records may be obtained by writing to:

> General Archives Division (WNRC)
> Washington, DC 20409

Naturalization Records can be obtained from the Immigration and Naturalization Service, Washington, DC 20536.

Passport information can be obtained from the Passport Office, Department of State, Washington, DC 20520.

MAKING A CLAIM FOR SURVIVOR BENEFITS

Once you have collected the documents listed, you have all of the information you will need to complete the various forms.

Make an appointment to see a counselor by calling your local SSA office. They may send the forms to you in advance if you request them. This will give you a chance to see what will be asked. It is possible to complete the entire procedure without actually going to the SSA office. Documents must be mailed with the application. They will be returned after reviewing. If this appeals to you, inquire when you make the initial call. If sending these important papers through the mail concerns you, then make claim in person.

There are several forms that you may need to fill out,

depending on your circumstances. A brief discussion of each is included here to help you understand the paperwork.

Application for Lump Sum Death Payment — Form SSA-8-F5

This is the same form you would need to apply for insurance benefits payable under the Railroad Retirement Act. The form is five pages long. The last page is a Receipt For Your Claim. It lists a name and telephone number for you to call if you have questions.

Application for Mother's or Father's Insurance Benefits — Form SSA-5-F6

You will complete this form if you have children less than age 16, or disabled children whose disability began before age 22. This form is six pages and provides a receipt. In addition, it also lists the "Changes to Be Reported and How to Report." We will discuss these in depth later in the chapter.

Application for Child's Insurance Benefits — Form SSA-4-BK

If you have children under 18 (or 19 if still in secondary school), they may qualify for benefits. This eight page form contains the same information as Form SSA-5-F6, plus a description of conditions that would cause a child to become unentitled.

Application for Widow's or Widower's Insurance Benefits — Form SSA-10-BK

This is an eight-page form which contains provisions for applying for Medicare Supplementary Medical Insurance.

Application for a Social Security Number Card — Form SS-5

You will need to complete one of these for each person applying for benefits who does not already have a Social Security number. It is a simple four-page form, three of the pages being information and directions.

RECEIVING YOUR BENEFITS

After completing the paperwork, you wait for your first check(s) to arrive. Your first check will reflect any retroactive benefits. Be sure that you keep all of the receipts from the forms that you completed, so that you will have the name and number of someone specific to call if your checks do not arrive when expected.

Social Security checks are usually received on the third day of the month. If the third day falls on a weekend or Federal holiday, then you receive your check on the last day the bank was opened before the third of the month. Therefore, if July third is on Saturday, your check should arrive on Friday, July second.

Checks are issued following the month they are earned. If your benefits begin in April, you will not receive a check until May.

Should your check be more than a few days late, notify your post office. They will advise you. If the check appears to be lost or stolen, notify your local Social Security office immediately.

One method of preventing lost or stolen checks is to have checks directly deposited to your bank account. This is a voluntary program and may be accomplished by completing Form SF-1199 at your banking institution. It may take two or three months for the checks to by-pass your mailbox and go directly to the bank. If after this, you are still getting the checks, complete another form and try again. Should you want to discontinue Direct Deposit, notify your Social Security office.

Except in cases of federal taxes, child support, or alimony, Social Security checks can not be garnished or attached.

REPRESENTATIVE PAYEE

When you receive checks for a minor child or for a person unable to care for their affairs, their benefit check will be sent to you as the "representative payee." When receiving checks for children, the check will say, "Mary Smith for the children of R. Smith." You must endorse it as it is written.

There are certain duties required of representative payees. These include the following:

1. You must use the benefits for the care and well-being of the entitled recipient.

2. When asked to do so, you must be able to make an accounting of how the money was used. Each year you must complete a Representative Payee Report that shows the SSA how you spent funds. This is not a detailed report that requires itemization, but rather asks if any money is being held in savings accounts or being invested, or if all was spent on day-to-day living expenses.

3. You are responsible for reporting any changes that occur that might affect Social Security benefits.

4. If you become unable or unwilling to continue as representative payee, you must notify the SSA in advance so that they will be able to find an alternate.

REPORTING CHANGES THAT MIGHT AFFECT SOCIAL SECURITY BENEFITS

There are many factors that affect the eligibility of a claimant. When any of the following changes occur, it is the responsibility of the beneficiary or his/her representative payee to notify their local SSA office immediately. In certain cases, failure to do so could result in a conviction of fraud with penalties or fines and/or imprisonment. Reasons for reporting include the following:

■ Change in marital status — beneficiary marries, divorces, becomes widowed.

■ Living outside of the United States. If you are a U.S. citizen and plan to be gone more than three months, you may request that your checks be sent to your new address as long as it is not a restricted country. If you are not a U.S. citizen, your checks may stop after you are out of the country six months.

■ Change in employment. If you decide to begin working, or increase your work hours, or if for any other reason, your earnings increase, you must report.

■ If beneficiary becomes incarcerated in a prison or penal institution for a felony.

■ If beneficiary dies.

■ If beneficiary receives any government pension or annuity or any changes are made in a reported pension or annuity.

■ If beneficiary is no longer disabled.

■ Custody changes. As an example, a minor child goes to live with a grandparent, leaving his mother.

■ Beneficiary has any change in income or resources.

■ Beneficiary moves or enters or leaves an institution.

■ Beneficiary minor child marries or leaves full time school.

You are liable for any benefits received that you are not entitled to. You must repay any unentitled sums (or they will be deducted from future checks, if you qualify for any). The simplest way is to return the check with a note of explanation. In the case of direct deposit checks, simply call the bank concerned and have them return the check.

MEDICARE BENEFITS

Earlier in the chapter, it was explained that Social Security benefits are divided into the four categories of retirement, survivor, disability, and hospital insurance. Because many widows(ers) may be nearing the age requirement of 65, a discussion of Social Security insurance is included. For more detailed information, refer to the sources mentioned earlier in this chapter.

Medicare is administered by the Health Care Financing Administration. It is a Federal Health Insurance (FHI) program for persons 65 years or older, certain disabled persons, and persons with permanent kidney failure.

Medicare has two parts. Part A, which is hospital insurance, is funded through the Social Security tax (FICA). There is no charge to eligible recipients. You are automatically eligible for Part A if you are 65 and entitled to Social Security benefits, or if age 65 and your spouse is entitled to SS benefits, or age 65 and a widow(er) of a person entitled to SS benefits, or age 65 and have been entitled to SS disability benefits for 24 months, or if you are entitled to SS benefits because of permanent kidney failure and need dialysis or kidney transplant.

About three months before your 65th birthday, contact your SS office. Although you are automatically entitled under the conditions above, there may be cases when you need to apply. If you are *not* eligible for Part A hospital insurance, you may choose to purchase this coverage for $226 a month (1987). If you do make this choice, it is mandatory that you also purchase Part B, the medical insurance.

The list of covered services under Part A can be categorized into five areas: hospital coverage, post-hospital skilled nursing facility care, post-hospital home health care, hospice care, and blood. A list of specific coverage can be obtained by contacting your SSA office. Part A does not pay for all hospital charges. There are deductible amounts, depending on the length of your hospital stay. In 1987, 1-60 days, you pay $520; 61-90, you pay $143 a day; 91-150 days, $286 a day; beyond 150 days, you pay all costs. There is a sixty day lifetime reserve that may be used, but only once. There are other deductibles with some of the other services.

Congress has been concerned with the financial burden placed on the elderly and disabled should they suffer a long term illness. Because of this concern, catastrophic health insurance coverage has been explored. The expected plan for passage in Congress makes the following major changes (to be phased in between 1990 and 1993) in the current Medicare system.

1. The maximum covered stay in a hospital will be increased to 365 days.

2. The out-of-pocket costs on non-drug related services would be limited to $1,850 per year.

3. Medicare will pay 80% of outpatient drug costs in excess of $600.

Four dollars a month premium for the catastrophic coverage will be added to the 1987 premium of $17.90. The new drug benefits will add an additional 60 cents in 1990, $1.40 in 1991, $2.20 in 1992, and $3.30 in 1993. There are additional income related premiums based on federal income tax liability.

Part B Medical Insurance generally covers services outside of the hospital, such as a portion of the doctor bills, outpatient care, and other medical supplies and services. Part B is optional. If you do not want Part B coverage you must so state at the time you apply for Part A. Medical insurance is funded partially from the federal government, and partially through the premiums paid by those insured. The premiums are $17.90 per month (1987). These increase slightly each year.

Part B does not pay all charges. There is an annual deductible amount as well as the difference between eight percent of the "approved charge" and the actual charge. The approved charge is what Medicare determines, using the lesser of three criteria, to calculate an acceptable figure for services and supplies.

Because Medicare leaves many gaps in your medical and hospital coverage, it is strongly recommended that you have supplemental insurance to make up the difference. This will be discussed more fully in Chapter Fourteen, "Financial Planning."

MEDICARE PAYMENTS FOR A DECEASED PERSON

If your spouse died while covered by Medicare, you will want to file a claim so that his medical bills are paid. Call your SSA office and ask for Form HFCA 1660, Medicare Payment for Services to a Patient Now Deceased. Together with the completed form, send in all medical bills. Make certain that you have all charges before sending in the claim. After Medicare has paid their portion, either the estate or your supplemental insurance carrier will be responsible for the remainder.

THE APPEAL PROCESS

If you disagree with any decision by the Social Security Administration, do not hesitate to appeal. Many cases have been appealed and won. There are five steps involved in an appeal.

1. Request an explanation of their decision. It may be that their information is incorrect or that they are not aware of a particular fact. If you understand why they rejected your

claim, you may be able to offer information that clarifies your position.

2. Request reconsideration of their decision. The case will be independently reviewed to see if the original decision was correct.

3. Request a hearing. If after reconsideration you still are not satisfied, you have a right to a hearing before an Administrative Law Judge of the Office of Hearings and Appeals. If the case involves a Medicare determination, the amount in question must meet a set minimum amount. If the hearing is over seventy-five miles from your home, you are entitled to reimbursement of expenses.

4. Request a review. You are entitled to request that the Appeals Council review the Administrative Law Judge's decision.

5. Court Action. You may appeal your case to the United States District Court.

You have sixty days after receiving the SSA decision to file an appeal. The necessary form is at your SSA office. You are entitled to representation by any qualified person. This may or may not be a lawyer. While there is no cost for the appeal, you are responsible for attorneys' or other professionals' fees, which must meet with the approval of the Social Security Administration.

WHAT IS MEDICAID?

Medicaid provides assistance to low income and disabled persons and their families who have substantial medical bills. It is funded through federal, state, and local governments. It is administered by states through local county and city welfare programs or public health and assistance offices. Anyone receiving SSI (see below) is automatically covered by Medicaid.

WHAT IS SSI?

Although administered through the Social Security Administration, Supplemental Security Income (SSI) is actually funded from general revenues of the U.S. Treasury. It was established to provide a minimum monthly income for people over 65, or blind or disabled (no age limitation) and who are citizens or lawful aliens who have met permanent residence requirements in the United States.

To qualify for SSI, your income and assets must be minimal. There are specific rules that determine what is counted as income and what is not. Generally, income includes earned income and unearned income. The countable income for a single person may not exceed $336 a month; a couple's countable income may not exceed $504 a month. There is a long list of items not considered as income. Contact your local Social Security office for a complete list of these.

Assets (anything you own) must be valued at less than $1,700 if you are single. Combined assets for a couple must be valued at less than $2,400 (1987). Assets counted toward this total are real estate, personal property, life insurance, securities, and bank accounts. Assets not included are a home where claimant resides and is part owner, personal property with a total equity value of $2,000 or less (if over $2,000, the excess counts), an automobile valued at less than $4,500 (if over, the excess is counted. There are instances where a car is excluded regardless of the value. Check with your SSA office.) Also excluded are life insurance policies (if total face value is less than $1,500), burial plots for the immediate family, burial funds (with limitations), retroactive SSI or Social Security payments for six months after receipt, and any items needed by a blind or disabled person to maintain or establish self-support.

Besides monthly cash payments, SSI recipients may also receive Medicaid, food stamps, social services (housekeeping help, transportation, meal preparation, etc.), and assistance for those wanting to work.

To apply for SSI, you will need the following information:

1. Social Security card or number.
2. Proof of age.
3. Names of people who contribute to your support.
4. Automobile registration.
5. Medical records if you are claiming disability.
6. Your latest tax bill or assessment, if you own property.

7. Financial papers that show assets or income such as bank books, security certificates, annuities or pensions, and insurance policies.

The application form is twelve pages long and entitled "Application for Supplemental Security Income" Form SSA-8000-BK.

If you are approved to receive SSI, the 1987 maximum federal benefit is $340 a month for individuals and $510 per month for couples.

Changes in the Social Security system occur on a regular basis. This evolution is due to the constant changes in the workplace, the financial fluctuation of the world, political influence, and the population profile in the United States. It is important that you do not rely on Social Security to meet your retirement needs or to support you and your children if your spouse should die or become disabled. The system is overtaxed. While the recent changes have alleviated the immediate problems, there are still many questions to be addressed in the future. Get all that you are entitled to from the Social Security system. After all, you have paid into it for many years, but don't expect it to last in its present form for as long as you will need it.

It is important to your financial planning to stay aware of changes as they are made in the system. Your local SSA office is well supplied with pamphlets that they will send to you free. These are updated on a regular basis. Call and have them send the ones that contain the information you need.

11.

Obligations and Debts

Unfortunately for our survivors, the debts and obligations we incur during our lifetimes outlive us. Dying may relieve the deceased of financial obligations, but it does not absolve the heirs. Very few of us die without owing money to someone. It may only be a few dollars on a credit or charge card, or it may be millions of dollars in business loans. Whatever the amount, the process for satisfying these debts is basically the same.

Before you start writing checks to pay creditors, there are some questions you need to address.

1. Which are estate debts and which are personal debts? If you are the surviving spouse and sole heir, you might not think this is important because in the long run it all comes out of the same pocket, but it could become very important when you file tax returns.

2. In whose name(s) are the debts held? Determining this will help you decide whether the obligations belong to the estate or to the person.

3. What types of debts are outstanding? The type of debt you have determines how and when it must be paid.

4. Are any debts covered by insurance?

5. Is there enough money to satisfy all of the claims? If there isn't enough to pay all of the debts, what do you do?

6. Where can you get advice?

7. How do you keep records?

8. Where can you get emergency money? (While the other questions are covered in this chapter, you should read

Chapter Twelve, "Unexpected Expenses," to see where you can get emergency money.)

Once you can answer these questions, you will have the information necessary to pass through this phase of death with few problems.

Let's begin our probe by reviewing what constitutes an estate. When you are alive, everything you own makes up your assets. Assets include personal property such as clothes, jewelry, money, and cars. It also includes real estate, securities, royalties, and patents. All things you legally own are your assets. When you die, these assets become your estate. An estate is a separate entity. It has its own bank account to pay its own bills and to receive its own income. The estate is in existence until the administrator or executor has completed all of his duties and the courts rule that the matters of the estate are completed.

In Chapter Five, "Understanding Wills and Probate," we saw that one of the duties of the administrator/executor was to pay creditors who make claims against the estate. When the estate is admitted to probate, a classified advertisement is placed in the newspaper telling of the death and soliciting claims against the estate. Though it varies from state-to-state, the ad is generally placed two or three times. Creditors are then given a deadline for filing these claims. This deadline is as little as sixty days in some states, and as long as six months in others. If no notices are given to creditors, the deadline would be three years for most states, but can be six years as in the case of Michigan. After the deadline has passed, any additional claims on the estate can be ignored, as they are not legally owed any longer. One of the advantages of probate, as you will remember, is this very point. Without the "Notice to Creditors" stipulation and provisions, the heirs could be hounded for years to pay debts. Probate, in this sense, is a protection.

DETERMINING ESTATE v. PERSONAL DEBTS

As the claims and bills arrive, you will need to determine in which pile they belong. Which debts should be paid by the spouse and which should be paid by the estate? If you are the spouse and the executor(trix), you will be paying both. But remember, the estate is a separate entity and you are just writing checks for it because it can not literally write for itself. By now, you should have already opened a separate estate account from which to write these checks.

To help you determine which is which, you must go back to our discussion on how property is held. The same rules apply to credit and loans. If only the deceased's name is on the contract, then it is an estate bill. If both of your names are on the contract, then you will be responsible for payment.

Most of the bills you receive fit into five categories:
■ Credit card/charge cards
■ Installment credit
■ Notes payable
■ Taxes
■ Household expenses

Make a list as the bills arrive and categorize them under three headings: DECEASED'S (or HIS/HERS), OURS, and MINE.

Read the contracts to determine under which column each bill belongs. For instance, a credit card or charge card may have been in his name only, therefore it would go under DECEASED'S column. It may have been in both of your names or in his name only, but you had credit privileges. In this case, it should go under OUR column. If you maintained a card under your name only (a good idea), then it would go under the MINE column.

Installment credit or contract loans are usually used in purchasing big items such as automobiles, furniture, boats, and recreational vehicles. Again, check to see how the contract is signed to determine which column you will list these bills. One thing to remember, even if the installment loan was owned solely by the deceased, he may have used your home or some other jointly owned item as collateral to get that loan.

Notes payable are generally home mortgages, bank loans, credit union loans, or loans against profit-sharing plans. They may also include co-signed loans. Because some people do not understand the implications of co-signing a loan with someone else, let's deviate for a moment to discuss the provisions of a co-signed loan. If a person can not get a loan based on his own credit rating or income, he can find someone to co-sign the loan. The bank or loan institution then takes into consideration the co-signer's income and credit rating. If the co-signer qualifies, then the loan can be granted. Be aware of the following:

1. As co-signer, you are being asked to guarantee a debt. If the borrower does not pay the debt, you will have to.

2. You are not only liable for the full unpaid amount, but also any late fees and collection costs.

3. In most states, the creditor can collect from you without first trying to collect from the borrower. You can be sued or your wages garnished just as the borrower's. A default in the loan can appear on your credit record.

4. Even as a co-signer, the loan can be counted as loans payable on your account when you go to apply for loans or credit for yourself.

Taxes include federal, state and property. Be sure to include any past due tax bills. The way the taxes are filed determines in which column you would list them. If it is an estate form, then it goes under DECEASED'S column. If it is a property tax bill on property owned solely by the deceased, then it goes under the same column.

Household expenses include telephone, utilities, water, sewage, garbage, pest control, gardener, gas, repairs, and maintenance. Most everything in this category goes under the OURS column.

Any expenses incurred because of the death such as hospital bills, funeral expenses, and legal fees belong to DECEASED'S column. Many times, business expenses are his/her separate property and would also go under the same column.

When you finish, your list may look something like the following:

HIS:	OUR:	MINE:
VISA #1234567	AAA Mortgage Co.	VISA #987654
General Hospital	MasterCard #4567890	Credit Union
XYZ Funeral Home	City Utility Co.	
Z Equipment Leasing	Property tax	
	Auto loan	
	Bob's Furniture	
	Joe's Roofing Co.	

This visual picture illustrates what are considered to be estate obligations. Everything under HIS or DECEASED'S column is the estate's obligation. Everything under OUR column belongs to both of you. For accounting and tax purposes, one-half of the household expenses, mortgage and property taxes belong to the estate between the time the co-owner died and the close of probate. Because you want to maintain your credit rating, it is suggested that for practical reasons, you go ahead and pay the OUR bills out of your account, keeping accurate records of those payments for the IRS and courts. Any bills listed under MINE are of course yours, no matter what.

Wait! Don't pay that bill yet!

After you have established who is going to pay the bill, contact the creditors, tell them of the death, and tell them to whom and where to send the bill. This is especially important if the spouse is not the executor/administrator.

Wait until all claims are filed and the waiting period has ended before paying any creditors. Medical bills, funeral bills, and administrative costs generally have precedence over other obligations and may be paid sooner, if it is obvious the estate is solvent. The three to six month waiting period for estate claims is expected by the creditors, and it gives you time to obtain funds and benefits to pay your other bills.

Taxes due from the estate are high on your list of priorities. The tax collector is one of your most important creditors. The IRS says that if the executor pays other debts first (other than bills related to last illnesses, burial, and estate administrative costs), and there is not enough left to pay the tax obligation, then the executor/administrator is responsible for taxes owed up to the combined amount of the bills or heirs already paid.

Check to see if any of the debts are covered by insurance. Sometimes, as discussed in Chapter Seven, "Survivor Benefits," people purchase or have automatic life insurance on their accounts that pay off the balance of the account if the borrower should die. To find out, write a simple letter, make copies, and send to creditors where there is a chance this might apply.

Sample letter to creditors:

                                        1234 A Street
                                        Jasper, MO
                                        February 1, 1988

VISA USA
567 B Street
Anytown, NY

Dear (look on your bill for a representative's name):

My husband, John James Doe, had account #987654 with your company. He died on January 1, 1988. As executrix of his estate, I must determine whether he had any insurance with your company that would pay the outstanding balance on the account at the time of his death. Please advise me as soon as possible concerning this matter. You may send any information and bills to me at the above address.

Sincerely,

Jane Doe

For those where you know there was insurance, such as with medical bills, make claim after you are positive all of the bills have been submitted. In the case of Medicare, you do not file a claim with your supplemental insurance company until after Medicare has paid their portion.

Scrutinize each bill, especially claims against the estate and those that arrive unexpectedly. Any companies that are unfamiliar to you should be contacted asking for an explanation of the charges and a copy of the original bill. Make sure each claim is valid and correct. This may take some digging through your spouse's papers to compare invoices and receipts. Sending unfounded claims to widows is a long running scam among con artists. They look for the notices to creditors in newspapers and simply send out a bill. If you suspect a claim is phony, give it to your attorney.

Now you need to determine whether the estate is solvent. Is there enough money to pay the estate's debts? Is there enough money to pay personal debts that are not a part of the estate? One of the first jobs of the executor(trix), is to assemble a list of all of the assets. This shows how much the estate is worth. When it is obvious that the estate's assets are sufficient to pay its obligations, and after the waiting period for creditor's claims has ended, you may begin paying the bills. Probate can not be closed and the estate settled until creditors are satisfied.

If the estate is insolvent, there are complex means of dealing with the assets that do exist. Each state has, as part of its probate laws, an order of descent for creditors. Typically funeral costs, medical bills, and administrative costs are first on the list. Taxes would follow. Any money left after this would be distributed according to the state's laws. The residue could be pro-rated among the creditors, or it could be in order of claims, or any other method the law provides. You would definitely need a lawyer in such a case.

Another of the early tasks of the executor is to provide an allowance for the surviving heirs. If there is not enough money for you to meet the day-to-day expenses, then the court is petitioned to approve a living allowance. It will be necessary for you to come up with a list of expenses so that the court can determine an adequate amount. If the estate is insolvent or so small that it offers little relief, what can you do?

Although you may not be responsible for the debts of the estate, you are still responsible for those debts you held jointly and for your own personal debts. It is very important that you maintain a good credit record. Now that you are alone, your credit rating is your sole responsibility.

WHEN FUNDS ARE SHORT

Your intentions are to satisfy your creditors. Although your spouse's income has ceased, the bills have not. Now you are trying to pay the same amount of bills, with only a fraction of the income. This condition may be temporary while you are waiting for your Social Security checks to begin or for insurance benefits to arrive. If survivor benefits are slim, the con-di-tion may require more long-term planning and budgeting.

There are steps you can take to help you through this time of financial uncertainty. These are listed in the order of consideration.

1. KNOW YOUR RIGHTS. The Fair Debt Collection Practices Act was passed in 1977 to provide the debtor with certain protection under the law. One of its provisions says that a debt collector may contact you in person, by mail, telephone, or telegram but not at an inconvenient or unusual time or place. Very early in the morning or late at night is considered inconvenient. A collector may not contact you at work, if your employer disapproves. You may stop a debt collector from contacting you by writing a letter to the collection agency telling them to stop. The debt collector then may only contact your attorney. If you do not have an attorney, then other people may be contacted to ascertain your current address or place of employment, but they may not say that you owe money. The debt collector has five days to send you a written notice of how much you owe and to whom. It will also contain instructions for you to follow if you feel you do not owe the money. You have thirty days to respond. If proof is sent to you showing that you do indeed owe the money, then the debt collector may resume his collection efforts.

Debt collectors may not:

■ Threaten your person, property, or reputation.

■ Give your name to anyone except the credit bureau.

■ Speak obscenely.

■ Annoy you with repeated telephone calls.

■ Call without identifying themselves.

■ Advertise your debt.

■ Contact you by postcard.

■ Misrepresent their identity.

■ Say that you have committed a crime.

■ Tell you that you can be arrested for not paying your debts.

■ Misrepresent the amount of the debt.

■ Indicate that papers are legal forms when they are not.

■ Threaten you with seizure, garnishment, attachment, or forced sale of property or wages when in fact they do not intend to or are not legally able to do so.

■ Give false credit information concerning you.

■ Send you any documents that look like documents from a court or government agency.

■ Collect more than you owe.

■ Deposit a post-dated check before the date on the check.

■ Make you accept collect calls or telegrams.

Should you feel that your rights have been violated, you have one year to sue the debt collector in a state or federal court. Report any problems to your state Attorney General's office and the Federal Trade Commission.

2. LIST BILLS IN THE ORDER OF THEIR PRIORITY. Categorizing and listing obligations by priority puts them into perspective. Look at the contracts or terms on the billings to ascertain the interest rates, late charges, and date due. You need to know what action will be taken if you fail to make the payments. Are there late payments? How much? Can the creditor demand payment in full if the terms of the loan are broken? Is there a grace period? How long? Can property be repossessed? Is foreclosure a possibility? When?

Generally, after you have insured that the roof over your head is secure, make your utility bill payments, for it is easy for utility companies to disconnect your service. Next, your auto loan payments, because they can repossess your car with no advance notice and stick you with the towing and storage as well as the full balance if you want the car back. (Before you let this happen, try selling the car yourself. Take the equity and find less expensive transportation.) Insurance premiums should be high on your priority list. You can not afford to get further behind in debts should you become injured or ill or suffer losses of personal property. Credit card balances should be paid off as soon as possible because of the high interest rates on unpaid balances. Some credit cards have interest rates as high as twenty-two percent.If you have more than one credit card, compare interest rates and pay off the highest one.

3. CONTACT CREDITORS. Don't wait until your account is turned over to a debt collector. As soon as you see there is going to be difficulty making the usual payments, call or write the creditor. If you have been current in the past and have a good record with the company, they will probably be willing to work with your current situation. Explain the change in your circumstances and ask if they can adjust the payment schedule, refinance at a lower interest rate, spread out the payments over a longer period of time, or work out a modified payment plan (pay interest only) until conditions improve.

4. SEEK COUNSELING. There are agencies that provide services for people in financial trouble. Some are privately owned and charge fees based on set rates or percentages. Debt counseling, debt consolidation, and debt reorganization are some of the advertising terms to lure those in need to their offices. Please investigate these types of businesses thoroughly before you sign any contracts. Check them out with your Better Business Bureau. Find out exactly what they are going to do for you and get it in writing before you agree to anything. Usually, they can do little more than you can do. They might contact your creditors for you and try to work out a deal as discussed above, or they may just put you in contact with a bankruptcy lawyer. Both of these you can do for yourself at no cost.

Your financial planner should be able to give you some sound advice and offer some guidelines. Utilize the time wisely by having all of your assets and obligations down on paper so that your situation can be analyzed more quickly.

Alternatives to the professional agencies are numerous. Ask your banker for advice. He deals with these types of problems constantly and can give you information and ideas.

Counsel with a person that you respect in the financial sense. They didn't get to be successful without a lot of knowledge concerning debt payment.

There may be help within the community. Senior citizen groups often have financial counselors. Church congregations in all likelihood have someone who would be willing to help you for a nominal fee or without charge. Credit unions often offer credit counseling.

Legal Aid and Legal Services help people who cannot afford the services of lawyers. You must meet eligibility requirements in order to receive this free legal service. There are over 1000 offices across the United States. Attorneys, law students, and paralegals can assist you with all sorts of problems including credit, social security, utilities, welfare, and landlord-tenant disputes. Check your phone book under federal, state, and local governments.

If you have a VA or FHA loan and can not make the payments for reasons beyond your control, these agencies have a mortgage assistance program. Contact your local offices for information.

Consumer Credit Counseling Services (CCCS) is a non-profit organization supported by banks, credit card companies, finance companies, and other credit offering organizations. It has over 200 offices in forty-four states. It provides educational programs, money management techniques, and assists in debt payment plans. Counselors will help you set up a realistic budget. They will help you plan for future expenses. They will work with you and your creditors to establish a mutually acceptable repayment plan.

Services may be offered without charge or for a nominal fee. To locate your nearest CCCS, contact:

> National Foundation for Consumer Credit, Inc.
> Suite 507
> 8701 Georgia Avenue
> Silver Spring, MD 20910
> (301) 589-5600

5. DECLARE BANKRUPTCY. This is a last alternative after every other avenue has been explored. This is a very serious matter and should only be considered after trying all of the suggestions above. Bankruptcy will leave a mark on your

future credit rating for years to come. Consult an attorney for information.

Staying ahead of the game

After getting a handle on your obligations, you will want to maintain your hold. This can be very difficult for someone not accustomed to having complete and sole control over all financial decisions. It takes discipline. First, you must set priorities. Decide what is most important to you. Everyone's priorities are different and can not be judged by other people. You can tell if something is a priority by your willingness to do without something else to have it. You may need to cut expenses to maintain your priorities.

Avoid getting back into the debtor's corner by running up your credit and charge cards, once they are paid off. With the Tax Reform Act of 1986, it is more important than ever that consumer debt be minimized. Before 1987, the interest paid on credit cards, automobile loans, student loans, and other types of consumer debt was deductible. Beginning in 1987, these deductions will be phased out over a five year period. Only 65 percent will be deductible in 1987; 40 percent in 1988; 20 percent in 1989; 10 percent in 1990; and 0 percent in 1991.

Credit cards are undeniably convenient. Just make sure that you are master over the card. Don't charge more than you can pay off each month. A rule of thumb used by many advisors is limit your debt — excluding house and car loan — to less than twenty percent of your after-tax income. A more in-depth discussion of credit cards and managing money will be covered in Chapter Fourteen, "Financial Planning," and Chapter Fifteen, "Building Credit On Your Own."

HOMESTEADING YOUR RESIDENCE

Most states have laws that protect a homeowner from having to sell his home in order to satisfy certain kinds of debts. In some states, the homestead is automatic. In others, it must be applied for and recorded with the county clerk's office. Not to be confused with the same term applying to claims on federal lands, where a person acquires title to land by establishing residence or making improvements, homesteading in this sense means protecting the equity in your home.

Homestead laws vary state-to-state. The amount that one can protect under homestead laws goes from $1,000 in the states of Tennessee, Ohio, and South Carolina to $80,000 in North Dakota. Some states, rather than giving a specific dollar figure, limit amounts of land, i.e., Kansas exempts 160 acres if rural or one acre if urban. States that have no homestead protection laws are Connecticut, Delaware, the District of Columbia (although widow(er) is entitled to $10,000 debt free), Indiana (spouse is entitled to portion of real property debt free), Maryland, New Jersey, Pennsylvania, and Rhode Island.

In most states, the homestead exemption continues for surviving spouse or children. Those states in which it does not are Alaska, Arizona, Missouri, Oklahoma, and Oregon.

Typically, homesteads may be filed only on the principle place of residence and do not protect against any claims filed before the homestead went into effect against mechanic, contractor, materialman, laborer, or vendor liens. In addition, homesteads do not protect against debts secured by a mortgage or deed of trust.

In order to invalidate a homestead claim, you must file a declaration of abandonment with the county recorder.

The disadvantage of a homestead is that a homesteaded property cannot be used as collateral for a loan. Therefore, if you intend to borrow money and need the equity in your home for collateral, homesteading would not be a viable alternative.

A Declaration of Homestead is not a difficult form to complete. You can get all of the information that you need from the Grant Deed or Deed of Trust. Make certain that the description of the property is accurate and complete. Most states require that completed forms be notarized.

The proper form can usually be found in stationery stores or at the county clerk's office. You do not need a lawyer to complete the form, but you should consult with him to find out your state's limitation. With this information,

you can decide whether homesteading is something you want
or need to do.

RECORDKEEPING

It will be important for you to keep accurate records of the
bills you pay for the estate as well as for yourself. The courts
will ask to see them if there are other heirs besides yourself
and you may be called upon by the IRS to show proof of some
transactions. You might need to justify why a particular bill
was put in the estate pile instead of the personal pile.

Don't be frightened. You needn't run off to the nearest
CPA. Unless the estate is large and complex, you will be able
to maintain adequate records yourself.

A basic recordkeeping system can include four large
manila envelopes and a notebook for notes. There are many
fancier systems that can be found in any stationery store.
These can include plastic file boxes, cancelled check files,
and prepared bookkeeping books with spaces for entries. All
of these extras do not insure a better record system, but if
that is your style, check them out and purchase what you
think will best suit your needs.

As you receive bills, sort them according to personal or
estate. Put them in separate envelopes labeled accordingly.
When you pay them, always use a check. This acts as a receipt and proof of payment. After they are paid, put them in
separate envelopes labeled "Paid Estate Bills" and "Paid Personal Bills." When the cancelled checks arrive each month,
staple the check to the bill stub that you have retained for
your records. Make any pertinent notes in your notebook. Be
sure to date the entries and make the notes complete enough
that you can jog your memory years from now. So often, we
think our memories are much better than they are. One note
that a widow came across said, "Paid Frank $1000 for ser-
vices." It took her three days to figure that one out. Make
your notes complete enough so that they will be able to help
you when you need them.

Recordkeeping, while necessary, needn't be elaborate. As
long as another person can see how much you received, how
much you spent, what you spent it for, who you wrote the

check to, and when the transaction took place, your bases are covered.

Paying debts can be one of the most discouraging processes even in the best of times. Try to focus your energy on streamlining your expenses until you have your obligations met. Pamper and reward yourself with simpler pleasures instead of expensive tickets to the opera or a sporting event, until your situation improves. With discipline and planning, you gain the satisfaction of knowing you are master of your finances instead of a slave to them.

11.

Real Estate

Real estate or real property consists of land, anything affixed to the land that can be regarded as permanent, that which is incidental or appurtenant to the land, and that which is immovable by law. Land includes all of the materials that make up the substance of the earth as well as the space above and below the earth. Permanent fixtures of the land include buildings, foliage, bridges, and anything permanently affixed to these items, such as built-in appliances, attached cabinets, and installed carpets. Easements and waterways are an example of that which is incidental or appurtenant to the land, and therefore considered real estate. Finally, anything that is prohibited from removal by law is real property.

For many, real estate accounts for the bulk of their estates. It may come in the form of a personal residence, a vacation home, and commercial or industrial property. It may have been purchased as an investment, in which case it could be any of the above. It may simply provide a roof over your head. Large or small, elaborate or simple, real estate is an important aspect of one's estate.

Volumes have been written concerning real estate. It is not the purpose of this book to tell you everything about buying and selling property. Real estate laws and regulations are ever-changing and vary from state-to-state, so the task would be monumental and fruitless. This chapter is intended for a select group of individuals, the widow(er) who has inherited real property from a deceased spouse. The information is basic to any decision you make concerning your inherited holdings. It contains ideas for you to ponder and alternatives you may not have considered.

If you do not own any real estate, nor heir to any, you may still benefit from reading the section on alternative living arrangements and/or the section on buying real estate.

TRANSFERRING REAL ESTATE TITLE

Real property, unlike personal property, is distributed according to the laws of the state in which it is located. Rules of descent to heirs are governed exclusively by the state in which the real estate lies. Therefore, the transfer of title must subscribe to the laws of the state even if domicile (place where deceased claimed residence) is governed by contradictory laws. If you are heir to out-of-state property, and your spouse left no will, you need to contact a lawyer within the state where the property exists for information about the intestate disbursement laws of that state.

For property willed to you, or property inherited within your state of domicile, you will need to look at the deeds to see how title to the property is held. By now, it is beginning to sound like a broken record, but how the deeds are held will determine the process of having title transferred to your name. A quick review of Chapter Five tells us that property may be commonly held in six different ways.

1. Joint tenancy provides for owners to hold equal shares. Upon death of one of the owners, his share passes directly to the other joint tenants.

2. Tenants in Common may or may not own equal shares. When one owner dies, his share passes to his heir(s), not to the other tenants in common.

3. Tenants by entirety are married couples who do not live in community property states. Upon death, the surviving spouse receives the property, unless by prior agreement by both parties.

4. Community property states (Arizona, California, Idaho, Louisiana, Nevada, New Mexico, Texas, and Washington) provide that each spouse has an equal interest in property that was acquired after marriage or voluntarily designated as such. Upon death, the deceased may dispose of his

share by Will in any manner he likes. Failure to do so will result in spouse receiving it through intestate succession.

5. Separate property is owned entirely by one spouse. This may be inherited property or property owned before the marriage. Without a Will, it will be dispersed according to the state laws of descent.

6. Common Law property exists in those states that are not community property states. Property is owned by whomever earns the wages to buy it. Without a Will, property is dispersed according to the state laws of descent.

With the exception of joint tenancy and tenancy by entirety, property held in other forms will go through probate. (Community property, in some states, can pass to a spouse without going through probate if the proper petitions are filed and the court approves the action). During the period of probate, titles will be cleared and transferred to the rightful heirs under the supervision of the courts. You will be informed of the exact information required, and your attorney will complete the necessary criteria for accom-plish-ing title transfer.

In the cases of joint tenancy and tenancy by entirety, the property automatically passes to the survivor. For record title purposes, you must record, in the county where the property is located, a certified copy of a court decree determining the fact of death and describing the property. Documentation to accomplish the recording and transfer typically includes a certified copy of the death certificate, a notarized Affidavit — Death of Joint Tenant, and tax lien releases from the state controller and IRS. You can accomplish this without the aid of an attorney. Call the county clerk's office and ask what you need and where you can get it. They can instruct you as to your state's requirements.

REAL ESTATE APPRAISALS

It is improbable that an heir to real property can get through the process of a spouse's death without needing the services of an appraiser. Property appraisals will be needed to determine the value of the estate not only for the probate court, but also for the state and federal tax agencies.

An appraisal is an estimate of the value of a property. Many things are taken into consideration to determine this value. An appraiser will measure the entire house to get the square footage. Any special equipment or features, such as built-in microwave, swimming pool, decking, awnings, and so on will be noted. The general condition of the property is noted. The types and conditions of surrounding homes will be included. Pictures are usually taken of several views of the home. Through county records, the appraiser will compare the selling prices of similar homes in the neighborhood. Often, the appraiser will include maps and building sketches.

Appraisal reports can be very detailed or more general, depending on the purpose of the report. When an appraiser is given the assignment, the reason for the appraisal is explained, i.e. market value, sale price, or loan value.

When all of the data is assembled, the appraiser makes a value conclusion. Remember, this is one person's subjective estimate based on a specific time, the current real estate market, and the current conditions of the property. If you should disagree with the appraiser's conclusion, get a second opinion. If you are wanting a selling price valuation, it would be wise to make repairs and improvements before you hire the appraiser. If you want a low valuation for tax purposes, don't make improvements until after the appraisal.

Finding an appraiser

Making an appraisal is exacting work. It demands someone who is accurate and thorough. For you, a lot is at stake, so you want someone who is fair. Good appraisers are in demand and it may take you a week or more to schedule an appointment. The appraiser will need time to make the report. Therefore, don't wait until you need the appraisal before you call an appraiser. As with many other professions, appraisers specialize. Make sure that the person you select has experience in appraising the type of property you have. You may need to employ more than one appraiser. Examples of specialization include jewelry, real estate (commercial, residential, industrial), machinery and equipment, automobiles, stamps and covers, Indian artifacts, antique furniture, fine art, oriental rugs, businesses, and even retirement plans.

The best places to find the names of appraisers is from people or businesses that use them frequently.

■ Insurance companies

■ Mortgage companies

■ Banks

■ The American Society of Appraisers (ASA) tests and certifies its members. Ethical standards are adopted by the ASA and members are screened. Look in the Yellow Pages for ASA members or contact American Society of Appraisers, P.O. Box 17265, Washington DC 20041. Their phone number is (703) 478-2228.

■ Real estate companies. Agents often do an informal appraisal by using computers to do a market analysis. This gives you a ball park selling price for your property. Depending on the purpose of the appraisal, this may adequately suit your needs. If you decide to go this route, get the opinion of several agents employed by different brokers, before you commit to a selling price.

Real estate improvements

It is important that you keep records of any improvements you make to the property you own. While our discussion focuses mainly on your residence, the rules apply to any type of land.

Capital gains is the difference between the price you paid for your house and the price you sold it for. You are taxed on any profit. You are allowed to subtract the cost of any improvements that you made while you owned the home, from the profit, thus lowering your capital gains tax. While this is a simplified explanation of the tax law, it does demonstrate the importance of keeping receipts and records.

Knowing how much you have spent on improvements will also help you determine a selling price. To be accurate, you must allow for depreciation of those improvements unless they are very recent.

Don't confuse improvements with maintenance and repairs. Planting a tree may be an improvement, but pruning it is not. Improvements must be permanent, not portable. A hot tub permanently placed in the ground is an improvement, one sitting on the deck that is movable to another location is not considered an improvement. The same holds true for swimming pools. The ones with plastic liners that sit on the lawn are not improvements, while the one that requires excavation is. Remodeling the kitchen with built-in appliances is an improvement. New bathroom fixtures qualify. Building a fence is an improvement, while replacing a few boards is not. Installing ceiling fans or skylights are improvements. Fixing a leaky faucet or shampooing the carpet go under maintenance and repair.

The easiest way to keep records of your home improvements is to get a large manila envelope and label it "Home Improvements." If you have more than one piece of property, get a separate envelope for each and label with the address of the property. Keep all receipts in this envelope. Either on a sheet of paper or on the envelope itself, list the date, amount, and improvement made. Try to keep in chronological order. Always pay for improvements with a check, if possible. If not, be sure to note on the receipt that you used cash or a credit card. This will help you should you ever need to substantiate your claims.

DOES YOUR HOME STILL MATCH YOUR NEEDS?

Sooner or later, all widows(ers) must ask themselves whether they should stay where they are, or move to another location. There are many factors involved in this major decision. You will need all of your faculties to make a wise decision, so try when possible, to delay a decision of this magnitude for at least one year after the death of your spouse.

When you feel ready and capable of investigating the many possibilities for living arrangements, take into consideration the following:

1. Your budget. If your income has been lessened dramatically by the loss of your spouse, it may become a hardship for you to maintain the mortgage payments. Be realistic. Don't do without other things that you want, just to keep a home that may no longer suit your needs. The rule of thumb is that your monthly house payment should not exceed one week's earnings. The total amount you spend on a place to live should not be more than thirty to thirty-five percent of

your income. This includes the taxes, insurance, repairs, and maintenance.

2. Your plans for the future. By now, you are giving some thought to what you want to do with the rest of your life. These plans will affect what type of housing is most suitable. Do you want to travel often? Do you want to live nearer your relatives? Do you want to go to work? Do you want to retire? Do you want to go to school?

3. Your priorities. What is most important to you? Being near old friends and/or relatives? Being close to your work? Being near your place of worship? Being near medical facilities, shopping centers, or the beach? Do you want the hustle and bustle of a large city, or the quietness of the country? Is climate a priority? Is cost a major factor? Make a list of everything that is important in the place you choose to live. Put them in order of their importance. To get everything you want would be near impossible, but to find a place that meets your priorities is obtainable.

4. Your health. If you need frequent medical attention or a certain climate to maintain your health, then this must certainly be a determining factor for your living arrangements. Do you need a home accessible to wheelchairs? Are you unable to climb stairs? Are high altitudes uncomfortable for you?

5. Your emotional well-being. What makes you feel good emotionally? Do you like to have lots of people around you or do you prefer solitude? Are you frightened when you are alone in your home? Do you like to garden and work in the yard? Do you need to have the security of owning the place you live? Is it difficult for you to leave or to live with the memories of your spouse?

6. Your physical needs. What does it take to make you physically comfortable? Do you need a yard for children and/or pets? Do you need more than one bathroom? How many bedrooms do you require? Are nearby recreational facilities important? Do you need room for entertaining?

As you can see, there is a lot to consider before you call the moving van. You need to have a clear understanding of what your needs are and the options available to meet these needs. Know what motivates you to make a change. Many widows(ers) think that if only they leave the home that they shared with their spouse, where so many memories linger, just waiting to jump out and torture them, then they could stop hurting. They try to escape pain by fleeing the scene. Unfortunately, it doesn't work. The memories follow you wherever you go. Often, the escapee feels lonelier and more isolated in strange surroundings. If this is your reason for wanting to move, please wait. Deal with the pain and loneliness where you are. Seek professional help if necessary. Make a decision when your reasons are based on sounder principles.

If you are at the point where you feel confident that a change is in order, then you are ready to look at the many varied living arrangements available. Never before have there been so many choices.

■ Buy a smaller house. If you are at least 55 years old, you may exclude up to $125,000 of profits on the sale of your personal residence. This is a one-time opportunity. To qualify, you must have lived at least three of the last five years in the home.

■ Rent a house. It is cheaper today to rent than to buy. Remember, the monthly mortgage payment is only a fraction of the true cost of buying a home.

■ Rent an apartment. If you are tired of the yard work and want to shed the responsibilities of maintenance and repairs, an apartment may just be the place. They come in all shapes, sizes, locations, and price ranges. You can get them furnished or unfurnished. Some are for adults only. Others cater to singles, the elderly, families, or young professionals. Many come with swimming pools and recreational rooms.

■ Purchase a manufactured house (mobile home). The advantages of living in a manufactured home are many. The cost is much less than a comparable conventional home. Down payments are more reasonable. You can choose the location within the limits of city zoning ordinances. There are many "mobile home parks" in the sun-belt states that cater mainly to retirees. The residents plan many opportunities for activities such as card games, trips, dances, dinners, movies, and parties. They provide access to recreational rooms and swimming pools. Many are located near golf courses and waterways. If you have not seen a mobile home lately, you are in for a surprise. They come with every amenity you can think of. If you are worried about the construction or safety of manufactured homes, set your fears to rest. In 1976, the federal government set standards for the industry with the Housing and Urban Development's National Manufactured Housing Code. In many instances, the codes for manufactured housing are more strict than for conventional houses.

■ Share a house. There are many ways to do this. If your present home is large enough, you might want to take in a boarder. Perhaps you want someone your age, sex, or religion. Then again, maybe you want a college student or a young couple. Be specific with your ad and ask for references when you interview prospects. Be sure that you contact each reference. Even if you know the person beforehand, put an agreement in writing. Anyone renting from you should know what you expect from them. What are the rules and limits?

Another alternative is for you to move in with someone else. Make sure their restrictions are within your tolerable limits.

A third idea is for two or more of you to find a place that you can rent together. Be sure that everyone understands the division of labor and shares the expenses equitably.

■ Create an accessory apartment. An accessory apartment is a small apartment accessible to the main house. It might be over the garage, in a basement, or added on to the side or back of the house. You could either rent an accessory apartment to live in yourself, or you could rent out the one attached to your home to someone else. If this sounds interesting to you, check your city and or county zoning laws to see if it is possible and get an estimate for any remodeling or additions from a contractor to see if it is feasible.

■ Consider ECHO housing. ECHO stands for Elder Cottage Housing Opportunity. A variety of other names includes Granny Flats, Granny Annexes, Portable Living Units for Seniors (PLUS), Granny Units (Australia), Garden Suites, and Garden Units. While there is a new interest in this housing option, the concept has been around for years. The Pennsylvania Dutch in the mid-1800's called them Gros Doddy Houses. Many communities are making allowances in their zoning codes for this type of housing. An ECHO home is a small, portable, self-contained unit that can be placed on the property of an existing residence. The exteriors can be matched to the main house for aesthetic purposes.

ECHO houses enable a person to live near friends or relatives, yet maintain privacy and independence. The homes are barrier-free for those in wheel chairs and energy-efficient and therefore inexpensive to maintain. Because they are portable, a special-use permit is required. Each time the permit expires, you have to apply for renewal, showing the still existing need for the ECHO housing.

There are one-bedroom, two-bedroom, and efficiency sized units available. Prices range from $16,000-$25,000 depending on the size of the unit. Some companies will lease the cottages. Their price includes the delivery and removal of the house when it is no longer needed.

Perhaps the most extensive study done on this type of optional housing was done by the Ontario Ministry of Housing in Canada. They ran a pilot program in which they purchased twelve homes and rented them out to qualified persons. Their evaluation showed it to be a viable housing option to meet the needs of their senior citizens. For information on their findings, write Ministry of Housing, Housing Conservation Unit, 7777 Bay Street, 2nd Floor, Toronto, Ontario M5G 2E5 or phone (416) 585-6514.

The Australian government leases Granny Units to its elderly. The program is so popular that there is a long waiting list for the units.

For further information on ECHO housing, you may contact these manufacturers:

Garden Units Leasing Limited
P.O. Box 971
Oshawa, Ontario
Canada L1H 7N2
(416) 725-0726

Coastal Colony Corporation
Box 797, R.D. #4
Manheim, PA 17545
(717) 665-6761

HCR Development, Ltd.
109 West Ninth Street
Leon, IA 50144
(515) 446-6888

■ Live in a boarding or rooming house. This is a little different than shared housing. Typically, the boarders rent a bedroom and share bathrooms and sitting room privileges. Meals are often provided and shared together in a central dining room. This could be ideal for someone who is not able or chooses not to cook and would enjoy the company and security of having others around.

■ Buy a condominium. This gives you the advantages of care-free living while still having the pride of ownership. Like apartments, condos come in many configurations and locations. Unlike apartment living, condo owners have more say in the policies governing the rules of the condominiums. There is usually an owners' association who makes decisions and handles problems. Because of ownership, you are free to decorate (at least the interior) any way you like. Except for a private patio or garden area, the grounds are maintained for you. Security patrols are often provided. Swimming pools and common recreational rooms are most often part of the package. Typically, there is a monthly charge in addition to your mortgage payment to cover these services.

■ Invest in cooperative housing. Cooperatives are much like condominiums except that you own shares in the corporation that owns the condos, rather than owning an individual unit. As a shareholder, you take an active part in the decision making of the corporation.

■ Be a caretaker. Sometimes people are looking for someone to live on the premises to watch over their property. Duties may or may not include handyman abilities. Often, a small salary is included along with living accommodations.

■ Congregate housing is for persons who would enjoy living in a group situation. You live in the privacy of your own apartment, but meals (served in a central dining room), transportation, and heavy housekeeping are provided. Staff are available to organize social and recreational activities. Some of these facilities are privately financed, while others are publicly assisted. If you need subsidized rent, make application through your local Housing Authority.

■ Consider a live-in companion, housekeeping, or babysitting position. With the two-career families of today, many people are looking for someone to take care of their homes and/or children. There are also many elderly or disabled people who would like to stay in their homes, but need assistance to do so. Room, board, and a small salary are usually offered for these positions.

■ Rent a single room. There are places that rent rooms without meals or kitchen privileges. This would necessitate your eating out, but if you do not plan to cook anyway, then this may not cause a problem.

■ Life Care or Continuing Care Communities are available in some parts of the country. In these communities, the resident, upon application, makes a one-time payment and agrees to pay a monthly fee for services provided. Fees cover maintenance, chore services, housekeeping, meals, and other personal care services. Many of these facilities have a "graduated care" arrangement which permits the resident to move from their own apartment into a nursing home unit, which includes skilled nursing home care, if needed. Frequently, these units will arrange for basic medical services. State and local regulations and requirements governing the operation and financing of these facilities vary considerably. Some states have no regulations or requirements regarding such facilities, while other states prohibit the development of such facilities.

The American Association of Retired Persons (AARP) has two books that will be most helpful if you are considering this option. One is the National Continuing Care Directory and the other is Comprehensive Information on Retirement Facilities and Communities Offering Prepaid Contracts for Long-Term Care. Your library or bookstore should have these available.

■ Nursing homes provide round-the-clock medical care for those who need such care. For persons unable to care for themselves, this is a viable option. You can be admitted to a nursing home only by directive from a physician. Intermediate care is a level of care extended to those who are unable to live independently, but do not need consistent, intensive care. Skilled nursing is for those who need intensive care. Most nursing homes are operated for profit, but there are those that are run by non-profit groups such as religious groups, fraternal organizations, and local governments. In 1978, the federal government mandated the ombudsman program, which provides information to the public and resolves complaints on behalf of the nursing home residents. Look in your phone book under local government to get the number of your ombudsman.

The above list gives you numerous options to consider. Which fits your income, personality, social needs, and physical needs? Choose two or three that sound the most appealing and start your investigation. You will want to visit any facility under consideration. Talk to other residents. Ask questions of the owners and managers. It is helpful if you develop your list of questions ahead of time so that you don't forget anything. The AARP, in cooperation with the Federal Trade Commission, offers a booklet entitled "Your Home Your Choice" that gives you detailed information about many of the options mentioned above. It contains excellent lists of questions for you to ask. To obtain a copy contact AARP, Consumer Affairs — Program Department, 1909 K Street, NW, Washington DC 20049 or FTC, Office of Consumer and Business Education, Bureau of Consumer Protection, Washington, DC 20580. Review contracts. Do not sign anything until an attorney or trusted advisor has reviewed the document. Discuss your plans with family members to see how they feel.

If you are considering a move out of your immediate locale, consider climate, state laws and taxes, and the cost of living of the area. Many states offer tax breaks to senior citizens, others do not. Before moving to an unfamiliar state, check the sales, income, property, excise, death/gift, and investment taxes. AARP publishes an excellent booklet entitled "Your Retirement State Tax Guide" that can give you all of this information.

Familiarize yourself with the area by reading local newspapers, obtaining information from the local Chamber of Commerce, skimming the local Yellow Pages, touring the town, and if possible, spending a vacation or two in or near the area.

Think hard before you pull up roots to move near children or other relatives. What guarantees do you have that they won't be transferred or move to another area because of a job change or better employment? It may be wise to make a trial move. You can rent your house or have someone stay in it until you see whether your new arrangement is going to work out.

Making a decision about where and how to live should be a head and a heart decision. Moving could be the most practical solution, but make you very unhappy emotionally. Try to balance your decision with facts and feelings.

Remember, you can change your mind. Perhaps you feel one way today; two years from now, your situation could be different. It took Vivian three years to decide to sell the beautiful home her husband had built for them. It was on ten acres of producing orchard, which made it expensive and very difficult for a single mother of young children to maintain. When Vivian decided she was ready to leave the isolation and hard work for a life in a city fifty miles away, she felt good about it. If she had acted sooner than when she was emotionally ready, it could have been devastating.

If your new change doesn't work out, you can try something else. Changes are not permanent. But you probably won't be able to buy back the home you sold, so consider keeping it until you are positive that you will not want to return, before you sell it.

STAYING IN YOUR HOME

Perhaps, after examining your options, you decide that you want to stay in your present home. Health considerations are the only motivation you have for leaving. Your family thinks you need help or companionship.

There are over 8,000 agencies in the U.S. that provide home care services. The purpose of these agencies is to provide services that enable you to stay in your home for as long as possible. Their services are diversified. We will discuss the most common ones.

1. Home Health Care. If your doctor feels that you need medical care that can be accomplished through regular visits from a registered, licensed practical, or vocational nurse, or home health aid, or therapist, then home health care may be for you. Your insurance may cover fees for these services. In thirty-eight sates, Medicaid benefits are approved for home care. Medicare pays a portion of these services if they are certified and approved agencies.

2. Meal Services. Many communities have a "Meals on Wheels" program for those unable to cook for themselves. Hot meals are delivered once a day. Some communities have transportation services to centers where meals are served. Look in your phone book under Community Services.

3. Homemaking and Chore Services. You can have someone come into your home on a regular basis to do cleaning. There are government agencies and private businesses that provide these services. Besides house cleaning, some provide laundry services, food shopping, and personal care. Gardeners can be hired for lawn maintenance.

It may be that you just need to modify your home in order to remain there. Perhaps you need to move your bedroom downstairs so that you do not have to climb stairs. A microwave oven may eliminate your need to light ovens or burners. A wheelchair ramp could make the home accessible. Removal of loose rugs could make your home safer. Grab bars in the bathroom may be the additions you need in the bathroom. Changing door knobs to lever types can make opening doors easier. Additional telephones in rooms most frequently occupied can be helpful. There are many modifications that you could make in order to live more comfortably in your own home. Some may be costly, others not.

Should you need to hire a contractor, be sure to ask for the names of people for whom he has done work. Call them to verify their satisfaction. Ask if they had any problems with the contractor fulfilling his agreement. Get several estimates for the same work. Cheapest does not always mean the best deal. The quality of materials or workmanship may be cheap also. Get everything in writing and read the contract carefully. Although you may be asked to pay for materials in advance, don't pay for work that has not been completed. This may be your only leverage in getting the job finished. Established contractors have accounts at building supply houses and usually don't need money for materials until they deliver them with a receipt to show you the exact amount of purchase. Then make sure you get everything listed on the receipt.

Widows are viewed as easy prey in areas where men traditionally take control. These areas include home repairs, automobile purchases and repairs, investments, insurance sales, and others, so be cautious. Have an attorney look over large purchase contracts. For smaller items, ask a trusted friend who has a knowledge of the subject to advise you.

If financial reasons indicate the necessity of your selling your home, investigate the Reverse Annuity Mortgage (RAM). Introduced by the Federal Home Loan Bank Board, it allows federally-chartered savings and loans to purchase your home. They make monthly payments to you and do not take over the house until you die. Not only are you assured an income, but also a place to live.

Property tax exemption and/or deferrals are available in some communities to persons over 65 who have limited income. Taxes are not payable until the property is either sold or upon your death, in which case it is paid by the estate.

Home equity conversion is a program which enables the owner to utilize the equity in a home for purchase of needed services. Some banks participate in this type of program and will arrange to free up these often overlooked resources to help cover the costs of services needed by the older person. The AARP maintains a Home Equity Information Center to educate both consumers and professionals of the merits and risks of home equity conversion. Contact them for information by writing:

> Consumer Center on Home Equity Conversion
> Consumer Affairs Section
> 1909 K Street, NW
> Washington, DC 20049

BUYING AND SELLING REAL ESTATE

After taking everything into consideration, and for whatever reasons, you decide that you want to sell a property (your residence, a rental, a vacation home, etc.). Or, perhaps you want to take a portion of your inheritance and buy a property (a condo, a rental, a smaller home, a cabin, etc.). Depending on the type of property you want to buy or sell, procedures and contracts will differ somewhat. Assuming that if you are involved with business property, you have an advisor in this specific field to guide you, this discussion will be limited to non-commercial residences.

Before you call a real estate broker, make an appointment with your financial advisor or accountant to determine the tax implications of buying or selling property. Seek advice on down payments and monthly payments. Your advisor can show you how much you will be able to afford and give you information on seeking financing. If you bypass this step, you could be asking for a lot of heartache later.

Selling Your Home

In 1986, over 3,500,000 homes were sold. Seventy-one percent of all home sales occur between early April and the end of July. If possible, put your house on the market in early spring to take advantage of the boom time. The winter months of November, December, and January are very slow for real estate sales.

Be realistic in setting your selling price. You were advised earlier to get the opinion of several real estate brokers who do market analysis or to hire an appraiser to give you the current market value. Seldom do you get your asking price, so set your price high enough so that you can compromise a little.

Give your house a facelift. There are many things you can do that will increase the desirability of your home. Don't spend a lot of money on expensive items. The return is seldom worth it. But there are lots of things you can do with a little time and elbow grease.

■ Painting is one of the most important things you can do to enhance the salability of your home. A few gallons of paint go a long way toward making your house look clean, fresh, and well cared for. HINTS: 1. Use neutral colors. No matter how stylish the shade, if it clashes with the buyer's furniture, it will be undesirable. 2. Choose a shade as near the existing color as possible. This makes it easier to cover and you can usually get by with one coat. 3. Measure your walls and buy what you need to do the entire project at one time. Often, it is hard to match colors exactly if you run out.

■ Get the yard in top shape. If necessary, hire a gardening service to come in and do a one-time spruce up job on your lawns. Trim shrubs; get rid of weeds; plant some flowers (get annuals about ready to bloom from your nursery); fertilize to make your grass a rich green; haul away all trimmings.

■ Wash windows inside and out. While you're outside, sweep away cobwebs. Put snail and earwig bait out, where there is a problem.

■ Clean out your garage. Men especially like roomy places to park the cars, store things, and work. You want it to look spacious. Clean up any oil stains in the driveway and garage. If the front of your house looks like a used car lot, find a place to stash the cars when you show your home.

■ Walk around the outside of your house. Look up and down. Is there a picket missing in the fence? Is the antennae straight? Are the toys put away? Have the dogs been cleaned up after? Are old lawn chairs put away? Does the swimming pool sparkle? Do all of the sprinklers work? Invite a friend over to make the inspection with you. Often one set of eyes, especially when they are accustomed to looking at it, miss something.

■ Shampoo carpets and clean drapes. This not only improves the looks, but also the smell of your home.

■ Clean out cabinets and closets. You want it to look like you have room to spare. This is the perfect time to get rid of everything not important enough to pack up and move. Have a garage sale. You'll make enough to pay for your paint.

■ Repair any holes in the walls, doors, or ceilings. If they are small, a little spackle will do the trick. Larger holes may require a new piece of sheetrock or paneling. Ask advice from a knowledgeable person at the local home building store.

■ Eliminate any bad odors caused by pets, soiled laundry, garbage, etc. Put out some potpourri; open the windows; bake some cookies. Make the house smell inviting.

■ Repair any built-in appliances, if necessary.

Now you are ready to locate a real estate agent or if you are adventuresome, you may choose to sell your house without the help of a professional. There are books at your bookstore that tell you how to go about selling your own property. You may also be able to find a continuing education class that will teach the points of selling your home. Many areas have real estate companies that assist you. For a flat fee (based on the value of your home), they place an ad in the paper, loan you the FOR SALE sign, and do all of the paperwork. Additional charges are made for the multiple listing service, if an outside agent sells your home. Your responsibility is to show the home.

If you feel less inclined to take on the task yourself or if you will not be in the area, you will need to find a real estate agent to help you. Chapter Five, "Team Up With Professional Advisors," told you how to find and what to expect from your real estate salesperson. After choosing your agent, you will be asked to sign a contract giving the agent the right to sell your property. An "Exclusive Authorization and Right to Sell" (or similarly named) contract states that this person is your representative in the sale of a particular piece of property. The second item generally lists the terms of the sale, i.e., purchase price and how it is to be paid. The contract should include a statement that the property will be in multiple listing (unless agreed otherwise). Multiple Listing Service (MLS) is a cooperative listing service conducted by a group of brokers. Details about your house are published in a book or catalog every week, and placed in the computer daily, so that all agents can be informed about your property. The advantage of MLS for the seller is greater exposure. Another aspect of the contract is the agreement on the real estate agent's commission. Real estate fees are negotiable. Make sure that your agent's fee is commensurate with others in your locality. The length of time the contract is valid is stated. This is negotiable and left up to you. Agents want as much time as possible, but you may feel that ninety days is sufficient. Keep in mind that the agent will be less inclined to spend their money on advertising and showing the property if it is felt the length of time is insufficient. Typically, agents will want six months. Bare lots or acreage usually take longer to sell than residences.

You may be asked if you want a home protection plan which provides protection for major systems and appliances during the listing and for a specified period after the sale (usually one year). Systems and appliances included are typically plumbing, heating, hot water heaters, electrical systems, and all built-in appliances. Additional coverage is available for swimming pool equipment, domestic use well pumps, and central air conditioning systems.

You will also need to approve a FOR SALE/SOLD sign being placed on your property, and the installment of a "lock box" or keybox on your door, enabling agents to enter your home when you are not there.

By signing the contract you agree to pay any taxes due and attorney fees that arise pertaining to the agreement. It is stated in the contract that the house is offered under the provisions of the Equal Housing Opportunity Act, meaning that you can not discriminate because of sex, creed, religion, marital status, race, age, or national origin.

Once this contract is signed and dated, the agent is free to begin advertising your property.

Before leaving the subject of agent contracts, mention should be made of the different types of listings you might encounter. The most common listing is the Exclusive Right to Sell Listing. With this listing, the broker named in the contract is entitled to a commission no matter who sells the property, if it is sold within the life of the contract or for a period of time after. Should another agent become involved in the sale, i.e. he notifies your agent that he has someone who wants to buy your house, then the commission is divided between the two brokers.

Open Listing basically says that whoever effects the sale gets the commissions. You can give an open listing to as many agents as you want. It is a simple authorization to sell your property.

Net Listings leave the agent's commission open. It basically says that the agent gets anything over the seller's asking price. An example of this would be your asking $100,000 for your home and the agent selling it for $110,000. You would get the $100,000 and the agent would get $10,000.

When you find an agent you can work with, it is very important that you be honest about the house. Go over every inch of your home, pointing out the pluses as well as the minuses. It is better for your agent to be ready than to be caught off-guard by a potential buyer who notices something wrong. You will probably be asked to sign a Real Estate Transfer Disclosure Statement. In it, you will disclose the equipment and systems, etc., that are part of the real estate. You will also inform the buyer of any significant defects or malfunctions in the house. Consumer rights have made great strides in recent years. They have made it very difficult for sellers to hide anything.

Be receptive to any suggestions the agent makes about improvements. This is their business and they know what buyers want. Hold up your end by having the house clean and ready for viewing when the agent makes an appointment to show it.

Help your agent by doing everything you can to make the house appealing. Some fresh flowers not only brighten the room, but smell delightful. Open curtains and turn on lights, so the house appears light and airy. Play some soft music to create a relaxed mood. Then, disappear. Real estate agents can do their job better if you aren't around. The prospective buyers feel freer to ask questions and open closets if you aren't watching.

Once the agent has found someone interested, they will be encouraged to make an offer. The offer is written in contract form and signed by the buyer(s). The amount of deposit or earnest money is stipulated.

Upon receiving the offer, you have three choices--accept it, reject it, or make a counter-offer. Your decision, written in a formal contract, is taken back to the prospective buyer who has the same three choices.

The agreement reached between buyer and seller is a legal binding document. Its name "Receipt for Deposit" or offer to buy, as it is often called, is sometimes misleading for the signers. When both buyer and seller attach their names to this document, they are both committed to the transferral of the deed. Contrary to the sound of the name, this is not a mere receipt for a down-payment.

The broker will prepare for the seller an "Estimated Seller's Proceeds" sheet. This lists all of the estimated costs such as escrow fees, recording fees, transfer taxes, title insurance, notary fees, appraisal, home warranties, broker's fees, structural pest control inspection and repairs, taxes, pre-payment penalties, reconveyance fees, and so on. After all of these items are subtracted, you get a net to seller figure.

A termite inspection is conducted, not only for the purposes of insect destruction, but also to determine if any preventative measures need to be taken (boards and scrap material removed from under the house) and any repairs need to be done (roof repair, cracked foundation, etc.). The inspecting company will give your real estate agent a complete list of items that need attention. The buyer is also entitled to this information. They will also give you an estimated price for doing the work. Almost always, you can either do the work yourself, or hire someone for less than the inspecting company charges. Be sure to get several estimates.

If your home is serviced by a well or septic tank, then usually the well water will need to be tested and given clearance by the health department.

What is escrow?

After the preliminaries have been accomplished, the seller and the buyer deliver to an escrow agency (may be a title company, real estate agent, lender, attorney, or escrow company representative) their "instructions." Instructions include such items as a property description, conditions of the sale, information about the deed, time limits and closing cost information. These instructions, along with the buyer's deposit are held by a disinterested third party (the escrow agency such as a title company) in escrow until the property transfers title. Escrow is a transaction whereby a deed is given to a third party to hold until certain conditions are met or fulfilled, at which time, the deed is transferred to the obliging party who fulfilled those conditions. Escrow provides a safe place for documents and monies until all necessary procedures have been completed to facilitate the sale of property. The title company assures the buyer that the title to the property is clear and that there are no liens against it. A title insurance policy is issued to insure against any mistakes made by the title company. It assembles all pertinent information for the buyer and seller as it pertains to the property, such as the termite report, fire insurance policy, new loan documents, demand for pay-off or beneficiary statement, and tax reports. It holds the deposit and disburses the funds to the seller when the transaction is finished or closed.

Not all states use the same settlement procedures described above. Your real estate agent will advise you of your area's practices. If you have a choice of settlement agents, shop around for the most complete service at the best price.

Buying real estate

If you are on the other end of the stick and looking for property to buy, you need some additional information. Know what you want. Make a list of all the things your new house should have. Include size, location, price range, financing, age, landscaping, and condition of property. Put the items in the order of importance to you. Make notes to the agent, such as "must be close to shopping areas, would like a pool, lawn maintenance must be minimal, need an assumable loan, must be near public transportation lines." The more specific you can be about what you want, the better. The agent can then eliminate the inappropriate houses, thereby saving your time and theirs. Don't expect to get everything you want. That's why you put the list in the order of its importance. Decide what you can't live without. The rest is icing on the cake.

One way to locate a broker is to drive around in the area in which you are interested. Take down the names and numbers of brokers you see on FOR SALE signs in the yards of homes that look interesting to you. Give them a call for more details about the property. When they find out you are a potential buyer, they will do all they can to fill your needs.

Some areas now have "Video Home Buying." Area agents get together and produce a video of homes they have for sale. These are aired on television and/or the real estate agent's office. As it is said, "A picture is worth a thousand words." This is especially true when looking at property. It gives you a better idea than a written description which often sounds better than it looks. If your locale has the video service, avail yourself of it and save some time and mileage.

Be finance wise

A few hours of homework will save you a lot of money.

1. Consult your financial advisor for information on home mortgages. It is important that you know for how much of a loan you can qualify. She can tell you about interest rates, down payments, monthly payments, and tax implications and how they fit into your financial plan. Remember, unless you are over 55 and have not used your one-time capital gains tax exemption of $125,000, you will be subject to a capital gains tax if you do not reinvest in a more expensive home within one year (two years, if you are building) after the sale of your residence.

2. Generally, you will want to make as small a downpayment as possible. If you invest the difference, then the interest earned will offset some or all of the interest paid. Inflation rewards those who owe money. You will be paying back the mortgage with cheaper dollars in the future. Mortgage interest is deductible from your taxes. All of these make good reasons for paying out as little as possible when you buy your home.

3. Shop around for the best terms. There are several places where you can look for mortgage money. Check out several and compare their terms (how long you have to repay) and the interest rates (how much it costs to borrow). The institutional lenders include insurance companies, savings and loan associations, mutual savings banks, and commercial banks. Noninstitutional lenders include mortgage companies, individuals and nonfinancial institutions.

TYPES OF LOANS

ASSUMABLE MORTGAGES are often the most appealing, because you assume or take over the loan from the seller. The advantage is often a lower interest rate. If you bought your house years ago paying an interest rate of six percent, there will be many eager buyers, provided they can assume the same rate. Veterans Administration (VA) loans and Federal Housing Administration (FHA) are assumable loans as long as the borrower qualifies.

GRADUATED PAYMENT MORTGAGES (GPM) start out with lower monthly payments that steadily increase with time. These were designed with the young professionals in mind. As their careers advance, so does their earning power and thus their abilities to pay increased monthly payments.

ADJUSTABLE RATE MORTGAGES (ARM) or Variable Rate Mortgages (VRM) have interest rates that fluctuate with certain economic indicators. Your interest rate can go up or down. Your monthly payments may reflect the difference, or payments remain the same, but different amounts are allocated to the principal or interest.

BALLOON MORTGAGES require that you make payments each month with the balance of the loan being paid at a specified date. These loans are usually short-term loans averaging three to five years.

FIXED-RATE MORTGAGES retain the same interest rate for the life of the loan. This is the traditional type of loan that makes assumable loans so attractive.

RENEGOTIATED-RATE MORTGAGES can have interest rates revised every three to five years, depending on your contract.

PORTABLE MORTGAGES are fixed-rate home loans that allow homeowners to transfer their mortgage to a new home without paying higher interest rates or points. Designed for the person who moves often, this is a new concept. It is currently being offered by one company nation-wide. There are certain fees involved and a one-quarter percent premium over the current fixed interest rates. For information on portable mortgages, contact a Chase Home Mortgage Company.

Location, location, location

Real estate experts have emphasized that the most important consideration in buying a property is its location. A beautiful home in an undesirable neighborhood or a no-growth town will not appreciate adequately to make it a desirable investment. It is much better to buy the smallest house in the best neighborhood than the largest house in the worst neighborhood.

Make sure that the location fits with your needs and priorities. Look at the list you made before you started your search to see how well each house compares.

Eureka! (I have found it!)

After you have found the place you want to buy, you will make an offer through the real estate agent, provided there is one, or to the owner, if there is not. After the terms of the sale have been negotiated and finalized, the same procedure is followed as described above for selling a residence.

You will need to seek financing at this point and the sales contract should reflect enough time for you to do so. It should be stated in the contract that the sale is contingent on your ability to find financing and that your deposit or earnest money shall be returned if you fail. In some cases, the owner may be willing to finance all or part of the mortgage. If this is the case, you will probably be asked to fill out a financial disclosure statement which lists your assets and liabilities. You will give the potential lender (owner of the property) permission to investigate your credit standing.

The lender you are consulting should furnish you an "Estimated Buyer's Cost" sheet that shows you your expenses and the total you owe at closing. These fees may include charges for appraisal, credit reports, notary, fire insurance, prorate taxes, escrow, and home warranty contract (warranty for appliances the first year you own the house).

Settlement costs

Settlement is the formal process of transferring title from seller to buyer. The Real Estate Settlement Procedure

Act (RESPA) provides that your lending institution give you a copy of "A Home Buyer's Guide to Settlement Costs." Be sure that you receive yours. This booklet contains a complete explanation of all costs pertaining to settlement. The payment of settlement costs is negotiable. Sometimes, either the buyer or the seller pays all costs. Other times, they negotiate to divide the costs, each paying equally. Whatever the agreement, make sure that it is decided and put in writing long before closing.

The final walk through

At least one week before the closing date, walk through the home you are purchasing and look for anything that needs to be repaired or replaced. Your real estate agent probably has a standard form that is used for this procedure. If it is a new home, contact the builder for anything that is incomplete. Once escrow closes and you have moved in, it is much more difficult to get the contractor to your house to fix something.

Even though you may be eager for escrow to close so that you can move in, resist the temptation to start packing until everything is right. Use your leverage wisely.

Once you have determined where and how you want to live and followed through with the appropriate action, be assured that you have crossed one of the major hurdles in dealing with the details of death. You have planned and researched this independent gesture and can feel good about what you have done. As stated earlier, if you find you made a mistake, then do something different. Just give yourself time for adjustment. It takes a while to feel "at home" even in the most wonderful place.

12.

Unexpected Expenses and How to Meet Them

Even in normal times, it is the unexpected expenses that play havoc with people's budgets. Just when you think everything is planned for and there is enough left over for a weekend getaway, little Johnny gets a tooth knocked loose at school and requires a $150 dental procedure.

Unexpected expenses deliver an especially hard blow to widows. For one thing, their incomes may have suddenly become fixed. There is no longer a spouse's monthly paycheck in the mail. For another, they may be so emotionally low that even a small decision seems monumental. If they are unfamiliar with the financial aspects of the marriage they may not know where to find the money to pay the bills. Finally, the assets they do have may be tied up in the courts for a long period of time.

For some widows(ers) the problems of unexpected expenses will be only temporary until the life insurance proceeds arrive or probate is completed. For many others, unexpected expenses are only the beginning to a long term condition of struggling to make ends meet.

As was discussed in Chapter Ten, "Obligations and Debts," there are some debts that you can and should delay. These include all creditor's claims against the estate. There are others, that if you do not pay, can hurt your credit rating, or worse, result in repossession or foreclosure.

Protecting your credit rating is very important. It is very difficult to manage in today's world without access to credit. You will need to establish credit for your "alone" self if you

189

have not already done so during your marriage. More on this subject is found in Chapter Fifteen, "Building Credit On Your Own."

By becoming aware of some of the unexpected expenses that bombard the surviving spouse, you can prepare for them mentally. Another shock is the last thing your system needs at this time. Use your energy and strength to figure out solutions, don't waste it on worry. Just as you found a way to pay for Johnny's tooth all those years ago, you will find a way to meet these new unexpected expenses.

The following list includes expenses that many people encounter after a death. Some of these are not created by nor incidental to the death, but merely come due at an inconvenient time. So that you don't forget about them, an easy thing to do during this time of your life, they are included for your perusal. Fortunately, not all of these will apply to your situation. Unfortunately, you may have additions to this list. If this is the case, make notes in the margins so that when you share the book and your knowledge with another newly widowed friend, you'll have a more complete list.

UNEXPECTED EXPENSES

■ Telephone Bills. Because telephoning is so easy and convenient in the United States, we have the tendency to overuse it in making long distance calls. We don't have to pay for the call at the time we make it, so it is easy to become oblivious of the amount of time we spend talking. It is not uncommon for a survivor to have a phone bill of several hundred dollars the month a spouse dies. It usually comes as a shock at a time when money is short.

■ Flowers. The floral arrangement that drapes the casket is usually paid for by the survivors. In the absence of a casket, other types of arrangements may replace the casket "blanket" or wreath. These sprays can be very costly ranging in prices up to hundreds of dollars.

■ Travel. It may be necessary to travel to other areas for burial or to pay the way of a mother, father, or child who could not afford to come otherwise. Airline tickets bought on short notice when you cannot take advantage of special rates can be very expensive.

■ Food. Although it is the custom in many regions for friends and family to provide meals for the bereaved, this arrangement usually extends only through the time of the funeral. If you have family that stays beyond this time, your food bill can escalate quickly.

■ Child Care. Small children will need a place to stay while you conduct all of the necessary business meetings with your professional advisors. Don't try to drag your youngsters with you. They will be bored and your power of concentration will be lessened. There are good child care centers that accept drop-in children if you do not have a regular babysitter.

■ Mortgages, notes, and loans that have "Payable -On-Death" clauses. Some contracts have stipulations that say the loan is due if the borrower dies. Look over any contracts to see if they include this clause. Depending on the contract and the type of loan, you can probably submit this as an estate bill, giving you additional time to pay more urgent bills.

■ Hired Business Help. If your spouse owned a business, then you may need to hire someone immediately to take over the deceased's role in the company. This is especially true if it is a small concern or where there are no employees capable of handling business matters.

■ Personal Help. If you were dependent on your spouse for personal care, you will need to employ someone to do those tasks that the deceased once did. This might be driving you to places you need to go, cooking, shopping, giving medication, etc.

■ Repayment of Direct Deposits. Although this is not an immediate worry, be aware that any unentitled checks you receive that are directly deposited to your bank account must be repaid. Social Security checks are paid one month behind your entitlement, i.e., a benefit due April 3 is not paid until May 3. Government checks are not prorated for the days during the month that your spouse lived. If he died the 30th of the month, he is not entitled to any benefits for the entire month in which he died.

■ Balloon Payments. Some loans have balloon payments

where you must pay the remainder of the loan off in one final payment. Check your records to see when any of these payments are due. If it appears there is one in the near future, call the company, explain your circumstances and see if they will extend the time limit until you receive survivor funds.

■ Counseling Services. You may want to talk to a professional counselor about your grief soon after your loss. If needed, don't skimp on this kind of help.

■ Wardrobe. If you are going out into the business world to look for a job for the first time in years, you will want to update your wardrobe. How you look and dress can be a determining factor in hiring. While not being extravagant, you will need one or two appropriate outfits to wear for interviews. With the price of clothes today, this can amount to hundreds of dollars.

■ Transportation. This is included because it seems that a disproportionate number of newly widowed persons end up needing a new car. It is as though the old auto senses that the master mechanic is gone and that it can give up and die, too. If you had a husband who kept the car running with a few dollars and a lot of experience, you are fortunate. Repairs in a mechanic's shop may soon make it unfeasible for you to keep the old car going.

■ Con Artists. A discussion of unscrupulous people who take advantage of widowed people is included here because it can be very expensive and very unexpected if you fall prey to their con games. Do not think that only naive or ignorant people are game for these well-seasoned experts. They get the names and addresses of their targets through death notices and obituaries that appear in the newspaper. They know that you are vulnerable and that they must act swiftly to catch you off-guard. One of the most common schemes is the delivery of a product or service that the deceased spouse supposedly ordered before his death. The con artist will try to collect from you. Do not let him perform any service. Do not accept any product that has not already been paid for. If he persists, give him the name of your lawyer and tell him to file a claim with the estate. If one is filed, alert your attorney of your misgivings about the claim.

Be careful of home repair schemes. A "contractor" will

offer to inspect your home for insect damage, foundation problems, etc., free of charge. He then discovers a problem that is nonexistent and charges you to fix it.

Another home repair scheme involves giving you an oral quote for doing the work, then when the job is finished, delivering a final bill that is much higher. Get quotes in writing and keep a copy.

Many warnings have gone out recently about giving your credit card number over the phone. In the hands of a disreputable business, your number could be used to charge all sorts of unauthorized goods and services.

Be wary of any deal or contract that must be signed immediately. Any legitimate business will give you time to think about it.

Check with the Better Business Bureau for complaints against anyone you are considering doing business with. It is safest to stay with established firms.

Always ask questions — lots of them. Ask for names, addresses, and phone numbers. Ask for and contact references. You can't be too cautious.

HOW TO MEET UNEXPECTED EXPENSES

Even though you make claims for your survivor benefits (see Chapter Seven, "Survivor Benefits,") soon after the death of your spouse, it will take several weeks, or even longer in some cases, to collect. In the meantime, bills arrive that need to be paid. There are many sources for emergency money. Some may be available to you, while others are not. As you read over the list, keep in mind that many of these are extreme measures for dire emergencies and not to be used without forethought. In the case of loans, it should be your intention to repay the borrowed amounts as soon as other monies become available to you. This is the wrong time for you to increase your debt with long term loans, so borrow only what you know you can safely repay.

Liquid assets

Liquid assets refer to those items and property that can be easily and immediately turned into money. When looking at investments, the investor often considers the liquidity of the investment vehicle. If you and your spouse owned any of the following, they can be a ready source of income in an emergency.

■ Regular Passbook Savings Accounts. That money you've been saving for a rainy day may be in your savings account.

■ Money Market Mutual Funds. There are no penalties for withdrawal; you simply write a check for the amount needed. Some mutual money market funds have a withdrawal minimum.

■ Bank Money Market Accounts. You can write a check for any amount without withdrawal penalties.

■ Credit Union Accounts.

■ U.S. Savings Bonds Series E and EE provided you are the beneficiary.

■ Marketable Securities while uncomplicated to sell, may take seven to ten days to convert into cash. If you do not wish to sell your stocks and bonds, you may borrow against them.

Other immediate sources, though less desirable because of interest and/or penalties include the following:

■ The line of credit on your checking account. This is often called "overdraft protection." Depending on your bank and your account, this can amount to thousands of dollars. While withdrawal is as easy as writing a check, interest rates on this money are usually high.

■ Credit card limits. You can withdraw money up to the amount of credit available on most credit cards. The interest may be high and you will have to make minimum monthly payments on the amount you use.

■ Hardship withdrawals on IRA and Keogh accounts. You may make a once-a-year, sixty-day withdrawal of your retirement account funds, without penalty, as long as the withdrawal and re-deposit is documented. Beyond sixty days, you will be penalized ten percent on the entire amount in the account and will have to pay taxes on the withdrawn amount.

■ Certificates of Deposit are readily available, but the penalties are high if you withdraw before the date of maturity. Compare these penalties to the cost of borrowing money before you make a decision.

Selling personal property

Depending on what you have to sell, selling personal property can be an excellent way to convert items into cash. Keep in mind, in most cases you will not be able to replace an item for what you sold it for. Therefore, where possible, sell only those items you no longer want or need.

■ Vehicles such as a second car, motorcycles, recreational vehicles, and boats are a ready source of cash. You can get an idea of the value of your vehicles by talking with your banker. They have books such as the Kelly Blue Book that place values on such items. Also, you can look in the classified ads of your newspaper to check the selling prices of similar vehicles. Always ask more than you expect to get. It is easier to go down than it is to go up.

If you prefer not to sell these items, often you can secure loans against them.

Now is the time to sell all of the things you've been accumulating for years in the garage and spare room. Furniture and working appliances move quickly. Tools are a big item. Old jewelry is easy to sell to collectors. Rifles and guns find ready markets. Shop equipment and machinery is usually easy to sell. Musical instruments are popular. Furs should be appraised with an asking price based on the appraisal.

Large ticket items can be advertised individually. Combine many small items into a single ad, or have a garage sale. Avoid the temptation of telling strangers your spouse died. While most people are honest, it only takes one to exploit your vulnerability.

Selling hard tangible assets and collectibles

You may have valuable collections or hard tangible assets that are easily converted to cash. For collectibles, there are clubs that cater to every sort of collection imaginable. Ask around or check with your librarian for a club that emphasizes what you have. Their members are all potential buyers and/or sources of information on value and buyers. The better-known collectibles and those which bring the highest

prices include the following:
Rare Coins
Stamps
Antiques
Art
Oriental Rugs
Rare Books
Hard tangibles include:
Gold coin, bullion, mining ventures, commodity futures, or gold mining shares.
Silver junk coins, silver bars, and uncirculated silver dollars.
Gemstones such as diamonds, rubies, sapphires, and emeralds.

LOANS

Your only avenue to needed money may be through securing a loan. Be aware of the difficulty women have in securing loans, especially if they are unemployed. Loan institutions are reluctant to loan money unless you have substantial collateral. Consider the different types of loans to see which would best suit your needs in regards to amount and time considerations.

UNSECURED LOANS are based on your promise to repay the lender. They may be formalized with a pre-printed or handwritten promissory note or IOU. There is nothing to back up this loan other than your promise to repay.

PAWNBROKER'S LOANS are obtained when you give the pawnbroker a valuable item and he loans you money until you can "buy" the item back. Interest rates, while they must be legal, are very high.

LIFE INSURANCE LOANS are a common way to obtain cash. Often, the ability to borrow against the policy is a selling factor in its purchase. You must have a whole life insurance policy. The cash value of your policy amounts to the total of the premiums paid plus any company dividends that you have accumulated.

CHATTEL LOANS are secured with personal property. You give the lender the right to sell the item you used as collateral if you fail to repay the loan.

MORTGAGE LOANS are secured with real property. You may have more than one mortgage on your property. Second and third mortgages usually command higher interest rates than first mortgages because the lender is at greater risk. You normally repay these loans with monthly payments just like your first mortgage. Because this increases your monthly living costs dramatically, you might want to consider this as one of your last resorts.

HOME EQUITY LOANS are a different name for the same type of loan. You can borrow amounts up to the equity you have in your property. Equity refers to the difference in the value of your home and the amount you still owe. The terms and interest vary among lenders, so shop around before you sign a contract.

Lenders

There are several lending sources available. Your choice should depend on how much it costs to borrow and how long you have to repay your debt. There may also be some emotional considerations if you are borrowing from friends or employers.

■ Banks offer a variety of loans. Ask to speak with a loan officer. Be sure to have the documentation needed for the type of loan for which you are asking. This saves time. Substantiate the value of the property you are using as collateral in as many ways as possible.

■ Credit Unions offer most of the same types of loans as do banking institutions, usually at lower interest rates.

■ Employers may be willing to advance you money on your wages. They know they can recoup their money from future paychecks. If you have a good record with your company, this may be a good alternative to borrowing from a traditional lending firm. Most employers will not charge you interest unless the advance is long term.

You may be able to borrow against your profit-sharing plan at your company. Consult your employer about this.

■ Friends and relatives may be willing to loan you money provided they are in a position to do so. It is strongly advised that you treat the loan just as though you were borrowing from a lending institution. Keep the loan businesslike. Complete promissory notes and IOU's. Agree on interest rates and terms. Abide by the agreement, making payments when and in the amount promised. You need the support of all of the friends and relatives you can get right now. Don't alienate any of them by reneging on an agreement.

OTHER SOURCES OF INCOME

If it is just a matter of needing money until the estate is settled, the executor of the estate should petition the court for an allowance for the surviving spouse and children. Present the executor with a list of the bills and an estimate of what you need to live. After court approval, the funds will be released to you.

Collect any money owed you by others. This is a perfect time to ask that loans you have extended be repaid. Debtors may feel more obligated and sympathetic and try to cooperate in every way they can.

Keep any direct deposits that are coming to your bank. You will have to repay any unentitled amounts, but a month or two may be enough to see you through the hard times. Don't try this for more than one or two checks as there are laws against not reporting changes that affect entitlement.

Mortgage Refinancing is an option if you can obtain a lower interest rate than you are currently paying on the existing mortgage. There are expenses and costs involved and it will take several weeks for you to get any money. You can usually get up to eighty percent of the value of your home refinanced.

Finally, there are the gifts and donations of money from people who care. Monetary gifts to the families of the deceased are becoming more and more common. Accept these gifts graciously and appreciatively. As the recipient of over $800 in gifts at the time of Roland's death, I can testify how that money benefited us by taking away many of the immediate financial pressures. If you do not have an immediate need, place the money in trust funds for your children's education, or give to your favorite charity.

13.

Death and Taxes

Never pleasant, but always necessary, is a discussion of "death" taxes. Death taxes fall into two categories, Estate Taxes and Inheritance Taxes. Remember, that an estate is a separate entity. It must pay its debts just as an individual. One of the most important debts of the estate is its taxes — its debt to the country and state in which the estate lies. Inheritance Taxes, on the other hand, are paid by those who benefit from the estate — the inheritors.

The Internal Revenue Service and the individual states have prescribed methods of reporting and filing tax returns for deceased persons. The first part of this chapter deals with the federal tax requirements. It is recommended that you prepare the various forms at the same time, as much of the information is duplicated. In some instances you have the discretion of choosing where you want to take a deduction. If all of your forms are together, it makes it easier to see and decide.

The purpose here is not to teach you how to complete tax forms, but rather to give you a working knowledge of the procedures, familiarize you with terminology, and guide you in a greater understanding of the system. In some cases, you will be able to do everything necessary to satisfy the government without the help of a professional tax consultant. Most often, the knowledge you gain by reading this chapter will enable you to work more efficiently with the accountant or tax consultant.

The IRS holds the executor, administrator, or personal

representative responsible for the proper and timely filing and payment of taxes. The ultimate responsibility lies not with the tax preparer, but with you, provided you have been appointed the executor/administrator. Therefore, you owe it to yourself to gain as much knowledge as possible in the areas of taxation, so that you can understand the procedures and give intelligent input into the tax returns to which you will affix your signature.

The scope of Death Taxes is broad and ever-changing. New tax reforms are always in the works, trying to close the loopholes that ingenious tax experts wriggle their ways through.

If you are dealing with a large estate, seek the most expert advice you can find for the process can become overwhelmingly complicated. For the purpose of this book, the focus will be on the average estate, with average holdings. "Average" is defined here as less than one million dollars.

Each federal return will be discussed, highlighting important and most often needed information. If your situation has peculiar aspects that are not addressed, contact the IRS who can furnish you with free helpful publications, or contact your accountant. At the end of the explanation of the federal returns, you will find a checklist to aid you in preparing and submitting your returns. Whether you are working with a tax consultant or going it alone, use this list for double checking your tax preparation.

MINIMIZING TAXES

It is your right and your responsibility to exercise any legal vehicle at your disposal to pay as little in taxes as possible. While there are some decisions that the executor can make that will lower the tax burden of the estate, most of the avoidance or reduction of taxes lies with the decedent before death. It is everyone's prerogative to plan for their own estates through Wills and trust agreements before their deaths. Failure to plan effectively and wisely is irresponsible. See Chapter Fourteen, "Financial Planning," for ideas on how to save your estate for your heirs.

For those of you already saddled with the responsibility

of trying to make the best of inadequate planning, there are some things that you can do that will protect portions of the estate assets. Take notes so that your tax consultant is certain to address these measures.

GENERAL INFORMATION FOR FILING IRS FORMS

As mentioned earlier, it is the responsibility of the executor, administrator, or the personal representative to report and pay when due, the proper income and estate taxes to the government. Any fees paid the executor(s) for this service must be reported in their gross income when filing their personal income tax returns.

The IRS makes it very clear that the Federal government is among the first in line when it comes to collecting on the decedent's debts. The executor is held liable for any prior distributions that don't follow the probate code, if the estate becomes insolvent before all taxes are paid. Be certain that tax obligations are or can be met before settling with any of the heirs.

It is the duty of the executor to apply for an identification number for the estate. This number is necessary on all forms and returns dealing with the estate. It must be provided to anyone who must submit a report with respect to the estate, such as banks, savings and loans, and credit unions. Failure to include the number on required documents is $50 per document. Failure to provide the number to required persons is $50 per occurrence. To make application, request Form SS-4, Application for Employer Identification Number. Call your IRS office for an application or go to your local Social Security office. Because all forms require this number, you should apply for it immediately.

Anyone acting in a fiduciary capacity for another must serve the IRS with written notice. This is accomplished with Form 56, Notice Concerning Fiduciary Relationship. Fiduciary refers to persons who hold something in trust for another. This could apply to attorneys, bank officers, executors, or anyone else responsible for making decisions on another's behalf. Include a copy of your order of legal appointment by the court. Form 56 is filed as soon as you have the identification number and all the other necessary information. After receiving Form 56, the IRS can send you tax notices and information concerning the estate you represent.

The fiduciary notice remains in effect until you notify the IRS that you have been relieved of your duties. When this happens, you must make notification checking the appropriate box on Form 56. Proof of termination is required and must be included with the completed form. If someone else is assuming your duties, you must give the name and address of that person.

Form 4810, Request for Prompt Assessment Under Internal Revenue Code Section 6501(d) may be filed by the executor to reduce from three years to eighteen months the time IRS has to charge additional taxes determined due by the taxpayer. This enables a faster settlement of the tax liabilities of the estate, which in turn, makes distribution of the assets to the beneficiaries more timely. This request can be made for any income tax return of the decedent and for the income tax return of the estate, but not for the estate tax return. File Form 4810 as soon as possible after filing Form 1040 or Form 1041.

Federal tax returns

As the person responsible for making sure all tax returns are filed and tax liabilities are met, you need to be familiar with the various forms. It will be your job to determine which returns are necessary. Provided that the decedent is current in filing all past returns required before death, there are three returns that must be examined.

Before examining the "Big Three" (Final, Fiduciary, and Income Tax Returns), you need to know what to do if the decedent died before being able to file a current tax return, for you must also see that this is done. Example: John Jones died January 5, 1988. He did not have time to file his 1987 tax return. The method for calculating taxes is unchanged and would be treated accordingly. Remember, John was alive the entire year of 1987 so his deductions, exemptions, and income are unaffected. The 1987 return will appear different in only two places: Where the name and address is located at the top of the 1040 return, you will write "Deceased" and the date of death beside John's name. The other difference will be in the signature. Obviously, John cannot sign the return. The surviving spouse will sign and write "Filing as Surviving Spouse" after her name. If there is no surviving spouse, the executor would sign and write "Executor" after his name.

The three returns that may affect a decedent are the Final Income Tax Return (Form 1040, 1040A, or 1040EZ), the Income Tax Return of the Estate (Form 1041), and the Estate Tax Return (Form 706). A discussion of each will help you to decide which ones apply to the estate for which you are responsible.

Final income tax return

What forms are used to file the Final Income Tax Return?

There are three forms available for your use — 1040, 1040A, and 1040EZ. The one you choose depends on how complicated your return will be. The 1040A is a simplified version of the 1040 and can be used for married filing jointly, married filing separately, or head of household. You are entitled to all exemptions. To use this form, taxable income must be less than $50,000 with interest income less than $400. Only income from salary, wages, unemployment compensation, tips, interest, and dividends is acceptable. Adjustments and credits are limited. The 1040EZ is even more limited than the 1040A. It can only be used for single filers with no dependents with a taxable income of less than $50,000 and interest income less than $400. Credits and adjustments are similar to those of the 1040A.

There is also a 1040X which is used to amend a 1040 in case any deletions or mistakes are made. You have three years to file these corrections.

When must a Final Income Tax Return be filed?

A Final Income Tax Return must be filed if the combined gross income of a married person filing a joint return is $7,560 (1987); $8,900 (1988). If one spouse is 65 or older, the combined gross income is $9,400 (1987); $9,500 (1988). If both spouses are 65 or older $10,000 (1987); $10,100 (1988).

An unmarried person must file if his gross income is $4,440 (1987); $4,950 (1988). If 65 or over it rises to $5,650 (1987); $5,700 (1988).

Qualifying widow(er) with a dependent child must file if his gross income is $5,660 (1987); $6,950 (1988). If 65 or over, it increases to $7,500 (1987); $7,750 (1988).

Married but filing separately, filing a joint return but did not live with spouse, or when a decedent or spouse is being claimed as a dependent on the return of another, the gross income is $1,900 (1987); $1,950 (1988). No further adjustments are made for persons over 65.

A Final Income Tax Return must be filed if the decedent had net earnings from self-employment of $400 or more, regardless of the amount of gross earnings. However, for record keeping purposes to close out a business, a final return is recommended whether mandatory or not. You may be due a refund or be able to claim losses.

A Final Income Tax Return must be filed if the decedent owed any taxes such as Social Security taxes.

When are Final Income Tax Returns due?

A final return is due on the same date that the decedent's return would have been due had he not died. For calendar year taxpayers, this would be April 15 following the year of death.

How are final returns signed?

The final return must be signed by the executor/administrator/personal representative of the estate. He/she would sign their name where it says "Your signature" and write the appropriate title after.

If filing a joint return, the surviving spouse would also sign, and write "surviving spouse" after his/her name.

The word "DECEASED" should be written across the top of the final return.

After the name of the deceased which appears with the address at the beginning of the return, write "deceased" and the date of death.

How do you apply for a refund for a deceased person?

If the person claiming the refund is the surviving spouse, then nothing other than showing the refund amount on the 1040 form is necessary. If someone other than the surviving spouse is making claim, Form 1310, Statement of Person Claiming Refund Due a Deceased Taxpayer must be completed.

What income is included in the final income tax return?

For decedents who used the cash method of accounting, only income actually or constructively received before death is included. For decedents who used the accrual method, only income accrued before death is included.

Any partnership income from the date of the tax year until the date of death is includible. Self-employment income must be included.

In community property states, one-half of income received may be considered income of the deceased or the surviving spouse and may be claimed by either.

Interest and Dividends earned prior to death are includable. Request of those paying interest and dividends, a completed Form 1099. You will need one 1099 to show monies earned before death and another to show earnings after death. Those received after the death will be claimed on the fiduciary return.

Any income that applied to the individual before death will apply to the final income tax return of that individual.

What income is deductible on the final return?

Generally, any allowable deductions, exemptions, and credits due an individual are also allowed a decedent.

Any income taxes withheld from salary, wages, pensions, annuities, etc. are claimed on the final return.

The zero bracket exemption has been replaced by the standard deduction and is allowed no matter what day of the year the person died.

Net operating losses from business operations and capital losses sustained during the last tax year are deductible only on the final return.

At-risk losses are deductible up to the amount of cash and the adjusted basis of property contributed by the decedent.

Medical expenses of the decedent and/or decedent's dependents are deductible if itemized and incurred before decedent's death. Those medical expenses not deductible on the final return may be deductible on the estate return. Where medical expenses are paid out of the estate during the one year beginning after death, the executor may elect to treat all or part of the expenses as paid by the decedent at the time they were incurred. By making this election, all or part of the expenses may be deductible from the final return. This applies only to the expenses of the deceased, not to his dependents. Should you decide to take the deduction on the final return, you must make a statement saying that the deduction was not taken on the estate tax return.

Any credits due the decedent before death may be claimed.

This includes earned income credit, credit for the elderly or permanently disabled, residential energy credit carryforward, credit for political contributions, and business tax credit.

Income tax return of the estate

What form is used to file the income tax return of the estate?

Form 1041, U.S. Fiduciary Income Tax Return is the form used to file the income tax return of the estate.

When must a fiduciary return be filed?

To understand the answer to this, a review of what an estate is and how long it is in existence is necessary. An estate is a separate taxable entity. It comes into existence upon the death of an individual and exists until all the assets of the estate have been distributed to the heirs and beneficiaries.

Any income earned by the assets of the estate during the time it existed, such as interest on bank accounts and dividends on stocks, is reportable.

If the gross income of the estate is $600 or more, then a 1041 must be filed.

When is the Fiduciary Income Tax Return due?

The executor has a choice of due dates. He may either use the calendar year or the fiscal year for reporting. As executor, you indicate which accounting period you will use when you file the first income tax return of the estate. Once your choice is made, only the IRS can grant permission to change the accounting period.

The first return must be filed by the last day of any month within twelve months. After the first return, subsequent returns would be due the 15th day of the fourth month after the end of the estate's tax year.

When must tax liabilities be paid?

The full tax liability must be paid when the return is filed. After 1986, no installments payments are allowed.

Pre-payment of estimated taxes are necessary if it is expected that the estate will owe $500 or more in taxes. There are exceptions depending on the past year's returns. Estimated tax payments are due in quarterly installments throughout the year.

What happens when there is property in different states?

When the decedent owns property in more than one state, there may be an executor appointed for each property. If this is the case, each executor must file a separate 1041. The executor of the domicile (principal place of residence) property will include the entire income of the estate in his return. The executor of the ancillary (secondary) property will file with the IRS office in his location and include with his return the name and address of the domiciliary representative, the amount of gross income received by the ancillary representative, and the deductions claimed against that income.

What constitutes the taxable income of an estate?

The gross income of an estate includes all income received or accrued during the tax year. Income from businesses, partnerships, capital gains, dividends (over $100), interest, royalties, trusts, rents, etc.

What may be deducted from the estate income?

Deductions include contributions (only if provided for by the Will and not a political contribution), losses incurred from the sale of property other than stock, net operating losses, casualty and theft losses (provided they have not been claimed on the federal estate tax return), alimony, and separate maintenance. Expenses of administration may be deducted either from the 706 or the 1041, but not both.

NOTES:

1. It is not necessary to include a copy of the Will unless asked to do so by the IRS.

2. Concerning signatures on the 1041, the executor or the authorized person for the organization having control over the income of the estate must sign the return. In addition, the person preparing the return for pay must also sign.

3. Schedule K-1 (Form 1041) must be filed by the executor for each beneficiary. The schedule must include the beneficiary's taxpayer identification number or be subject to a $50 fine. Each beneficiary must be furnished a statement containing the information on the 1041 or the executor is subject to a $50 fine.

4. You may file for an extension of time on Form 2758. It will be required that you include a portion of the estimated tax with this request.

The estate tax return

What form is used to file the estate tax return?

United States Estate Tax Return, Form 706 is the proper document for filing the estate tax return.

When must an estate tax return be filed?

An estate tax return must be filed only if the value of the gross estate exceeds $600,000 (1987 and thereafter). This means that $600,000 can be transferred to your inheritors tax-free.

When is the estate tax return due?

The estate tax return is due nine months after the date of death.

What documents must be included with the return?

Certified copy of the Will

Form 712, Life Insurance Statement.

(You will need one for each life insurance policy listed in the return. These are obtained from the insurance companies who hold the policies.)

Form 709 or 709-A which are gift tax forms.

Trust and power of appointment instruments.

State certification of payment of death taxes.

Form 706CE

How does the executor file for an extension of time?

Time extensions for filing the estate tax return are not automatic. You must make a request that is supported by sufficient cause. Application for Extension of Time to File U.S. Estate Tax Return and/or Pay Estate Tax, Form 4768 is the correct form for requesting an extension for time to file and an extension for time to pay. Being granted an extension for time to file does not extend the time for payment unless properly requested and approved by the IRS.

Time extensions for filing are limited to six months unless the executor is out of the country. Time extensions for payment are usually granted for up to twelve months. Extensions for payment of estate tax can be as long as ten years if there is reasonable cause.

What is included in the gross estate?

The gross estate includes the value of all property in which the decedent had an interest at the time of death. This would include real estate, stocks and bonds, mortgages, notes, cash or cash equivalents, life insurance policies on decedent, and other policies where decedent had an interest. Also included is jointly owned property (minus any amounts paid for by the other joint owners), one-half of qualified joint interests, miscellaneous property such as furs, jewelry, furnishings, and collectibles. Any gifts that are reportable, powers of appointment where the decedent had the right to designate a beneficiary under another's Will, any annuities, retirement plans such as IRA's, Keogh's, TSA's, and corporate plans, interest in any tax refund, and the interest in any business must be counted.

Includible in the gross estate are certain property interests transferred before death. These include transfers with retained life estate, those taking effect at death, and revocable transfers.

Use your attorney's prepared statement of "Inventory and Appraisement" required by the courts to cross reference your gross estate assets.

According to tax laws, every person is entitled to make tax-free gifts up to $10,000 per year to any individual. You may make as many of these $10,000 gifts as you wish and can afford. Gifts exceeding this tax-free amount are subject to tax and must be listed on the estate tax return Form 706. Other reportable gifts include those in which the decedent retained or controlled the income for life, or to which the right to designate the ultimate donee was reserved. Gifts that are effective only at the death of the decedent and gifts that can be revoked or amended during the lifetime of the decedent must be claimed as part of the gross estate. All gifts from one spouse to another are exempt from gift taxes.

If the decedent owned the life insurance policy, the proceeds are includible in the taxable estate. If someone else owned the policy, the proceeds are not subject to federal estate taxes, but may be subject to state estate taxes. The decedent is considered to have owned the policy if he had the right to change or name beneficiaries, was able to borrow against the policy, was able to use the cash value as collateral, or was able to cash it. Also, he owned the policy if he had rights of cancellation, could select a payment option, or could make payments on the policy. Any life insurance policy transferred or given to another individual less than three years before death is considered owned by the giver and must be included in the gross estate.

Social Security and Railroad Retirement Act benefits are not includible.

How is the valuation of property made?

Valuation of property is based on the fair market value at the time of death. However, the executor may elect to use an alternate valuation method of six months after the decedent's death, if it is advantageous to the estate. If, within the six months, any property is sold or distributed, then the fair market value is established at the time of the sale or distribution.

What is included in the taxable estate?

The taxable estate is the net value (market price less all amounts owed at time of death). It consists of the gross estate MINUS the following items:

■ Expenses and debts of the estate such as funeral expenses, administration costs of the estate, mortgages and other debts on property, and certain other claims against the estate.

■ Casualty and theft losses that occurred during estate settlement and not already claimed on the estate income tax return.

■ Charitable deductions transferred by Will or during the life of the decedent.

■ Any property passing to the surviving spouse.

■ One-half the value of certain proceeds from sales of employer securities.

■ Medical and dental expenses of the decedent paid by

the estate. You have the option, under certain conditions, of including these items as part of the 1040 return. See discussion in the section on final income tax returns.

■ Unified tax credit which amounts to $192,800 for 1987 and after.

■ Taxes (federal and state income and real estate taxes only) that are legally owed by the decedent at the time of death.

■ Gift taxes paid on gifts made after 1976, or those listed under Taxable Gifts where applicable.

■ Credits for foreign death taxes, federal estate tax previously paid, and state inheritance or death taxes.

NOTES:

1. If your taxable estate is worth more than the federally exempted amount ($600,000), the amount in excess will be taxed at the rate applicable to the total value of the entire estate. Therefore, it is very desirable to find methods to reduce the estate to a point below the exempt amount.

2. The unlimited marital deduction enables tax-free transfer of unlimited amounts of property to a spouse. Be aware that when the second spouse dies, all property exceeding the federal exempt amount is then subject to estate taxes.

3. The rate of tax on the first nonexempt dollar in 1987 and 1988 is thirty-seven percent. The tax rate rises to fifty-five percent on monies over $3,000,000 in 1987, and fifty percent on amounts over $2,500,000 in 1988.

4. One type of marital bequest is called the "Qualified Terminable Interest Property" or "Q-Tip." It is a trust set up by the testator that enables the surviving spouse the income from the trust while the spouse is alive. Upon death, the trust assets pass to whomever the testator chooses.

5. Any appreciation in value of gifts that occurs between the time the gift is given and the death of the decedent is not taxable to the estate of the decedent.

6. You cannot take double deductions. If you claim an item on one return, you may not claim it on another. In cases where you have a choice, you may claim the item wherever it is most advantageous.

7. Property inherited by the estate within the last ten

years has probably had the taxes paid on it already. You are allowed a tax credit that can be substantial, depending on how long the property has been an asset of the estate. The tax credit decreases until the tenth year when it diminishes to zero.

THE TAX RETURN OF THE SURVIVOR

There are some points that you should be aware of when filing your own personal tax return for the IRS, as you may be entitled to certain benefits.

■ You may file a joint return the year of your spouse's death.

Sign the return as "surviving spouse" and put "deceased" and the date of death beside your spouse's name at the top of the form.

■ You may file a joint return for two years after the death provided you were entitled to file a joint return the year of spouse's death and did not remarry before the end of the year.

You must have a child, stepchild, or foster child for which you provide more than one-half the cost of maintaining the principal residence of the child for the entire year.

■ After the two years, you may file as Head of Household as long as you have a dependent child at home.

■ You may claim a full exemption for the deceased no matter when during the year your spouse died.

■ Income in respect of the decedent refers to any income the decedent would have received had he lived. You or whoever receives this money must report it on their personal income tax return.

■ Property received by inheritance, gift, or bequest is not included as income. Any profit such as interest or dividends made from such property is considered income and is taxable.

■ Lump sum life insurance proceeds are not taxable, but interest obtained and installment payments are.

■ Veteran's Insurance proceeds and dividends are not taxable. Interest and dividends left on deposit with the VA are taxable.

■ Salary and wages of the decedent received after death are taxed as ordinary income.

■ Pensions and annuities are taxable, subject to certain exclusions.

■ IRA's are taxed as ordinary income to anyone except a spouse who can receive them under the unlimited marital deduction clause.

■ The tax basis of property you inherit is "stepped up" either at the time of decedent's death, or at the time of the alternate valuation date, or in certain instances at the time determined under special-use valuation. An example illustrates this: Your husband bought a painting for $1,000 in 1980. At the time of his death in 1985, the painting was worth $1,500. If you sold the painting in 1987 for $1,750, your taxable profit would be $250 ($1,750-1,500=$250).

If the painting was owned jointly by the two of you, only his half would receive a new tax basis. Yours would remain the same until your death. Therefore, his half ownership at the time of his death is stepped up to $750, while your half continues to be $500. If you sold the painting in 1987 for $1,750, your profit would be $500.

If, at the time of your death, the painting is valued at $2,000, this would be the new tax basis for those inheriting the painting.

In community property states, both halves of the property are stepped up at the death of the first spouse.

The federal Ways and Means Committee is examining this "loophole" and may make some changes in the near future. It is estimated that five billion dollars is being lost to the federal treasury annually through the stepped-up tax basis on capital gains. Watch for possible changes in this law.

■ Concerning federal taxes, there is never a double tax. Once the tax liability is met on one federal return, it does not have to be claimed on another federal return.

You now have a basic understanding of what is expected of the executor of an estate in regards to the IRS. This discussion did not include information for every circumstance that you may face. It is not intended to replace the advice or information available from a tax consultant, but simply to help you communicate more effectively and knowledgeably with your advisor. You now have a basis for questions and the groundwork for understanding the answers.

CHECKLIST FOR EXECUTORS/ADMINISTRATORS/ PERSONAL REPRESENTATIVES

____ Apply for a taxpayer identification number immediately using Form SS-4, Application for Employer Identification Number.

____ Notify the IRS that you will be filing the tax returns of the decedent using Form 56, Notice Concerning Fiduciary Relationship.

____ Inventory all assets of the estate. You want the "fair market" value of all assets at the time of decedent's death. This may require the hiring of professional appraisers.

____ Determine the gross income (combined gross income if filing a joint return) of the decedent the year of death for the final income tax return Form 1040, U.S. Individual Income Tax Return. This return is due April 15th the year after death.

____ If there is a refund due and person claiming the refund is someone other than surviving spouse, file Form 1310, Statement of Person Claiming Refund Due a Deceased Taxpayer. Include Form 1310 with the 1040 return.

____ Determine whether or not all tax liabilities are current. If not, file past year's return.

____ If the gross value of the estate exceeds $600,000, file Form 706, U.S. Estate Tax Return due nine months after date of decedent's death.

____ Determine the valuation date to be used by the estate, i.e., the date of death or six months after the date of death.

____ Include Form 712, Life Insurance Statement with the estate tax return (Form 706).

____ If the gross income of the estate is $600 or more, file Form 1041, U.S. Fiduciary Income Tax Return.

____ Choose either the calendar year or the fiscal year date for filing the 1041 return. The first return is due the last day of the month within twelve months of decedent's death. Subsequent returns are due the 15th day of the fourth month after end of estate's tax year.

____ File Form 4810, Request for Prompt Assessment Under Internal Revenue Code Section 6501(d) as soon as possible after filing Form 1040 or Form 1041. This may not be filed for Form 706.

____ Decide the accounting method to be used i.e., accrual or cash method.

____ File Schedule K-1 (Form 1041) for each beneficiary. Include a taxpayer number for each beneficiary, and give the information included in Form 1041 to each of the beneficiaries.

____ File for any extensions necessary.

____ Form 2758, Application for Extension of Time to File U.S. Partnership, Fiduciary, and Certain Exempt Organization Returns

____ Form 4768, Application for Extension of Time to File U.S. Estate Tax Return and/or Pay Estate

____ Form 4868, Application for Automatic Extension of Time to File U.S. Individual Income Tax Return

____ From 2688, Application for Extension of Time to File (to be used after Form 4868)

____ File your own personal income tax return (Form 1040) taking advantage of any allowable survivor's benefits.

____ Report the termination of the estate to the IRS using Form 56, Notice Concerning Fiduciary Relationship.

The Internal Revenue Service has over 100 publications to help the taxpayer better understand the tax regulations. These are offered free by simply calling the Internal Revenue Service listed under United States Government in your phone book. It takes about two weeks for delivery. Those most helpful to the survivor include Tax Information for Survivors, Executors, and Administrators (Publication 559) and Federal Estate and Gift Taxes (Publication 448). Upon receiving these, check the last page for other helpful publications that apply to your particular circumstances.

To understand the newest tax laws, ask for Publication 920, Explanation of the Tax Reform Act of 1986 for Individuals, and Publication 553, Highlights of 1986 Tax Changes.

STATE DEATH TAXES

So far, our discussion has centered around federal taxes. A look at state taxes shows that they vary considerably. Some states have inheritance taxes, others have estate taxes, most have state income taxes, and still others have all three. Only the state of Nevada has none of the above.

In dealing with taxes due the state in which you live or own property, you will (depending on the state) be chiefly concerned with four returns: state income tax return, fiduciary state income tax return, state inheritance tax return, and the state estate tax return. Most of the information on your federal returns is similar to the types of information required on the state returns.

State income tax return

Except for the states of Alaska, Florida, Nevada, South Dakota, Texas, Washington, and Wyoming, all other states enforce a state income tax.

Individual state income tax laws are as varied as the states themselves. The state of Connecticut only taxes capital gains, interest, and dividends. Tennessee and New Hampshire tax dividends and interest only. You will have to contact your state tax offices to receive the proper returns and information booklets to help you complete the returns.

Fiduciary state income tax return

For those states that have estate taxes, you will probably have to file a fiduciary form just as you must file one for the federal government. The gross income necessary before filing may be more or less than that of the IRS, so be sure to check with your state tax board before filing.

State inheritance tax

Inheritance taxes are levied on the person inheriting the property of the decedent. Those states having an inheritance tax are Delaware, Idaho, Indiana, Iowa, Kansas, Kentucky, Louisiana, Maryland, Michigan, Montana, Nebraska, New

Hampshire, New Jersey, North Carolina, Oregon, Pennsylvania, South Dakota, Tennessee, Texas, and Wisconsin.

Some states impose different rates of taxes on different classes of heirs. Those heirs closest to the decedent such as a spouse, child, or parent pay a smaller percentage, while siblings and non-relatives pay a higher rate. The type of property inherited, whether it be real or personal, also makes a difference in some states.

State estate taxes

All states with the exception of Nevada levy an estate tax. The names for these taxes vary, sometimes called transfer taxes, gift taxes, or legacy taxes. In most states, the amount of the state estate tax is equal to the amount that is credited toward your federal tax liability (line 13 on Form 706), therefore, costing you no additional taxes. Sometimes referred to as a "pickup tax," the state collects a portion of the revenues that would otherwise go to the federal government. The amount of the tax is based on the federal estate tax credit allowed for state death taxes.

States typically allow the same types of exemptions and deductions as the federal government, but not always in the same amounts. That is why you may have to pay state estate taxes even when you do not have to pay federal estate taxes.

Those states that do not take the maximum allowable credit against the federal estate tax are Connecticut, Ohio, and Oklahoma.

If you have property in more than one state, you must be sure to establish which is your domicile (where you vote, go to school, have a job, etc.), to avoid being taxed twice. You will still have to pay estate taxes on the real estate of the ancillary state, but not on the entire gross estate except in the domicile state. The amounts paid to each state are prorated. Property often cannot be distributed or transferred to the heirs until all state tax liabilities have been met. If a state estate tax is paid, it can be credited against your federal tax.

Most states require that a declaration concerning residence be attached to Form 706 along with a short state estate tax return. This makes it unnecessary to repeat the information required on the IRS Form 706.

GETTING HELP WITH YOUR TAXES

Chapter Four, "Team Up With Professionals," gave you information on how to find help with your taxes. An additional resource for elderly persons is Tax-Aide consisting of American Association of Retired Persons (AARP) volunteers who have been trained in cooperation with the Internal Revenue Service. They provide free tax service at 8,000 sites nationwide. They also publish two booklets that are outstanding, Your Retirement Income Tax Guide (C175) and Your Retirement State Tax (C182). To order these write All About AARP, AARP Fulfillment Section, 1909 K Street NW, Washington, DC 20049, if you live east of the Mississippi River. If you live west of the Mississippi, the address is Box 2400, Long Beach, CA 90801.

The IRS publishes a comprehensive guide entitled, Guide to Free Tax Services (Publication 910). It includes information about Volunteer Income Tax Assistance (VITA), Tax Counseling for the Elderly, Student Tax Clinics (volunteer law and graduate students), and Community Outreach Tax Assistance.

A REMINDER ABOUT TAXES: Tax laws can be complicated and are ever-changing. You must stay abreast of these changes for the good of your estate. The business section of your newspaper and all of the news magazines often carry articles concerning tax law. Most larger newspapers have an advice column where you can write and have personal questions answered. Clip articles throughout the year that might pertain to your situation. When you prepare or have your returns prepared, use the information you have gleaned from the articles to ask questions. Every time major tax legislation is passed, a slew of new books hits the bookstores that explain the reforms in layman's language. You may want to invest in one of these.

Stay current and informed. Taxes are always a topic of conversation and with your new knowledge, you will be able to contribute what you have learned.

14.

Financial Planning

Financial planning for the widowed person involves a unique set of circumstances. For many varied reasons, planning the financial future of a recently widowed person can be frustrating and challenging. First of all, widows(ers) are having to deal with the important issues of money and taxes at a time when they are least able to concentrate. Their grief makes it extremely difficult to get through even the routine tasks of the day. This makes them exceedingly vulnerable to smooth talking shysters who want to "invest" their money for them. Even legitimate businesspersons may encourage taking, or not taking, lump sum benefits without knowing the whole picture concerning taxes or the circumstances of the widow. Then, there are the loving friends and relatives who are always ready to tell the surviving spouse what to do.

Another unique circumstance of the widowed person is the fact that they may be receiving a large sum of money, more than they have ever had to deal with, at one time. For those not accustomed to wealth, receiving $100,000 or more in life insurance benefits can be overwhelming.

A third unique aspect of financial planning especially for the widow is the fact that the income that the family has grown accustomed to is cut off suddenly, and usually without much warning. In the traditional American family, the man usually is the larger wage earner. Even in dual professional families where the wife earns as much or more than her spouse, a sudden drop in income can play havoc with present obligations and future goals. For the homemaker who brings in no outside outcome, this may mean some radical changes in her lifestyle.

The fourth distinct factor facing a widow is her too often lack of knowledge about financial matters. Widowers, while often as much or more distraught, usually have a working knowledge of their finances. Although changing rapidly, the woman who leaves all financial decisions to her husband is still too common. Many of those who lead the "traditional" lifestyle (hubby brings home the bacon and wife raises children) will learn too late that they should have taken an active role in financial matters. Unfortunately, because of a lack of knowledge about taxes and inflation, there are many well-meaning husbands who think they have provided adequately for their wives, only later to find an estate worth little or nothing.

Because you may now be on a fixed or shrunken income, it is more important than ever that you preserve your inherited assets. You want what you have to last you a lifetime, if possible. You need to learn the means of stretching and increasing dollars. It is the goal of this chapter to give you information that will point you in the direction of achieving financial independence and maintaining it throughout your lifetime.

You *must* resist the temptation to let someone else be responsible for making the decisions concerning your financial future. The persons who ill-advise you will not likely support you or repay any mishandled money that you entrust to them. As miserable and incapable as you might feel at this time in your life, you must take action to protect what you have.

Achieving financial independence puts a direct responsibility on you. You may have to find employment, which could mean learning new skills. College campuses are filled with middle-aged persons who are going back to obtain degrees for new jobs.

Even if you don't have to change or find a job, you will still need to educate yourself about the financial world. There are continuing education classes in almost every community that deal with investments, estate planning, taxes, and budgeting. Hundreds of books have been written that are available at your local library. Magazines and newspapers include updated articles on the financial scene. For your own well-being, you must become informed.

As we discussed in Chapter Four, "Team Up With Professionals," it will be your responsibility to choose a financial advisor. This may or may not be the one your spouse used. After all, his reasons for investing may constitute an entirely different approach to financial planning than yours. Use the guidelines presented in that chapter to find someone with whom you can communicate your new needs.

If you are among the fortunate ones who played a part in the financial decisions of the household and have a speaking knowledge of finances, then this stage of growth will be easier and quicker. Your goal will be to increase your knowledge and to stay current of the changes in laws and regulations. This is no easy task, considering the laws are constantly in motion.

Money management is making your money work for you. To be successful, it will take homework, good advice, discipline, and a clear idea of what you want to accomplish. Anyone can do it, if they are willing to incorporate the following good habits in their daily lives: plan for taxes, reduce spending, invest wisely, plan for retirement, shop wisely, pay bills promptly, save, balance the checkbook regularly, budget wisely, maintain good records, and control debt. It is the job of the financial planner to show you how you can do all of this.

A financial planner will ascertain your goals and appraise the methods available for reaching them. Not only will the planner need information on what you already have, but also your temperament for risk and your attitude about spending, saving, and investing. With all of this information, along with training and knowledge, your financial planner will be able to tailor a plan that will help you achieve your financial goals.

In her book *The New Financial Planner* (Dow Jones-Irwin, 1986), Cathey Bertot lists twelve steps that are essential in effective financial planning:

1. Identifying and clarifying objectives.
2. Analyzing current financial position.
3. Quantifying financial objectives and comparing them

to present position.

 4. Reviewing and evaluating risk requirements.

 5. Reviewing tax status and computing projections.

 6. Examining the estate plan.

 7. Identifying problem areas.

 8. Considering how future and present assets will be positioned.

 9. Determining what special circumstances may apply.

 10. Recommending specific actions

 11. Implementing changes.

 12. Reviewing the situation periodically.

Bertot points out, as evidenced by this list, that there are no quick answers to solving financial problems. It takes a lot of analytical work on the part of the planner, and a lot of cooperation and determination on your part. It may mean some sacrifices now, for some gains later. It may entail forming more realistic goals.

Even if you have carefully selected your financial planner and have confidence in the recommendations, be certain that you understand the investments and feel comfortable with the level of risk involved. Ask questions about terminology you do not understand. Plan *with* the financial advisor; don't let the advisor plan *for* you. This is where your responsibility for increasing your knowledge about financial matters becomes important. The more you know, the better able you are to contribute to the decision making process.

Although applicable to a majority of persons, the following Seven Step Plan is tailored for the widowed person. Each step will be approached from the widowed person's perspective. Your financial plan will be most effective when you work with a professional in this area. The money you spend on a good financial planner will come back to you many times.

STEP ONE

The first thing a widowed person should do is to get a *tax projection*. You need to know what the tax implications are for your new situation. How much are you going to have to pay in taxes this year? How much do you need to save to be able to pay next year's tax liability? To get a handle on your financial situation, you need answers to these questions. Preferably, this is done even before you make a decision on how to receive any large life insurance benefits. Unless you need the proceeds immediately, let them sit until you have discussed the best method of collection with your planner. The insurance company will encourage you to leave your money with them and take an annuity. They have several plans of distribution. They may not tell you that you will be taxed on life insurance proceeds other than lump sums. Whether you elect the interest only, fixed amount, fixed period, lifetime income, or lump sum payment option (discussed in Chapter Seven) will depend a lot on your age, needs, tax bracket, and health.

Figuring your tax bracket not only helps you know the level of taxes you are going to pay, but it also helps you in the budgeting and cash flow process. You need to know how much you are going to spend on taxes, so that you can budget that amount. The new IRS penalty and interest charges discourage anyone from being delinquent with their taxes.

There are many misconceptions about how to determine the tax bracket you are in. Look at the tax rate tables that follow.

1987 TAX RATES		
Married Filing Jointly or Qualifying Widow(er)		
Taxable Income		**Tax Rate**
Over	But not over	
0	— $3,000	11%
$3,000	— 28,000	15%
28,000	— 45,000	28%
45,000	— 90,000	35%
90,000		38.5%

1988 TAX RATES

Taxable Income	Tax Rate
Married Filing Jointly or Qualifying Widow(er)	
0 to $29,750	15%
Over $29,750	28%
Single	
0 to $17,850	15%
Over $17,850	28%
Married Filing Separately	
0 to $14,875	15%
Over $14,875	28%
Head of Household	
0 to $23,900	15%
Over $23,900	28%

For tax years beginning after 1988, the income brackets will be adjusted, if necessary, so that inflation will not increase taxes. In addition, persons in higher income brackets will be taxed an additional five percent to phase out the fifteen percent tax rate. See IRS Publication 920 for specifics. However, it is important to remember Congress can change these tax rates at any time in the future.

To determine your tax bracket, look at the tax schedule on the previous page. As an example, we will use the case of Mary Johnson. Mary's husband died in June of 1986. Because she has one minor child, she is entitled to file as a qualifying widow on her 1987 tax return. Her taxable income (gross income minus deductions and exemptions) amounts to $50,552. Her tax would be computed as follows.

Income in the 11% bracket	$ 3,000 x 11% =	$ 330.00
Income in the 15% bracket	25,000 x 15% =	3,750.00
Income in the 28% bracket	17,000 x 28% =	4,760.00
Income in the 35% bracket	5,552 x 35% =	2,109.76
TOTAL	$50,552	$10,949.72

For those who have incomes of less than $50,000 you must use the Tax Table, while those with incomes over $50,000 use the Tax Rate Schedule (above). Both of these are found at the end of Publication 17, Your Federal Income Tax.

Knowing your tax bracket will show you how much a deduction is worth. Let's say a person is in a thirty-five percent tax bracket. If they can find $500 in tax deductions, it means a tax savings of $175 (amount of tax deduction x tax bracket = tax savings). In this example, $500 x .35 (35%) = $175. This gives you a feel for whether it is worth your effort to look for more deductions. It also shows you how painful or expensive additional income will be should you decide to go to work, sell property, cash in bonds, etc.

One of the most important questions to ask your planner at this time is, "Is there anything in the tax law that could really impact me in the future?" You need to know what is going to happen next year so that there aren't any surprises. The more advance notice you have, the longer you can plan. You have time then, to find more deductions or make tax-deferred investments. Tax liabilities can become personal assets with proper planning and action.

What will your financial planner need to make a tax projection? To estimate your taxable income, the planner will probably ask for the following items:

■ Estimated gross income. Look at your benefits receivable (including any taxable life insurance proceeds), your expected income from salaries or wages, income from interest and dividends, and any other sources you can think of.

■ Past tax returns. Even though your returns may look dramatically different now that you are widowed, they can still be a good indication of the types of income sources you have.

■ The number of dependents you will be claiming. You are given a tax exemption for each dependent. In 1987, that amounts to $1,900 each, in 1988 — $1,950, and in 1999 — $2,000. Once you have a handle on your estimated taxes and know your tax bracket, you are ready for the next step.

STEP TWO

Your next job is to prepare a *net worth statement*. Your net worth is how much you *own*, minus how much you *owe*. Another way of saying it is your liabilities subtracted from your assets. When listing your assets, include lump sum pensions and IRA's, tax sheltered annuities (TSA's), notes receivable, securities, personal property, cash in checking and savings accounts, cash value of insurance policies, certificates of deposit, credit union funds, government securities, real estate, investments, and any business interests. On the minus side, you must include the mortgage, credit card and charge card balances, all loans, installment contracts, tax liabilities, and any judgments against you. The purpose of the net worth statement is to see where you are, so you can map out where you are going. The financial planner uses this statement to assess your position in terms of your goals. It is essential that you give the planner all of the information required, so that a more accurate job of plotting your way to financial independence can be done. Many of the planner's recommendations are based on your balance sheet. Your balance sheet shows the strength or weakness of your position. It tells you if your assets are situated where they can provide you with income or growth. It shows how much cash flow you can expect. After getting a composite of what you own, you can see what your debts are like. What debts need to be paid off? Can these debts be restructured? Check the interest rates and payment schedules. Can any be refinanced to a lower interest rate? Would this be a wise move? Your planner can determine all of this by analyzing your net worth statement.

Be sure that you qualify any figures that have time limits. Identify when a benefit will start and how long it will last. To prepare a net worth statement, you can use a data sheet provided by your financial planner. Banks also have net worth statements that you can use. You will need much of this information for your spouse's tax returns, so you will get double benefit for taking the time and effort to prepare them.

STEP THREE

Make an accounting of your *income and expenses*. You need to know how much you are bringing in and where it is going. Without knowing how you are spending the money, you can't make any changes. The first few months after a death are very transitional. Cut expenses and limit spending until you know what the overall picture is going to look like.

You need to determine how consistent and stable are your income sources. How long is the income expected to last? Will there be cost of living increases? Concerning expenses, you need to determine whether they are fixed or discretionary, how often they move up or down, and what you can do to minimize them. Determine how much control you have over your expenses.

Begin step three by listing all of your income sources. Include salaries, tips, wages, self-employment income, Social Security payments, child support from a previous spouse, dividends, interest, trust accounts, retirement plans, net rents, royalties, and any other income sources.

Continue this step by listing all of your expenses. You want to track where the money is going. A good way to do this is to write down every penny you spend for a couple of months. Include your rent or house payment, food, baby sitter, automobile expenses (loan payments, maintenance, fuel, oil), telephone, utilities, taxes, insurance premiums, recreation, gardener, school expenses (lunches, books, and supplies), pet care, medical and dental bills, gifts, clothing, laundry and cleaning, alimony and child support from a previous marriage, debt repayment (loans, credit and charge cards), retirement contributions, and any other expenses.

After tracking the expenses, *categorize* them. On one side, put the fixed expenses and on the other put the discretionary expenses. Discretionary expenses are those that we enjoy, while not being necessary for survival. They are the expenses we can choose whether or not to have. Eating out, going on vacations, and giving to your favorite charity are discretionary expenses.

It is also helpful to categorize expenses in a way so that you can see where the bulk of your money is going. Is it on living expenses such as food and utilities, or house payments, travel, child care, or transportation? After tracking and categorizing, the next step is to prioritize your expenses. Which ones do you have control over and which ones do you not? Do you want to keep things the way they are or do you want to make changes? Which expenses are absolutely necessary and which ones could you omit or decrease? What is most important to you? Maybe a week's vacation is more important to you than new living room furniture. It is up to the individual to decide what changes they are willing to make. By listing your expenses by priority, it shows not only you, but also your planner, what needs to be done.

You can't create something from nothing. It may be necessary for you to seek employment either part time or full time. This may be a temporary measure until you start receiving Social Security or a pension check; or it may be a long term solution if your sources of income are just not adequate to meet your living expenses. Perhaps wise investing of your assets will be enough to meet your needs without having to find a job. Cutting expenses may be enough to cure the problem. These and other alternatives can be explored with your financial planner.

STEP FOUR

After completing step three, you are ready to revise and plan your spending strategies. But first, you need to create a new budget. Creating a new budget that reflects your new circumstances enables you to see what is left over for investing. It makes it easier to anticipate that extra money, thereby setting goals for future investments. You've got to know how much money you need. It's too hard to get to that new cash flow system until you know where you've been. Budgeting takes time and discipline. The fact that you have already recorded your expenses in Step Three will simplify the task tremendously. To make the job easier, and to make sure you don't leave out anything, check at your stationery store for a budget-keeping book. There are many varieties, so pick one that seems to meet your needs. A *Survival Kit for Wives* (Villard Books, New York 1986) by Don and Renee Martin, has some excellent material to help you plan your budget. It contains five separate work sheets to guide you through the process. One is a "Daily Cash Budgeting Worksheet" which helps you see where the day-to-day expenditures are going. Then there is the "Monthly Expense Budgeting Worksheet" and the "Annual Expense Budgeting

Worksheet." The "Discretionary Expense Worksheet" lists your nonessential expenses. After accumulating all of this information, you are ready for the "Monthly Budget Control Worksheet" which summarizes your goals. Your financial planner can also assist you with ideas and forms for creating your new budget. Whichever forms you use, make several copies so that you can make changes and adjustments as needed. You are in the experimental stage of feeling your way through new territory. Don't discourage yourself by becoming too inflexible.

Keep in mind that some expenses such as taxes and insurance premiums are annual. Others occur unexpectedly, such as doctor bills, vet bills, and auto repairs. By the same token, some of your income will be lump sum once in a lifetime, such as life insurance proceeds, burial allowances, and some bequests and gifts. Others will be semi-annual such as dividends and interest. The non-recurring expenses and income are often the most difficult to budget. It necessitates putting money aside to pay for those expenses when they occur. It's all too tempting to spend all of the money in the account each month and forget about a large payment that will come due in six months. This is where budgeting plays an important role. It helps us to discipline ourselves. After working with your budget for a few months, you will see where your weaknesses lie. You will begin to see where you can save money for investment purposes. Readjust amounts where needed, always looking for a way to squeeze one more dollar out of the expense column and into the income column.

One word of caution. Do not sacrifice to the point you feel a sense of deprivation. You need to be good to yourself. Treating yourself to an occasional expensive dinner or a new coat can be uplifting. You deserve it, but try to control impulsive spending. By planning your outings and your rewards, you are less likely to overindulge. Think about doing recreational activities that don't involve a lot of expense. Ask your single friends, they are probably experts on the subject.

STEP FIVE

Reviewing your insurance is the next critical step in a widow's(er's) financial planning. The most obvious reason for this is that because your situation has changed, there is a possibility your insurance needs have changed. Do you need additional coverage, or less coverage? Do you need a different type of coverage? It is important that you examine what you have to determine what changes, if any, you need to make. Gather all of your policies and read them. Some are so filled with legalese that you may have a difficult time understanding them. If so, contact your insurance agent and ask that your coverage be explained. A good insurance agent will be happy to help you. There is insurance available for everything and every contingency imaginable. You can get health insurance for your pets, burial insurance for yourself, and life insurance for your children. You can insure your house, jewelry, auto, stamp collection, and even your legs. For a price, you can insure your belongings against flood, tornado, hurricane, earthquake, fire, and theft. The only thing you can't get coverage for is acts of war.

For the purposes of this book, we will discuss the more common types of coverage and how they pertain to the circumstances of widowed persons. You are encouraged to obtain any and all insurance that you need, without overbuying, thus becoming "insurance poor." One insurance company owner was asked the question, "If a recently widowed woman came to you seeking advice and help with her insurance needs, what would you tell her?" His reply, "I'd ask her what she could afford to spend after all of her other bills were paid each month. Then, I'd give her the best and the most coverage I could for that amount." A good insurance agent is not going to push you into anything. A plan will be presented that reflects and respects your economic circumstances. You will fare much better with insurance salespersons if you do your homework before you contact one. Do some reading to familiarize yourself with the terminology of the industry. Have a good idea of what you want and what is available ahead of time. Look over your budget to determine what you can afford to spend. Finally, comparison shop! Besides comparing prices, compare the policies to make sure coverage is similar. Among various companies, the differences can be significant.

Life insurance

There are records dating back to the fourteenth century that show that people insured their lives. The first life insurance company in the United States opened for business in 1759 in Philadelphia, Pennsylvania. Established by the Synod of the Presbyterian Church, it was called "The Corporation for Relief of Poor and Distressed Presbyterian Ministers and of the Poor and Distressed Widows and Children of Presbyterian Ministers." The name has since been shortened to the Presbyterian Ministers' Fund and has the distinction of being the oldest life insurance company in continued existence in the world.

According to the 1986 Life Insurance Fact Book published by the American Council of Life Insurance, Americans purchased $1,231.2 billion of new life insurance in 1985. Life insurance is owned by eighty-five percent of American families. Among insured families, the average amount of life insurance is $74,600.

The main purpose for purchasing life insurance continues to be for providing financial security for the surviving spouse and children. If you are the recipient of such proceeds, then you can attest to the importance of life insurance. It is a relatively fast and simple way of obtaining needed cash after a spouse dies.

At this point you will want to decide whether there is a need to insure your own life. You may already have an existing policy. If so, you must evaluate the coverage and answer the following questions:

1. Do I still need life insurance?
2. If yes, how much coverage should I have?
3. Do I need to change beneficiaries?

In order to decide whether or not you need life insurance, you should answer two questions. Is there anyone depending on you for their livelihood? Is there enough in your estate to pay all of your debts? If the answer to the first question is "no" and the answer to the second is "yes," then you probably don't need life insurance. If your purpose of having life insurance is to leave a legacy to your heirs, be aware that there are other ways of accomplishing this desire which will be discussed in Step Seven — Investments.

If you have dependents, then life insurance is a wonderful way to provide for their security, if you do not have other wealth to protect them. How much do you need? Some say five to seven times your annual salary. Another well-touted method is adding a zero to your annual salary, e.g., a person making $40,000 annually, would want $400,000 in insurance. Those methods are all too imprecise. The best way is to use your income and expenses figures to decide how much it takes for your family to live. Add any costs for services that will exist because you are not there to perform them, and any future expenses such as college educations. Subtract any benefits that your dependents will obtain because of your death. Decide how many years you need to provide for your dependents. The object here is not to make your dependents wealthy, but to maintain their standard of living until they are independent. A lot will depend on what has already been established in your estate for the support of your children. In the case of a disabled child, you will need to take many more factors into consideration. If there is the possibility that the child will never function independently, you must allow for an entire lifetime of care. If you have no dependents, but have debts that would not be covered by the assets of your estate, then you might want a life insurance policy to provide for these expenses. Don't forget funeral costs, medical bills that might not be covered by health insurance, outstanding loans to individuals and companies (credit cards and charge cards), legal costs involved in settling your estate, and tax liabilities. As discussed in Chapter Seven, "Survivor Benefits," there are a variety of policies available to you. Outline your needs and then go shopping. Compare coverage that fits your pocketbook. You can always add more coverage when your finances improve. By working with your financial advisor, you will know the best way to "own" the policy. Would it be wisest to retain ownership or to assign the policy to another? You will also discover who should be named as beneficiary. Should the estate be named, or your children?

Before leaving the subject of life insurance, you should be familiar with the term "life insurance trust." An insurance trust is created by naming the trust as the beneficiary. The trustee of the estate manages and disburses the insurance money according to the terms of the trust set forth by the owner of the policy. Insurance trusts have the advantage of estate tax savings while accomplishing the same thing as naming your estate as beneficiary.

Buying life insurance wisely requires team effort. Use the expertise of your insurance agent, financial advisor, and tax expert to arrive at the policy for you. Don't forget to revise your policy, if your needs or wishes change. This is especially important when it comes to naming beneficiaries. The company has no choice but to issue the proceeds to the beneficiary named.

Health insurance

With the high cost of medical services today, you cannot afford to be without health insurance. Yet, it is not uncommon especially for unemployed women, to go without even the minimal amounts of coverage. The cost of private health insurance is not affordable to many widows. If you are employed, be grateful for the health insurance benefits provided by your employer. Even if you must contribute a portion of the premiums from your check each month, be assured that the cost is a fraction of what you would pay outside of a group policy, and the coverage is probably better.

The federal government recognizes the plight of the medically uninsured person and has made strides toward alleviating the problem. One way is through providing the elderly with Medicare, Part A, through the Social Security Administration. Medicare, Part B, is made available at a reasonable price for further coverage. Medicaid is available to low income or disabled people through the cooperation of the local, state, and federal governments. Because both of these programs were discussed in detail in the chapter on Social Security, we will not repeat them here, but we do need to examine private "supplemental" health insurance, designed to pay whatever Medicare doesn't. A majority of those who have Medicare, Parts A and B, feel it wise to have another policy that bridges the gap in their coverage. At best, Parts A and B cover only seventy-five percent of your medical costs. That left over twenty-five percent in today's hospitals, could wipe out your life's savings in a short period of time.

Many companies offer supplemental insurance for this purpose. Some are good, many are not. You need to ask questions before you sign on the dotted line. Find out specifically what they will and will not pay. Find out if there is a deductible, and if so, is it per year or per claim? If, after your first illness, you find that you have made a mistake, don't hesitate to look for other insurance.

Another way the federal government has aided the widow is through the passage of the Consolidated Omnibus Budget Reconciliation Act of 1985, often referred to as COBRA. As of July 1, 1986, employers with twenty or more employees are required by law to offer continuing group health insurance benefits to former employees, their spouses, and dependents following termination of employment, death, or divorce. Widows(ers) who were members of the company group plan before their spouse's death are able to continue the same coverage (or choose alternate plans during open enrollment) for up to thirty-six months. The employer cannot charge more than 102 percent of the cost of the policy. Let's say your husband had a group plan at work that cost him $30 per month and his employer contributed $70 per month to make up the total cost of the monthly premium. If you elect to continue this insurance, it cannot cost you more than $102 per month ($30 + $70 + 2% = $102). This same coverage extends to your dependent children. After they reach an age where they become ineligible for coverage under your plan, they can elect to continue coverage for themselves up to a combined maximum of three years, e.g., your husband dies when your son is 20. He becomes ineligible at age 21 under the rules of your group carrier. The son elects to continue the coverage until he is 23, an additional two years after he was ineligible under your plan. In order to protect this option for yourself, YOU MUST notify the health plan carrier of your spouse's death. Within two weeks, you will be offered a continuation plan. You have sixty days to accept it. If you do not respond within that time limit, you lose your eligibility.

NOTE:

1. If your spouse retires on Medicare and you are under 65, you are eligible.

2. No medical examination is needed.

3. You will lose your eligibility if you fail to pay the premium, become entitled to Medicare benefits, become covered under any other group health plan, or if the employer terminates its group policy.

4. Federal employees and all people working in Washington, DC are not eligible. (Federal workers have a partial continuation plan of their own).

For a free brochure that explains your rights send a self-addressed, stamped envelope to:

The Older Women's League
Insurance Continuation
730 11th Street, NW, Suite 300
Washington, DC 20001
(202) 783-6686

Some state governments such as Massachusetts and California are introducing legislation that would help provide health care to every citizen of their states. It is expected that more states will follow suit. Hopefully, in the not-so-distant future, the problem of obtaining acceptably priced health insurance will be corrected.

Do not delay obtaining health insurance. Because of the affect of stress and depression on the physical body, survivors often find their immune systems depleted and become ill more often than before their spouse's death. Statistics show that they also become more accident prone, probably due to the temporary decrease in concentration.

Automobile insurance

Widows(ers) need to review their automobile coverage to make certain it still fits their needs. If you sell your spouse's car, be sure that you notify the insurance carrier so that it can be deleted from your policy. You should receive credit for the unused amount, if the policy was paid in advance.

If you no longer have a "second" vehicle, you may want to add coverage that pays for the rental of a vehicle while yours is being repaired after an accident. When buying a new vehicle, you will have to choose the type of coverage you want. If you have taken out a loan to pay for the car, then the loaning company will require that you carry collision as well as liability insurance. Collision insurance covers the repair of your car if involved in an accident, while liability (required in most states by law) covers injury to the occupants and repairs to the other car(s) involved in an accident. You may also get theft and vandalism insurance. You can choose your deductible amount. The deductible is the amount you pay per claim. For example, you choose the $100 deductible plan and are involved in a minor accident that does $300 worth of damage to your car. You will pay the first $100, the insurance company pays the remaining $200. The higher the deductible, the lower your premiums will be.

Homeowners and renters insurance

Review your policy to make certain that you understand what types of losses are covered and what types are not. A majority of persons wait until something happens, then frantically call their agent to see if they are covered. Ideally, you should know beforehand, so that you can make adjustments deemed necessary in your coverage.

You will need to add or drop coverage, if you buy or sell a home. If you elect to rent, you can get renter's insurance that will protect your personal belongings. You may even get traveler's insurance that covers the personal property you take with you on trips.

Be sure that you understand what replacement costs would be for your home and personal property. Some policies pay you what it would cost to replace a residence or personal item, while others pay you the value at the time of loss. Since used appliances are worth little, your washing machine may only have a value of $100, yet it would cost you $350 to replace it.

For valuable items such as furs and jewelry, you will need to have them appraised and then insure each item with a "floater policy" rider on your homeowner's insurance.

Otherwise, there may be reimbursement limits of amounts much less than the value of the item. Some companies automatically increase the amount of your coverage (and the amount of your premium) to keep pace with inflation and rising land values. If yours does not, you may want to increase the coverage on a periodic basis.

Mortgage insurance

In addition to the information on mortgage insurance found in Chapter Seven, you should know that not all mortgage insurance is the same. When you buy private mortgage insurance (PMI) it doesn't insure you against anything. It insures the bank that made the mortgage loan that they won't lose anything on you. The bank is made the beneficiary of the policy. You pay for PMI initially at closing of escrow and then as part of each mortgage payment. There are about twelve firms that offer PMI nationwide. Their rates vary as much as $400 for the same coverage. Comparison shopping can save you dollars.

More on insurance

As stated in the beginning, you can be insured for practically anything as long as you are willing to pay the price.

Some money-saving hints include:

■ Non-smokers can get reduced auto and homeowner premiums.

■ People over 65 can get a break on auto insurance.

■ Students who maintain a "B" or better average in school can qualify for lower premiums.

■ Car poolers can get discounts.

A final note before we go to step six. Be sure you understand when your insurance goes into force. You may have to wait until after you take a physical, in the case of health insurance; or until your driving record is verified, in the case of auto insurance. A company often will issue a binder that summarizes the protection you have agreed to purchase. Sometimes they will require the first payment at that time. This binder will protect you until you receive the policy.

STEP SIX

Plan your estate. Estate planning is done for those left behind. If your spouse left affairs in order at the time of death, then you are numbered with the fortunate few. Imagine how difficult it must be for the majority of survivors whose husbands and wives died without planning for that passage. As a surviving widow(er) it is your responsibility to "get your house in order."

Collect information

Make it easy on the fiduciaries of your estate by keeping current records of all legal and financial papers such as insurance policies, business agreements, deeds, birth certificates or adoption papers of children, automobile registration, military discharge papers, location and keys to safe deposit boxes, loans, bank accounts, names of organizations, friends, and clubs that you would want notified, securities certificates, burial wishes, recent tax returns, Social Security numbers and documents, and marriage certificate. The executor of your estate should have a list of where all of these items can be found in the event you die. Revise this list as often as needed.

Leave a list of names, addresses, and phone numbers of advisors whose services you have used. Because these people are familiar with your business, they can be a valuable resource for your executor. Make certain that you have discussed your desires concerning organ donations and prolonging of your death by use of extraordinary means with your family and friends. Complete the necessary paperwork discussed in Chapter Two to insure that your wishes are met.

All of this information can be compiled on sheets of paper or in an inexpensive estate planning binder that can be found at your stationery store. More detailed and elaborate notes and lists can be made in one of the workbooks on the market today, designed for that purpose. Four new marvelous manuals that can be found in your bookstore that will facilitate your record keeping are *A Survival Kit for Wives* (Villard Books, New York 1986) by Don and Renee

Martin, *Legacy of Love* (Shelter Publications, Bolinas, CA, 1986) by Elmo A. Petterle, *Your Family Records* (Nolo Press, Berkeley, CA, 1987) by Carol Pladsen and Denis Clifford, and *Answers* (Harper & Row, New York) by Becky Barker. While all four are similar in scope, the layout and approach in each is a little different. Any one of these offers you more than adequate coverage for your affairs.

Leave a valid will

A major factor of planning your estate is writing or updating your Will. Don't further complicate matters by leaving no Will, or a Will that is no longer in line with current laws or that no longer expresses your wishes.

Our discussion of Wills in Chapter Five was from the perspective of the surviving spouse. In this chapter, we will look at the other side and view it from the testator's (person who leaves a Will) angle. Many aspects of what constitutes a legal Will have already been explored, so this discussion will focus on how a Will can be an effective tool in estate planning.

Now that your spouse is dead, you may need to nominate new guardians for your minor children. This would also apply if you are responsible for an aging parent or other person who is incompetent to care for themselves. The court actually appoints the guardian, but your recommendations will almost always be followed. Guardians do not have to be members of your family. The circumstances may be such that the best people for the job are close friends. Be certain that whoever you choose is ready, willing, and able to assume the role. Alternate guardians should be nominated, in case your first choice is unable to comply. Do not hesitate to change guardians should circumstances warrant. Be certain, where possible, to give the guardian of your money (trustee) the power and authorization to make available the funds necessary to support your children. Take into consideration the changes in lifestyle for the family accepting your little (or big) ones. Let's say that you have three children, and have chosen as guardians your best friends Alice and Martin, who also have three children. Eight people are going to have a difficult time fitting into a compact car. If the children are young, Alice may need to quit her job to care for them all. Hiring a housekeeper may become a necessity. The food bill will increase dramatically. You get the picture. Be liberal with your instructions to provide money to assist the guardian family.

In assessing prospective guardians, take into consideration the following aspects:

■ Time. Do the busy lives of these people allow for your children? If both husband and wife have executive, high stress positions or jobs that require a lot of travel, then they may not have enough time to spend with your children.

■ Temperament. Are they patient, loving, and understanding? Do they like kids?

■ Similar Values. For some, being raised in the same religion is of utmost importance. For others, while religious teachings are not essential, they want a value system taught that is closely aligned with their own.

■ Stability. Is the guardian family stable? Is their marriage strong? Is their employment steady? Do they have a secure standing in the community? If it is important to you that your children remain in the same area (because of nearby grandparents or for other reasons), is it probable that the ones you have chosen are rooted in the vicinity? Health. Are they physically, mentally and emotionally healthy?

If your deceased spouse was executor of your old Will, then you will need to designate a new one. In Chapter Five you were given a list of the duties of the person chosen as executor. Obviously, you need someone who is capable of performing these tasks. The person must be a citizen of the United States and depending on the state in which you live, at least 18-21 years of age. They must be of sound mind and free of any felony convictions. It is advised that the person be familiar with your family and financial situation and have a genuine concern for the well-being of your family. Ideally, the executor should live near you, or at least within the same state. As with guardians, a substitute should be designated. It is not uncommon to choose co-executors to manage your estate. Often, people designate a friend or relative and a lawyer, bank, or accountant to work with them. This becomes more expensive, but may be justified. Writers often designate a literary executor, a fellow writer in whom they have confidence, to make decisions concerning their outstanding manuscripts, royalties, and contracts.

Executors should retain many of the same qualities as guardians. They should have the time, as well as the inclination, to take on the task. A general knowledge of financial matters is very helpful. Of course they should be honest and enjoy a good reputation among their peers. Overall good health is important, for it will take some stamina and alertness to accomplish all facets of the job.

Information the attorney will need to draw a will

Most of the information your lawyer will need can be found on the sheets you prepared in Steps Two and Three. An attorney will need a complete list of your assets, real property and personal property, and a list of your obligations. If you expect any inheritances, inform the attorney of the expected amount. If you have any powers of appointment over another's property, be sure the attorney is aware. A list of insurance policies should be submitted.

Know who you want to inherit your assets and establish when you want them to inherit. Specific bequests should be listed along with instructions for the residuary estate.

If you are leaving the bulk of your estate to your children and grandchildren, you should be familiar with two terms, per stirpes and per capita. Per stirpes provides that should your child die before you, his share of your assets would be divided equally between his children. Under the same circumstances, per capita would distribute the assets of your estate equally between all your grandchildren. A diagram explains this more graphically:

PER STIRPES
($300,000 Estate)

Son gets $150,000		Daughter gets $150,000	
Child 1	Child 2	Child 3	Only Child
$50,000	$50,000	$50,000	$150,000

Per Capita
Each Grandchild would receive $75,000

Decide how you want the assets divided and have it written in your Will.

Most attorneys will advise you to bequeath a percentage of your estate rather than a specific amount. Circumstances change and if your estate should be worth less at your death than when the Will was drawn, your intentions may be distorted. An example illustrates this best. When you made out your Will, your assets totaled approximately $200,000. You bequeath--ed $50,000 to your sister, and the residue to your son. After a lengthy illness and a poor stock investment, your estate dwindled to $75,000. Under the terms of you Will, your sister will get $50,000 and your son $25,000. It would have been better, had you said, "To my sister I leave twenty-five percent of my estate, with the residue going to my son."

Is there any property you cannot dispose of in a will?

Yes, you cannot will away those assets that are held in beneficiary form such as life insurance policies, pensions, or U.S. Savings Bonds. Neither can you dispose of jointly owned property with the right of survivorship, property whose disposition is governed by state laws, or property that you have yet to inherit. You may not assign any assets in which you lose control at your death.

Where should you keep your will?

The best place to keep your Will is in your attorney's safe. This makes it more accessible than a safe deposit box and safer than your home. Inform the executor of its whereabouts so that he can obtain it upon your death.

Consider forming trusts

If you find that the assets of your estate are considerable enough that the tax burden is going to be heavy, or that you need to delay the distribution of your assets, consider a more comprehensive plan that combines the formation of trusts along with your Will. Because many of the assets passed to you from your spouse will have to be re-titled anyway, this is an opportune time to have them re-titled and re-registered into the name of the trust. Because laws governing trusts are complex, and may vary slightly in different states, you must seek the guidance of an attorney.

A trust is a separate entity established by a person known as a trustor (also settlor, grantor, or donor) for the purpose of holding property for the benefit of a beneficiary. The beneficiary may be the trustor or any other person (or animal, on occasion). A trustee is one who is appointed by the trustor to administer the trust agreement. The trustor specifies in the trust instrument, the "terms" under which the assets must be held and distributed. It is the responsibility of the trustee to carry them out.

Trusts can be created during your lifetime (living trust or *intervivos* trust), or they may be created by your Will (testamentary trust). Trusts can be either revocable or irrevocable. Revocable means that you can change the terms of the agreement as much and as often as you like. Conversely, once an irrevocable trust is established, you lose all rights to make any changes. Only irrevocable trusts qualify as a tax reduction trust under IRS rules. There are several types of trusts designed to fit various needs. A discussion of the more common ones follows:

Living trust

Any time that you want to control when or how assets are distributed to your heirs, the living trust is a valuable tool. Assets can be passed immediately or their distribution can be postponed. This would be a valuable vehicle for delaying a child's inheritance until an age you deem sensible (children cannot own real property until they are 18). It can also be used to care for the needs of a handicapped child or elderly parent by instructing the trustee to provide money as needed for their care.

Property contained in a living trust is not subject to probate, thereby saving costs associated with the procedure.

Assets of the trust are not made public.

Living trusts may be made either revocable or irrevocable, depending on your purposes for establishing them. NOTE! Living trusts avoid probate, testamentary trusts (those established by the Will) do not.

Titles to property placed in the trust must be re-titled or re-registered in the name of the trust. Real estate deeds must be re-named and recorded and new stock certificates must be issued.

Typically, living trusts do not have to be recorded or filed with any public agency.

Trusts can be used to provide immediate money for funeral expenses, taxes, and administration costs.

Clifford Trust

Often used to pay for college expenses or to care for an elderly parent, the Clifford trust is an irrevocable short term (minimum life of the trust must be ten years plus one day) trust. It allows you to place property into a trust for the benefit of a child, for instance, who is in a much lower tax bracket. The Tax Reform Act of 1986 generally repealed this provision for trusts set up after March 1, 1986. Income from these trusts is taxable to the trustor.

Qualified terminal interest property trust

Mentioned in the last chapter, this trust (Q-TIP) is designed to care for a spouse during her lifetime, while allowing the trus-tor to determine who gets the estate upon her death. This is commonly used by men who have remarried, but have child-ren by a previous marriage, and who want to provide for their wives, but be assured that their children inherit the remainder.

Charitable remainder trust

These trusts are advantageous to the person who wants to give away an asset, yet collect earnings from it until the trust ends. The IRS calculates a tax deduction for the gift, based on the life expectancy of the donor. When the donor dies, the charity receives the assets of the trust.

Charitable lead trust

The charity gets all rights and benefits of the assets in the trust until the donor's death, at which time they go to the designated beneficiary.

Selecting a trustee

Trustees can be persons or institutions (banks or trust companies). If you choose the trust department of a bank to manage your trust, you can be relatively assured that your assets will be managed prudently. Trust officers have a working understanding of financial matters, and are under the scrutiny of an auditor. The biggest disadvantages of appointing an institution as your trustee are the expense (usually a flat annual fee, plus a percentage of the trust, and an hourly fee) and the lack of personalization. Trust officers are relocated regularly and it may be difficult to establish a long term working relationship with any one person. They are also regulated by procedure and may be inflexible to the needs of your beneficiaries.

If you choose an individual as trustee, be certain that the person has the time and knowledge to do the job. The duties of the trustee include investing funds, collecting income, distributing assets, recordkeeping, handling securities, keeping tax records, and providing beneficiaries with the necessary statements for their tax reporting.

Because they remain in the capacity of trustee for the life of the trust (either an established amount of time or until the death of the beneficiary), age of the designee may be a determining factor.

There are no established set fees for trustees. You should inform the person or institution of your desire to name them trustee before doing so, and work out a fee arrangement upon their acceptance. Be aware that some banks do not handle estates that are below a certain value. Therefore, it is important that you talk with a trust officer in advance.

As trustor, you may grant or deny beneficiaries the right to change trustees. This would depend on the confidence you have in the beneficiary to make good choices. If incompetence on the part of the trustee can be proven, the court may change trustees.

STEP SEVEN

The final step of financial planning involves *investing*. Investing simply means using your money to make more money. If this is a new phenomenon to you, then go slowly. Do your homework! Take a continuing education class on investments. They are offered by colleges as well as in workshops sponsored by senior citizen groups and women's groups. Often, large investment companies conduct seminars for the purpose of informing people, like yourself, about the various aspects of investments.

Read the business section of your newspaper. Visit your bookstore. You will be surprised at the number of books on the shelves pertaining to investments. The library is always a source of information. The government publishes helpful booklets that can be ordered free. See the "Sources of Information" section at the end of this book for suggested reading.

Until you can start to feel better about investing, and feel that you can cope with managing your money, put your funds in safe, secure instruments such as high-yielding certificates of deposit or Treasury bills.

Don't rush off into some super-fast investment. By the same token, it makes no sense, if after two or three years, you are still wondering where to put the life insurance proceeds. There is a reasonable time frame between procrastinating and making a hurried decision.

For many widowed persons, the lump sum life insurance proceeds represent the bulk of their inheritance. It may be more money than most have ever dealt with in their entire lives. They may also have other large sums of money from the sale of real estate or valuable personal property. Even mortgage insurance does not always have to be used to pay off the mortgage. You may have the option of collecting the proceeds and continuing your monthly payments. This could be a wise move if you have a low interest mortgage loan and can make more interest on your money through investments.

What do you want to do with your money? You may want to pay off some outstanding debts, especially if they carry high interest rates. First, determine with your financial advisor the answers to questions such as the following:

■ What is your after-tax rate of return on your other investments?

■ What is the after-tax cost of borrowing?

■ What can you make on life insurance money after taxes?

Once you have answers to these questions, you begin to see the wisest plan of action.

What are your goals?

One of the first questions an investment counselor will ask is, "What are your investment goals?" Why are you investing? What do you intend to do with the money? Answers are as varied as the respondents. One may need money to finance a child's college education. A young couple may want to buy a house. An older couple may want to retire with enough money to travel. A widow may need income to supplement her salary or Social Security benefits. A financially secure person may just want to keep pace with inflation. Decide what your reasons are for wanting to invest, and write them down.

How many years do you have to achieve your goals?

After determining your goals, you need to ascertain the amount of money needed to accomplish each one and how many years you have to obtain that amount. Let's say that your son John is 10 years old. It will cost approximately $8,000 per year to send him to the state college. He will enter as a freshman at the age of 19. That means you have nine years to accumulate $32,000, if John goes through a four year degree program. This gives you an idea of how much you would have to set aside each month to accomplish your goals.

What is your risk tolerance?

Some people love to gamble; others don't. Most people like to gamble a little. With any kind of investment there is inherent risk. Generally, the greater the risk, the higher the potential for gain or loss. Part of the investment counselor's job is to ascertain your risk tolerance and to plan an investment program with which you can feel comfortable. You need to determine the importance of each goal and decide how much money you can afford to lose in striving to obtain it. If your primary objective is to protect your money, even if it means lower returns, then you need to express this to your investment counselor.

The chart below classifies various investments according to their risk factors. After determining your tolerance for risk, you can get an idea of what types of investments would align with those feelings.

■ **Low Risk.** Treasury bills, notes and bonds, insured municipal bonds, U.S. savings bonds (Series EE and HH), certificates of deposit, savings/checking accounts, money market funds.

■ **Moderate Risk.** Municipal bonds (AAA, AA or A), corporate bonds (AAA, AA or A), blue chip stocks, universal life insurance, municipal bond mutual funds, fixed annuities.

■ **Moderate High Risk.** Municipal bonds (BBB), corporate bonds (BBB), growth stocks, growth mutual funds, income mutual funds, real estate limited partnerships, variable annuities, variable life insurance policies.

■ **High Risk.** Speculative stocks, junk bonds, stock options, commodity futures, financial futures, real estate development, raw land, collectibles, gold and silver, strategic metals.

Types of investments

The following section is a description of the various types of investments available to you. In no way should you interpret any information as a recommendation. It is the intention to make you aware of, not to give advice on, particular investments. That is left to the professional consultant who has the training, knowledge, and licenses to make recommendations.

1. Regular interest-bearing savings and checking accounts. These are hardly considered investments because they frequently do not keep pace with inflation. Checking accounts are necessary to pay bills and should contain only

enough to do so. Passbook savings accounts should contain small amounts for emergency purposes only.

2. Certificates of deposit require that you commit your money for a specified period of time. This can range from weeks to years. Typically, the longer you commit the money, the higher the interest you receive. Rates vary among institutions. There are early withdrawal penalties, if you withdraw the funds before the agreed date.

3. Stocks. When you purchase stocks, you become an owner of a portion of the company's assets. If the company does well, the value of your stocks increases. Conversely, if the company does poorly, the value of your stocks decreases. Some companies pay "dividends," a distribution of part of their earnings to the shareholders.

Some stocks are listed on an exchange. The better known exchanges are the New York Stock Exchange and the American Stock Exchange. The issuing company must meet certain requirements to qualify for one of these major exchanges. Securities not traded on an exchange are traded over-the-counter (OTC) through a network of securities brokers and dealers.

You will hear the expression "common stocks" and "preferred stocks." The preferred stock holders get a dividend of a stated amount, if earnings of the company are good. The common stockholder gets dividends only in the event one is declared by the issuing company. Preferred stockholders are also in a better position should the company go out of business.

4. Corporate bonds are different from stocks in that the investor holds a certificate of promise to pay (an IOU), and is not an owner of any portion of the company. The company promises to repay the loan (issued in denominations of $1,000) at a specified time, and at a specified rate of interest. Your investment is not dependent on the gains or losses of the company. Bonds are considered long term investments.

Bearer bonds may be sold by the person who has possession of them. This makes their safekeeping especially important. Registered bonds record the buyer's name with the issuing company.

Bonds are rated on a scale of AAA (the highest), to D

(the lowest), by independent companies who estimate the risk to the investor. Moody's and Standard & Poor's are two of the better known rating services.

5. Municipal bonds are issued by states, cities, and other local agencies. Although the interest rates are lower than those of corporate bonds, they have the advantage of being exempt from federal income taxes, and from state and local taxes, provided the buyer lives in the jurisdiction of the issuing authority.

6. Stock options give a person the right to buy (referred to as "calls") or sell (referred to as "puts") something at a fixed price, within a specified amount of time.

7. Real Estate Investment Trusts (REIT's) are composed of many investors who pool their resources and invest in real estate.

8. Mutual fund is a type of investment company that offers shares to the public and buys them back on demand. Investors pool their resources and professionals manage the account. The mutual fund industry ranks fourth among the nation's largest financial services institutions. The 1987 Mutual Funds Fact Book states that over 25 million investors contribute to 1800 mutual funds.

A no-load mutual fund does not charge a fee when you purchase shares. A load fund charges a fee not to exceed 8.5 percent of the purchasing price. Some companies charge an additional redemption fee when you sell your stocks back to them. All companies charge a management fee.

Read the mutual fund prospectus before you invest to determine whether there is a waiting period for redemption of shares and what the fee structure is like.

The type of mutual fund you invest in is determined by your goals. If you want your money to grow and don't need an income from it, then you will want to invest in a growth fund. If you need to supplement your income to pay your bills, then you will want either a growth and income fund, or strictly an income fund, depending on how much income you need. You will be able to determine this by looking at the work you did in Steps Three and Four.

9. Money market funds are a type of mutual fund that invests in short-term debt instruments such as large

denomination certificates of deposit, government securities, and commercial paper. There is no sales load (commission) and minimum investments range from $500 to $1,000. There are check writing privileges and withdrawals can be made at any time, usually in minimum amounts of $500.

10. Tax shelters and limited partnerships are formed for the main purpose of reducing tax liabilities. Investors form a partnership in a venture, but do not take an active role in managing it. There have been significant tax changes in this area, therefore you will need professional advice.

11. Government securities include Treasury bills, Treasury notes, and U.S. Government agency bonds. These debt securities (loans) can be obtained without paying a commission from a Federal Reserve Bank or the Bureau of Public Debt or they can be purchased from banks, dealers or brokers.

12. Real estate comes in all forms, from raw land to apartment complexes. Duplexes and rental houses are popular investments for middle income individuals, because of the tax advantages and the ability to offset mortgage payments by collecting the rents.

13. Individual Retirement Accounts (IRA's), Keogh's and Tax-sheltered annuities (TSA's) are vehicles for saving money for your retirement. You are not taxed on the interest earned in the account until you withdraw the funds between the ages of 59 1/2 and 70 1/2. The Tax Reform Act of 1986 made some changes in the amount of deduction allowed a person contributing to an IRA. Check with your accountant or the IRS for these changes.

14. Collectibles can range from antique jukeboxes to classic cars. The most popular are rare stamps and coins, which have both enjoyed a steady return over the years. Before investing in collectibles, it is recommended that you have a good knowledge of the item you are collecting, in order to get the best buys.

15. Gold can be bought in coin, bullion, commodity futures, mining ventures, or through mutual funds investing in mining shares.

16. Silver is bought in silver bars, junk silver coins, and uncirculated silver dollars.

17. Diamonds and other gems are considered long term investments. It takes a great deal of knowledge to invest wisely in this area.

18. Energy investments include oil and gas stocks, limited partnerships for drilling and exploration, and limited partnerships for obtaining producing oil and gas properties.

19. Equipment leasing, cable television, and cellular phone businesses are among the newest forms of investments.

20. Foreign securities are generally subject to the same rules and regulations as American companies.

Now that you have an idea of the kinds of investments available, and the risk rating of each type, you can begin to get a feel for your investment preferences. Most all investment counselors will recommend that you not put all of your eggs in one basket, but rather that you diversify. Your investment portfolio could contain several of the investment types listed above. This offers greater protection for your overall investing.

Investments can be made in lump sum amounts, or you can contribute periodically. Investing a specific amount each month is a good habit to embrace. You will be surprised how quickly your money grows when you contribute regularly and leave the dividends to accumulate.

Don't forget about the role taxes play in any investment you make. Some investments offer immediate tax savings, while others offer long term tax advantages. Work closely with your tax consultant and financial advisor to capitalize on investments that minimize your tax liabilities. This area is highly complex and you will need a qualified professional to help you.

Protection for the investor

The Securities and Exchange Commission (SEC) is the overseer of brokerage houses and other financial institutions that deal in public securities. Before a company can issue stock to the public, the proposed stock issue must be registered and approved by the SEC. This is done only after the company's prospectus is reviewed. A prospectus describes the nature of the business, its management, the type of security being offered, and a financial statement. The SEC requires that this prospectus also be available to all interested investors. Comprehensive reports (Form 10-K) must be filed annually thereafter. To obtain these reports, write SEC, Public Reference Room, 450 Fifth Street, NW, Washington, DC 20549, or phone (202) 272-7450. The SEC cannot assure the accuracy of all statements made in the prospectus, but it does impose stiff penalties for false and fraudulent statements.

There are several self-regulating organizations (SRO's) that watch over the conduct of those buying and selling securities. They establish rules, set qualifications, and regulate and discipline their members.

Most states provide further protection with laws designed to regulate the buying and selling of securities within the state. Before the SEC existed, it was the sole responsibility of the individual states.

Most securities brokers/dealers are members of the Securities Investor Protection Corporation (SIPC) which insures accounts up to $500,000 per customer (not more than $100,000 for cash claims). Many brokerage firms carry additional insurance for amounts that exceed the SIPC limits.

Even though there are protections for the investor, the ultimate responsibility lies with the investor. The SEC recommends that you do not buy securities offered by telephone; that you check the credentials of the salesperson; that you understand the risks involved; that you get advice about anything unclear in the prospectus; and that you not buy on tips or rumors.

Complaints may be registered with the:

> U.S. Securities and Exchange Commission
> Office of Consumer Affairs
> 450 Fifth Street, NW
> Washington, DC 20549
> (202) 272-7440

Commission rates

Commission rates are negotiable. Although firms have established rates, those rates may vary among firms. It is to your benefit to shop for the best rates. In this day of discount food stores, furniture stores, and drug stores, it is not surprising that there are also discount brokerage firms. They offer fewer services for a lower price. "Churning" is the expression used to describe the unlawful pressure on clients to trade securities so that commissions can be made. If you ever feel that your account is being manipulated for this purpose, report it to the SEC or one of the SRO's.

Where should you keep your securities?

The securities business is being handled more and more by electronic means. Computers store ownership information that can be retrieved in minutes. It is a matter of time before all certificates are handled electronically.

In the meantime, if you are holding certificates, keep them in a safe place such as your safe deposit box. Many brokers prefer that you keep them with the broker to insure ease of transfer.

A plan for success

By following the Seven Step plan, you have built for yourself a foundation for financial independence. Continue acquiring knowledge about the financial world and you will gain more control over your financial future. Few things are more gratifying than knowing you are master of your finances. Make decisions for your money, rather than letting money dictate what you will do. The more time and effort you spend in this pursuit, the greater will be your satisfaction and your profits.

15.

Building Credit
on Your Own

Credit is the ability to receive something now, by promising to pay for it later. That something may be a service, a tangible product, or money in the form of a loan. For better or for worse, the financial system of America is firmly established on the principal: buy now, pay later. Individuals, institutions, and governments all depend on credit to function.

When there is an emergency, the easiest way to meet the financial burden is to take out a piece of plastic called a credit card and buy the plane ticket, or pay for the mechanic's labor, or make a long distance phone call back home. It also enables one to carry small amounts of cash, which is especially important when traveling. With a credit or charge card, you can take advantage of sale items even though you may not have the cash during the period of the sale. Using your card, you can order almost anything from flowers to theater tickets by telephone. By charging items, you can write one check to pay several bills and still have an accurate record of your purchases for bookkeeping and the IRS.

Some businesses, such as car rentals, require that you have a credit card. Others require a credit card if you want to cash a check. Credit cards are often used to confirm your identification.

You'll certainly need to establish credit if you want a loan to buy a house, make home improvements, or purchase a new car. Starting a business will most likely require lots of credit. Many credit cards are interest-free thirty day loans, and using them as such makes good business sense.

Whether you need credit for convenience, safety, identification, or purchasing power, the steps to obtaining it and the laws governing it are the same. Rare is the American citizen who can live in today's society without getting caught up in the world of credit. It is therefore important that you learn about your rights and responsibilities.

TYPES OF PERSONAL CREDIT

The types of credit you will most likely want will fall into three categories — installment loans, credit cards, and mortgages.

Installment loans are used for large ticket items such as automobiles, furniture, vacations, college, etc., for a period of one to three years. You apply for these types of loans most generally from banks, credit unions, and finance companies. The loan may be either secured or unsecured. Secured means you have capital goods to back up the loan. If you default on your loan, the creditor can take the item you have pledged and sell it to recover the loss. Unsecured loans, often called "signature" loans, are based solely on your promise to repay the debt. It usually takes a long-standing relationship with a banker to obtain this type of credit. Once an installment loan is granted, you make regular (usually monthly) payments that include principal (the amount borrowed) plus interest (the amount it costs you to borrow the principal).

Credit Cards are a type of unsecured loan. They also come in various types — retail charge cards, bank credit cards, and travel and entertainment charge cards.

Retail charge cards are issued by department stores and oil companies and may be used only in the establishment of the issuing company. Some have limits on the amount you can charge, others do not. Typically, you are expected to pay the outstanding balance each month when you receive the bill. Some retail merchants offer a revolving account, where you pay a portion of the balance and the remainder is rolled over to the next month. In this case, you are liable for a finance charge on the unpaid amount.

Bank credit cards such as Visa and MasterCard may be used in a variety of places, from restaurants to craft fairs.

There is a maximum spending limit for each individual and you may either pay off the balance each month and incur no finance charges (in most cases — check your contract), or pay the minimum payment requirement and interest on the unpaid amount.

Travel and entertainment charge cards such as American Express, Carte Blanche, and Diner's Club charge an annual membership fee and expect payment in full each month. There is generally no maximum limit.

Mortgage loans are secured loans where the house itself is the collateral. If you default on the loan, the house (or other real estate) is forfeited to the loan institution. You commit yourself to the provisions of the loan when you sign the mortgage contract.

THE COSTS OF CREDIT

Because the cost of using credit varies from place to place, you need to shop around for the best terms. The Consumer Credit Protection Act of 1968 established Truth in Lending laws that require creditors (those extending the credit) to tell you, in writing and before you sign any agreement, the finance charges and the annual percentage rate.

Finance charges include interest costs, service charges, required insurance premiums, and/or appraisal fees. These costs must be totaled and written in your contract.

The annual percentage rate (APR) refers to the yearly interest rate (the cost of borrowing for a year) of the credit. Interest rates fluctuate constantly because of the national money supply. A fifteen percent loan may be a good deal the beginning of the year when interest rates are hovering around the 16.5 percent range, but much too high later the same year when interest rates have dropped to twelve percent.

Knowing your needs will help you when you are shopping for credit. Do you want the lowest cost loan or do you want the lowest monthly payments? A fifteen percent loan over a period of three years will have higher monthly payments than a fifteen percent loan spread out over five years, but the overall cost of the five year loan will be more than the three year loan. Looking at your budget will help you make these decisions.

Open-end credit

Credit cards, check overdraft accounts, and charge cards offer open-ended credit, which allows you to continue borrowing until you have reached your credit limit. Once you have reduced the amount you owe on your account, you can borrow again, repeating the process indefinitely. Your credit limit is usually dependent on how the issuing company views your ability to repay the borrowed amount. Often, they will begin your account with a small borrowing limit and increase it as you prove that you are a good credit risk.

Finance charges are calculated in three ways: the adjusted balance method, the previous balance method, and the average daily balance method.

The adjusted balance method subtracts any payments you made during the billing period from the total before they add the finance charges. When you get no credit for amounts paid during the billing period, this is called using the previous balance method. The average daily balance method takes the balance for each day and divides by the number of days in the billing period. Look at the following example.

	Adjusted	Previous	Avg. Daily
% rate (monthly)	1%	1%	1%
Previous Balance	$300	$300	$300
Payment (payment on 15th day)	$100	$100	$100
Interest Charge	$2.00 ($200x1%)	$3.00 ($300x1%)	$2.50 $250x1%) (avg. balance)

By law, creditors must tell you the way in which they arrive at their charges.

Creditors must also tell you when the finance charges begin. Many credit card companies give you twenty-five to thirty days before they impose interest fees, and an additional ten to fifteen days before tacking on a late charge. Others begin charging interest as soon as the charge is made.

Truth in Leasing laws are similar to those of the lending laws. They apply to personal property leased for more than four months. Apartments would not be included because they are not personal property. The written terms must include the responsibilities of the lessor as well as the lessee. It must state whether or not you have an option to buy the item at the end of the leasing period.

Creditors are also bound to disclosure in their advertising. They may not speak of low down-payments without also mentioning the APR and terms of repayment.

Shop around for the best terms

It is important that you are aware of the annual fee, the annual interest rate, and the cost of late charges when shopping for credit cards. When you receive offers for credit cards (it is against the law for a company to send you an unsolicited credit card), read the material carefully. You will usually find the disadvantages to a particular card contained in the fine print. The large or exaggerated print will boast of low interest, while the fine print at the bottom explains that you will be charged interest from the date the charges are made. Another ploy to get your attention is to advertise no annual fee for the card, while the fine print reveals there is a transaction fee each time you use the card.

To find out which banks are currently offering the lowest finance charges for credit cards send $1.50 check or money order to:

> BankCard Holders of America
> 333 Pennsylvania Avenue, S.E.
> Washington, DC 20003

Ask for the "Low Interest Rate List." If you would like a list of banks that offer cards with no annual fee, send $1.50 to the same address and request the "No Annual Fee List."

HOW THE CREDIT LAWS PROTECT YOU

In addition to the Truth in Lending and Truth in Leasing laws mentioned above, The Consumer Credit Protection Act went further to protect the consumer with various amendments. One of these was the Equal Credit Opportunity Act which went into effect October 28, 1975. This law made it illegal to discriminate in any aspect of a credit transaction on the basis of sex, marital status, race, national origin, age, religion, or color. It further states that you may not be denied credit because you receive public assistance, such as Social Security or Welfare.

Provisions of the Equal Credit Opportunity Act include the following:

■ Women have the right to obtain credit in their own names based on their own credit records and earnings.

■ Creditors may not ask about your plans to have children.

■ All income, even child support, alimony, Social Security, and retirement benefits must be counted as part of your income, unless you choose not to disclose it.

■ You may not be turned down or have your credit line reduced because of your age.

■ Creditors may not close your account or require you to reapply because of your age or change in marital status. There must be some indication that your creditworthiness has diminished.

■ Provided you are creditworthy, the creditor may not require a co-signer on your account.

■ When applying for credit, you do not have to answer any questions about your husband or ex-husband unless you are claiming income from child support, alimony, or separate maintenance, or unless you live in a community property state, or unless your husband will also be using the account.

■ Creditors must tell you why you are being denied credit.

■ Creditors must consider the credit history of accounts women hold jointly with their husbands. In cases where the account is held in the husband's name only, creditors must consider her credit rating, if she can prove it also reflects her creditworthiness. This is done by showing how you paid the bills or contributed to the income that paid the bills. If the husband's credit rating is poor, you can try to show how that is no reflection of your creditworthiness.

WHAT ARE CREDITORS LOOKING FOR?

When looking at a prospective borrower, creditors want to know if you have the three C's — capacity, character, and collateral.

Capacity refers to your ability to repay debt. You will be asked to fill out forms that ask about your sources of income and your obligations. They want to know how many people are dependent on your earnings and income. This information gives them a good indication of whether you can afford to tack on an additional obligation. On your credit application, be sure to include all annuities, retirement funds, certificates of deposit, mutual funds, stocks, etc., to make your resources of income look more substantial. You may be denied credit if your income is not adequate to repay the debt.

Character tells the creditor whether you are willing to repay the debt. They will look at your credit history to see if you have repaid other debt on time and how much and how often you borrow. They want to know whether you rent or own your home, how long you have lived there, and how long you have been employed. This type of information gives them clues to your stability. You may be denied credit if your bill paying record is poor.

Collateral provides security for the creditor if you fail to repay your debt. What do you have that can be sold to repay the creditor? A bank's favorite form of collateral is stocks and bonds because they can be easily converted if you default on a loan. Other acceptable property includes real estate, cars, certificates of deposit, and cash in a savings account. If you use your home as security for a credit transaction, you have three business days to change your mind. The cancellation must be given to the creditor in writing. The three day rule can be eliminated in the case of an emergency by signing a waiver and making a written explanation of the reasons. You may be denied credit if you lack sufficient collateral.

Determining your creditworthiness

You may wonder why one institution will grant you credit, while another will not. Largely this is because each company has its own measuring stick. Many create a "point" system, giving so many points for each factor in your favor. Because these rating systems differ, you may qualify one place and not another.

Mention was made of your credit history. You might wonder how a company gets information about your past credit experiences. There are agencies that keep records of your salary, your debts and how you pay them, your outside sources of income, and much more. When you apply for credit, the company you are applying to will pay a credit reporting agency to give them a credit profile of you. This helps them to determine whether you are a good credit risk.

The Fair Credit Reporting Act makes it possible for you to acquire the credit information in your file. There is a small fee (usually less than $10 for an individual) for this service. It's a good idea to check your rating every few years to make sure there are no mistakes. If you find that a mistake has been made, the credit agency (also called credit bureau) must investigate the matter with the creditor who gave them the information. If the creditor admits there has been an error, the agency must remove that information from your record and submit the corrected information to anyone who previously received the incorrect information. If the creditor adheres to the information with which you disagree, you may submit a statement that tells your side. This statement must be included with any reports that the agency gives out in the future.

The time limit for most unfavorable information in your file is seven years, except for bankruptcies, which are not removed for ten years.

Only those people with legitimate reasons may examine your credit files. You have the right to know who has received a report on you within the preceding six months or within the preceding two years, if the report was furnished for employment purposes.

In the case where you have been denied credit because of a poor credit report, you have the right to ask the name and address of the reporting agency. By making a request to see your file within thirty days after the credit rejection, you may get a copy free of charge. The agency has the duty to help you interpret any of the information found in the report.

Consumer credit agencies may be found by looking in the Yellow Pages under "Credit Rating" or "Reporting Agencies." Another way of locating a credit agency is to ask someone in business who they use for their reports.

How to start a credit history

You would think that with the proliferation of credit today, getting credit cards would be easy. For most people it is, but for the divorced or widowed woman who has never had credit in her name, it can be immensely frustrating. The many provisions under the Equal Credit Opportunity Act have gone a long way toward making it easier, but can still be difficult for the unprepared woman.

Ideally, a woman should establish credit while she is still married. This can be done by obtaining jointly owned credit cards with your and your husband's names on them (not just the right to make charges on his card), by requesting that credit information be sent to credit agencies in both of your names, by having a credit card in your own name, and by having a bank account of your own from which you can pay bills. Save cancelled checks where you have paid bills to show you are reliable.

If you did not establish a credit history before your spouse's death, then the task will take a bit more time and patience, but you can do it. The first rule is "Apply Now." Even if you don't need the credit (that's all the better) start making applications early, because it will take some time to build an adequate credit line. You may need readily available money when you least expect it. The second rule is "Don't Give Up." If one company turns you down, try another. The third rule is "Be Creative." There is "more than one way to skin a cat," as the saying goes.

Keeping the three rules in mind, here is a workable plan for creating your very own credit history:

1. Open a checking and/or a savings account. While bank accounts do not appear as part of your credit history, they do prove that you have money (capacity) and can manage it. As mentioned earlier, keep cancelled checks that

show bills you have paid (character).

2. Apply for easier to get credit such as department store charge cards and gasoline cards. Use them wisely and pay the balances off promptly each month.

3. Apply for a credit card with your own bank. Because they know you and your spending habits, your chances are increased.

4. Ask your banker for a line of credit. This is usually in the form of an overdraft checking account and is a type of unsecured loan.

5. Some banks will give you a credit card if you open an account with them. Your line of credit will be determined by the amount in your account (collateral). It works like this. You open an account by depositing $500 in a savings account. The bank will give you a credit card with a limit of $500. It is important that you do not withdraw the money, but maintain it as security. After several months of faithful debt repayment, ask the bank to increase your limit beyond the amount in your account.

6. Apply for a small loan, put the money into a certificate of deposit or some other saving vehicle, and repay the loan in installments. The loan must be in existence one year in order to appear on your credit rating. When you speak with the loan officer, have some project in mind, don't tell him that you are just trying to obtain a credit history.

7. As a last resort, ask someone with an established credit history to co-sign your credit request. By law, this does not have to be a spouse. After a year, ask the creditor to extend to you your own separate line of credit. Provided that you have paid the debts from your own account on time and satisfactorily, your request should be granted.

WHAT IF YOU ARE DENIED CREDIT?

The Equal Credit Opportunity Act says that the creditor has thirty days after you make application to notify you whether your loan has been approved. If credit is denied, they must either give you in writing the reasons for the denial or explain your right to request an explanation. These same rules apply if an existing account has been closed.

The first thing you want to do is to find out why you were denied credit. The reasons may stem from an unstable income, insufficient income to meet the loan payments, or a poor or non-existent credit history. If you were denied because of something on your credit report, you have the right to the name and address of the reporting agency. Contact them and follow the procedure mentioned above for correcting any mistakes.

HOW TO CORRECT BILLING ERRORS

Once you have established credit, it is very important that you protect it. Your credit history is like your good name. Because of the millions of credit cards in circulation being used by millions of consumers, billing mistakes can and do happen. Failure to follow the proper procedures for correcting these errors will not only lead to frustration, but could also affect your credit history. The Fair Credit Billing Act was established to provide a means of correcting billing errors.

When you receive your bill each month, check to make sure the arithmetic is correct, the totals on the bill match your receipts, all previous payments have been credited to your account, any returned items do not appear on the bill, and only items you purchased appear on the bill. If you find any discrepancies, there is a three step procedure to follow:

1. Notify the creditor *in writing* within sixty days after the bill was mailed. There will be an address and/or phone number on your bill to use if you have billing inquiries. Although not necessary, including a *copy* of the bill is useful. Be sure to include your name, account number, and why you think the bill is incorrect. You may telephone the company, but in order to be within the provisions of the law, the notification must also be in writing.

2. Pay any and all parts of the bill that are not in dispute. You do not have to pay the amount in question or any finance charges that apply to it. The creditor has thirty days to reply to your letter. Within ninety days, the account must be corrected or you must be told why the creditor believes the bill to be correct as stands. In the latter case, the

creditor is entitled to include any finance charges that have accumulated and any minimum payments you missed during the dispute.

3. If you still think the bill is incorrect, again notify the creditor in writing before the bill is due.

A creditor may not threaten your credit rating nor take measures to collect any disputed amounts until the issue is settled. Only after the creditor has completed the actions in step 2 above, can he report you delinquent if you do not repay the amount in dispute by the billing date. Upon doing so, the creditor must also report that you have challenged the bill (step 3). He must give you the names and addresses of each person that received information about your account and report to them the outcome of the dispute.

YOUR OTHER RIGHTS

Consumers have more rights concerning credit.

■ Creditors must mail their statements at least fourteen days before the payment is due, if your account is the type where finance charges aren't added before a certain date.

■ Payments must be credited on the day they arrive.

■ Credit balances must be made to you in cash no more than seven days after you request it in writing, or automatically after six months.

■ You may refuse to pay for defective merchandise that has been charged to your account, if you have made a good faith effort to first resolve the problem with the merchant, and the amount of the item is over $50 and within your state or within 100 miles of your residence.

COMPLAINTS

Occasionally, you may not be able to resolve your problem with the creditor. If you feel your rights under the Equal Credit Opportunity Act have been violated, then you should report the matter to the appropriate government agency.

If your complaint involves a Consumer Reporting Agency, then write to the:

Federal Trade Commission (FTC)
Division of Credit Practices
6 Pennsylvania Avenue, NW
Washington, DC 20580
(202) 326-2000

If your complaint concerns an oil company, credit card or charge card company, retail store, public utility company, small loan and finance company, state credit union, government lending program or department store, contact:

Federal Trade Commission
Consumer Inquiries
6 Pennsylvania Avenue, NW
Washington, DC 20580

If you have a complaint about the practices of a bank, you may direct your complaint in writing to:

Director of the Division of Consumer and
    Community Affairs
Board of Governors of the Federal Reserve
    System
20th and C Street, NW
Washington, DC 20551
(202) 452-3693

If your complaint does not fall within their jurisdiction, they will forward the complaint to the appropriate agency, informing you of where it has been sent.

If you feel your civil rights have been violated with any type of creditor, contact: General Litigation Section,Civil Rights Division, Department of Justice, Housing and Civil Enforcement Section, P.O. Box 65998, Room 7525, Washington, DC 20035-5998, (202) 633-4713

Consumers also have the right to bring litigation against any creditor they feel has broken the law. There are established limits for collection, depending on the laws violated. Check with an attorney or write for the booklet "Consumer Handbook to Credit Protection Laws," which can be obtained for 50 cents from:

R. Woods
Consumer Information Center-C
P.O. Box 100
Pueblo, CO 81002

PROTECTING YOUR CREDIT CARDS

There are certain steps you can take to protect your credit cards, thus protecting your credit. The United States Office of Consumer Affairs suggests the following:

1. Keep a record of your card numbers, expiration dates, and the phone number of each company in a secure place.

2. Watch your card, whenever possible, after giving it to a clerk. Retrieve your card promptly after using it.

3. Take the carbons along with your credit card receipt. Void or destroy incorrect receipts.

4. Avoid signing a blank receipt. Draw a line through blank spaces above the total when you sign card receipts.

5. Open credit card bills promptly and compare them with your receipts.

6. Never give a credit card number to a telephone solicitor unless you have initiated the call.

7. Never put your card number on a postcard or on the outside of an envelope.

8. Sign new cards and destroy unwanted cards as soon as they arrive.

9. Keep infrequently used cards in a secure place.

Should you lose your credit card, or have it stolen, report the loss to the issuing company immediately. Most companies have a twenty-four hour, toll-free number that can be found on your billing statement. As soon as the company is notified, they will close the account and send you a new card with a new account number. While inconvenient, the amount of liability is very limited because of the federal laws. You do not have to pay for any unauthorized charges made after you notify the company. If you didn't realize the card was missing before the thief ran up charges on your account, you are still only liable for $50 on each card.

ELECTRONIC FUND TRANSFER SYSTEMS

Because of the cost of processing checks through the banking system, banks are encouraging the use of electronic machines for transferring money from one place to another.

The most familiar method of electronic transfer to most people is through the use of the Automated Teller Machines (ATMs) found at almost every bank today. *Upon request*, you may be issued a plastic card that looks much like a credit card and is called a bank *debit card*. It differs from a credit card in that it merely transfers funds you already have, it does not extend you credit. ATM cards can be used to get cash, make deposits, pay installment loans, or transfer money from one account to another as in the case of taking money from a savings account and putting it into your checking account.

There is another type of transfer that is rapidly becoming part of our society, the Point-of-Sale (POS) transaction. You use your debit card to transfer funds from your account to the merchant's account. These are most commonly seen in gas stations and grocery stores. The potential for increased use is tremendous among other types of merchants.

One type of transfer that has been encouraged by the Social Security Administration for years is the electronic deposit of funds called "direct deposit" to your account. Employers, especially government agencies, use this system. Rather than getting a piece of paper (check) on payday, the transfer of your wages is made electronically to your bank. For some, this is a real convenience and safety factor. Whereas you may be required to receive your salary electronically, you do have the right to choose the financial institution.

Telephone and computer transfers are relatively new, but may see a rapid increase in use as the pushbutton phone and home computers become the norm for our society.

The Electronic Fund Transfer Act

Because electronic transfers are becoming an acceptable means of handling financial business, laws have been established to protect the consumer. The Electronic Fund Transfer Act provides for the same types of problems that the credit laws address.

All electronic transfers must appear on your monthly bank statement. You have sixty days to notify the bank of billing errors. The financial institution has forty-five days to investigate the error. If it takes longer than ten days to resolve the error, then the amount in question must be recredited to your account until the investigation is completed. After the investigation is completed, the bank must notify you of its findings in writing.

In the case of loss or theft, your liability is limited to $50 *if* you notify the financial institution within *two* business days after learning of the theft or loss. After the two days, your liability increases to $500. Notification of unauthorized transfers after sixty days after the mailing of the statement could result in your losing everything in your account and your overdraft line of credit.

WHEN SHOULD YOU USE CREDIT?

Perhaps the most important issue of any discussion on credit should address when you should use credit. For people with poor money managing skills, credit can dig them deeper into the pit of financial hardship. For those who can control spending, it can provide a convenient and safe method of shopping. Examine your motives for seeking credit. If you know you have a weakness for abusing credit cards, then leave them at home when you go shopping. Put them in a place that is hard to reach (like a safe deposit box), so that you will be more likely to use them only after a lot of thought or in the case of an emergency.

Venita Van Caspel, in her book *Money Dynamics for the New Economy* (Simon and Schuster, New York, 1986), gives four rules that everyone should follow:

■ Never charge anything you can't pay for in thirty days.

■ Never borrow for your daily living or luxuries.

■ Borrow only for long-term investing and only if you can sell your investment for as much as you paid for it.

■ Always be solvent.

Remember that interest on consumer debt will no longer be tax deductible after 1990, and will be greatly reduced between now and then. Learn to use credit without abusing it. Make it work for you, rather than against you.

16.

"Who Ya Gonna Call?"

Wouldn't it be great, if we could call in a team like Dan Aykroyd and Harold Ramis' "Ghost Busters" to eradicate our grief. "Grief Busters" definitely has a nice ring. While there are no machines or sprays to chase away your pain, there are some people and organizations that will share your burden. Somewhere along the way, some of us came to believe that persons always need to be strong, never showing emotion outside the privacy of their bedrooms, and persevering alone, neither asking nor needing the help of others.

One of the first steps to recovery after the loss of a loved one is giving yourself permission to accept help from others. Be assured, that as time goes on, you will be able to do more for yourself. A day will come when you will be able to guide others through the process of death. It is then that you see how rewarding the role of friend, helper, listener, and counselor can be. If you need help, don't cheat someone who knows what you are experiencing out of the chance to repay kindnesses that were once shown to them.

If you have maintained social contacts outside of your marriage, then it will be much easier to adjust to being alone. One of the hardest transitions for a newly widowed person is moving into a world of new social contacts. If you are fortunate to already have your own friends and clubs, continue to cultivate them. Don't drop your activities or contacts at a time when you need them most. It will be easier for you to participate in an atmosphere where people relate to you as an individual and not as the other member of a pair.

If you do not have outside contacts, or you need some additional support, there are four main places to find the help you need — individuals, support groups, professional counselors, and clubs and organizations. You may be more comfortable seeking help in one of these places than in another. A professional counselor may be a temporary source of strength, while an organization will give you friends for life. Decide where you can feel most open and get the most help at this time in your life. If one place doesn't seem right, try another and another until you find the right kind of help.

INDIVIDUALS

Linda J. Bailey, a counselor and author of *How To Get Going When You Can Barely Get Out Of Bed*, teaches that everyone should have at least three people they can call any time day or night. That way, if one friend is out of town or doesn't have the time or inclination to listen to you, you have two more to call. It's a good idea.

Where can you find people who will listen and sympathize?

Friends are a good place to start. You doubtless had several sincere people who attended the funeral tell you that if there was anything they could do to help, just call. If any of these individuals have experienced a similar loss, you can be assured that they are willing and eager to listen.

Relatives relate well for they also knew your spouse and are feeling a loss. Because the deceased was not a stranger to them, they can talk of personal remembrances. This is often comforting, when friends are afraid to even mention the deceased's name for fear of upsetting you.

Neighbors often form close relationships and are ready to help when the need arises. Having a neighbor over for coffee is an excellent way to make an outside contact.

Children, whether adult or younger, can be good company. You might be surprised at their insight and understanding. They love you, and that's an important thing to be surrounded with when you are grieving.

Ministers and lay counselors are excellent sources of help. Their experience and training can give you an outlet for your grief. They can often recommend reading material and other sources of help.

Most people want to help, but they don't know how. If you can tell them what you need, the battle is half won.

SUPPORT GROUPS

Often called self-help groups, support groups are alliances formed by individuals who share common experiences. The tie that binds members is mutual need. The first group of this type was Alcoholics Anonymous, formed in 1935.

Today there are self-help groups that address almost every contingency of society. The role these groups play is vital to their communities. Mental health facilities are often under-staffed and under-funded, leaving them able to help only the most desperate clients. Because most people just need a listening ear and reassurance that they are not alone, self-help groups fill a void that might otherwise stay vacant.

To locate a group that deals specifically with your situation, call your local Mental Health Association office. They have lists of groups in your area that provide relief to those facing personal crisis. Many publish directories that list the various support groups.

Many hospitals have bereavement programs. The discussion is often facilitated by a person in the human services field, but the crux of the dialogue is offered by the participants.

Churches are beginning to see the need for nurturing their single members, and are rapidly forming groups for widows(ers) and for other single adults. Although based in churches and often with church sanction, most groups are open to people of all (or no) religious affiliation. Generally, the meetings include group discussions, speakers, and a social time in which you have a chance to meet others. Social activities are usually planned on a regular basis.

The most progressive funeral directors are starting support groups by inviting clients to informal discussion groups. If your funeral director does not have such a group, he might know of someone who does. Because of their training, funeral directors can make excellent group facilitators.

National organizations such as the American Cancer Society with their "I Can Cope," have support groups all over the country. Contact local branches of these organizations to see whether they have any programs.

If you are a military wife, contact the:

National Association of Military Widows
2666 Military Road
Arlington, VA 22207
(703) 841-0121

Minister's wives have a group called:

International Association of Minister's Wives
and Minister's Widows, Inc.
609 South Davis Avenue
Richmond, VA 23220
(804) 359-0767

Many communities have local widowed persons groups. They vary in size and activity. Leadership comes from within the group, with different members taking responsibility for the organization. Ask around and look for notices of meetings in your newspaper.

If there is not a local widows and widowers group in your area, then think about starting one. Helen Krogh saw the need for a group after her husband's death. She began by inviting seven other widows to brunch in 1983. By 1987, the Widowed Persons Association of California, Inc. (2628 El Camino Ave., Suite D-18, Sacramento, CA 95821) grew to be the largest and most active club of its kind in the nation. Originally founded in Sacramento, California, it now has branches in several other cities and is still growing. The WPAC calendar is filled with activities every night of every month. They offer counseling groups and workshops for the newly widowed, and dinners, travel, game nights, parties, dancing, rap sessions, and much more for their members. Their motto is "A grief shared is a grief diminished." Perhaps you could do what Helen did in your own community. You could get names of widowed people from funeral directors, newspaper obituaries, and pastors. Almost everyone knows at least one widowed person to invite. Harriet Sarnoff Schiff has written a book entitled *Living Through Mourning* (Viking, New York, 1986). The first part deals with bereavement, while the latter part is a support group manual. It gives specific ideas and suggestions for forming your own support group, including detailed plans and objectives for the first eight meetings.

In 1957, Jim Egleson and Jacqueline Bernard began a support group for single parents called Parents Without Partners (PWP). It has grown to 180,000 members and has chapters in almost every community in the United States and Canada. For more information, call 800-638-8078 (or 301-588-9354 if you live in Maryland) or write:

Parents Without Partners
8807 Colesville Road
Silver Spring, MD 20910

Dr. Ethel Percy Andrus founded a support group in 1958. Today it has more than 25 million members. The American Association of Retired Persons (AARP) has 3,600 local chapters. Its membership is comprised of persons over 50 years of age. One AARP program is its Widowed Person Service (WPS) active in approximately 200 communities nationwide. Over 7,000 WPS volunteers who have been widowed at least eighteen months receive fifteen hours of training to help recently widowed persons. Each WPS chapter offers a variety of help in the form of visits, newsletters, social activities, and rap sessions. Recently widowed persons are encouraged to contact the organization for help by writing:

WPS-JD
AARP
1909 K Street, NW
Washington, DC 20049

The Theos Foundation is a church affiliated self-help organization for widows. To find out about local groups in your area, contact the Theos Foundation, 1301 Clark Bldg., 717 Liberty Avenue, Pittsburgh, PA 15222. (412) 471-7779

A source for educational and inspirational materials, as well as workshops and counseling for dying and bereaved persons is the:

Elisabeth Kubler-Ross Center
S. Route 616
Head Waters, VA 24442
(703) 396-3441

By joining a support group, you not only have an outlet for your grief, but you also have an excellent chance of meeting some new friends who are as lonely as you and would enjoy your company.

PROFESSIONAL COUNSELORS

Because of their education and training, professional counselors are often able to move us through the stages of grief at a faster pace. Once thought only for people who were mentally ill, they now play a vital and accepted role as purveyors of good mental health. Many widowed persons find it easier and less threatening to discuss their innermost thoughts with a stranger than with a friend or relative. Some counselors specialize in grief therapy.

Use the same guidelines in choosing a professional counselor that you used to find other professional advisors. Ask friends for recommendations. You will be surprised how many of them have seen counselors. Look in the Yellow Pages under Counselors and you will find a comprehensive list of various types of counseling services. While there are many to choose from, the most common are as follows:

Clinical psychologist — A master's degree, plus sixty semester hours of post-graduate work in psychology, three years of full-time experience, and a written and oral examination.

Marriage, Family and Child Counselor (MFCC) — A Master's or doctoral degree in the field of counseling, two years of internship, a written and oral examination.

Psychiatrist — a medical doctor with a specialty in psychiatry and licensed to prescribe drugs.

Licensed Clinical Social Worker (LCSW) — Master's degree, plus two years internship (3200 hours) in specified areas, and a written and oral examination.

Master's in Social Work (MSW) — completed a Master's graduate program in social work.

Licensing requirements may vary state-to-state. Check with your state Board of Behavioral Sciences for more detailed information.

You should seriously consider seeking professional help

if any of the following feelings persist: thoughts of suicide, panic or anxiety attacks, depression that keeps you from functioning at a basic level, insomnia, sleeping too much, inability to return to work, or loss of interest in any pleasurable activities. You may just need reassurance and help in understanding the phases of grief. If so, one or two visits may go a long way to put your mind at ease.

Many professional counselors form group therapy sessions where they bring together people with similar problems. These sessions are less costly than private sessions.

If money is a real concern, ask your counselor if there is a sliding scale for those who can not afford the full fee. Also, check with your insurance carrier. Many now make provisions for licensed counselors.

CLUBS AND ORGANIZATIONS

After the initial shock has passed, you will want and need to return to an active life. Clubs and organizations are an excellent way to reorganize your social life. Whatever your interests, you can find kindred spirits to share your passions. There are literally thousands of clubs such as photography, computer, cooking, book review, theater groups, bird watchers, etc. Some have national affiliations with local branches such as the Audubon Society, Toastmaster's, American Association of Retired Persons, National Organization for Women, and League of Women Voters. If you are looking for something that caters more to the single adult, check out Parents Without Partners, Sierra Club Singles, church singles groups, and the many local singles groups. Almost every community has a senior citizen group who has activities, programs, and workshops. To locate a club or organization that interests you, try these methods:

1. Look in the Yellow Pages.

2. Call the Chamber of Commerce. Many have directories of clubs and organizations in their cities.

3. Inquire in logical establishments. If you are seeking a group that goes bicycling, then ask in a large bicycle shop. If you want to join a stamp collectors group, ask in a shop which buys and sells stamps.

4. Ask friends and acquaintances.

5. Watch for newspaper ads and television public service announcements.

6. Look for locally published singles magazines at your newsstand. They usually have a list of activities and names of local groups.

Visit several different groups until you find one that meets your needs. Go to several meetings before you commit yourself or write it off. The speaker may not interest you the first time, but the next one may be dynamite. The biggest test is "Do you like the other members?" Remember, you are going to make new friends, not just to learn more about a hobby.

SETTING NEW GOALS

During marriage, a couple tends to set mutual goals. Somehow, our personal quests get preempted for undertakings that benefit the whole family. Husbands and wives make plans for trips together, additions to the house, and retirement. When one becomes suddenly single, these goals vanish with the deceased. Widowed people temporarily lose meaning for living. Having no goals can be very depressing, making lives feel empty. One widow felt this lack of purpose and knew she needed something to work toward. After weeks of trying to find some goal in her life, she decided to take piano lessons. It was a small first step toward establishing her own personal goals, something she had neglected for years.

You may need to start small, also. As you gain in confidence, you'll feel better and want to tackle bigger things. To give you some ideas to ponder, think about going back to school, employment, volunteer work, and traveling.

Going back to school

School is a wonderful place to learn fresh ideas and meet new people. Whether your purpose is to increase your knowledge about a subject you are interested in, or to sharpen skills needed to get a job, you will find that there are others in class for similar reasons.

Junior colleges are a good place to start, if you have been

out of academia for a length of time. Because they are smaller, they aren't so overwhelming. Most offer night classes, which tend to attract those employed during the day. It is a wonderful way to spend an evening that you would otherwise have spent at home alone in front of television. There are technical and vocational schools that may be what you need to fine-tune rusty skills. Start collecting school catalogs and look for announcements of special seminars in your community. There's certain to be something that interests you.

Finding a job

Those who have jobs to attend everyday seem to cope better with widowhood. They have established an identity outside of the home, have contacts other than through the marriage, and have less time to dwell on their loneliness. This is not to say that if you have not been employed, that you should dash out the door and find a job. In some cases, it may be financially imperative that you do just that, but if you aren't feeling the financial stress, take your time. Think about what your skills and talents are, and how you can market them. Looking for a job can be very stressful. You don't need to take any more upon yourself right now. If you think of finding employment as a goal, then you will plan the steps toward reaching that goal in a methodic way.

First, do you have skills already, or will you need to learn some? You may need to go back to school as discussed earlier, or you may be able to get on-the-job training.

If you are unsure where your talents lie, or what would be enjoyable, there are career centers with counselors that will help you discover talents and skills you were previously unaware of. There are tests that show your aptitude in different areas. A good career counselor can outline a program of training for you, if necessary. Career centers are often found in colleges and universities, women's centers, and private agencies.

There is a "Displaced Homemakers Network" that helps return homemakers to the working world. They provide job information and career counseling for the recent divorcee/widow who is having difficulty getting a job. For referrals to local programs contact the:

Network National Office
1411 K Street, NW
Suite 930
Washington, DC 20005
(202) 628-6767

An excellent tool to help you get started in your self-evaluation is a book by Richard Nelson Bolles entitled *What Color Is Your Parachute?* Revised annually, it is "A Practical Manual for Job-Hunters and Career Changers." It is filled with ideas about how and where to find jobs, how to decide what you want to do, and how to choose a career counselor.

One of the best ways to find a job is through friends and acquaintances. Let everyone you know be aware of the fact that you are looking for a job. Tell them what you want. You will be surprised how many people know of available jobs. Be open to all job offers. Something might come along that you had not considered, but could be very satisfied with.

You can also look in the classified ads of your newspaper, check with your state employment agency, or check with private employment agencies. The latter usually charge either a flat fee for their services, or a percentage of the first few months' paycheck. Be sure that you understand the fee basis before you sign any contracts.

There are books available that show you how to write resumes, how to fill out job applications, how to dress for the interview, and what to say and ask at the interview. Choose a couple of these and read for ideas. Most important, be sincere and be yourself.

Think about self-employment. You may be able to turn a favorite hobby or skill into a business of your own. It's been done many times. Check with your local Small Business Administration listed under United States Government in your telephone directory for workshops and assistance in getting started.

Traveling

Planning some trips in the future can be a wonderful goal. Today, there is no need to travel alone. Some travel agencies specialize in planning for single adults of all ages.

The Travel Industry Association of America has available a free listing of all the U.S. state and territorial travel offices.

Request a copy of the Discover America brochure by sending a self-addressed, stamped envelope to the:

Travel Industry Association of America
Two Lafayette Centre
1133 21st St. NW
Washington, DC 20036
(202) 293-1433

Not only are there tours available, but the extended vacation is becoming very popular. With extended vacations, you stay in one spot for a week or two. Sight-seeing excursions are extra, while air fare, transfers, and the services of a local tour guide are generally included in the package.

You can combine travel with learning and receive college credits for university sponsored programs. Check with your nearby university for their catalog on educational travel programs.

Volunteer work

Many people have found satisfaction and fulfillment volunteering their services to help others. There are hundreds of opportunities available in even small communities. They include hospitals, schools, senior centers, the YMCA, the American Red Cross, libraries, museums, the American Cancer Society, the American Heart Association, United Way, soup kitchens, churches, and many more. All of these would be grateful for your time and talents. Your choices are limitless. Because you are volunteering your time, you usually have the added advantage of flexibility in the hours and days that you work.

Many cities have a Volunteer Bureau that acts as a clearinghouse for groups that need help. These bureaus match your interests with available volunteer positions.

Volunteer work is another wonderful way to meet new people with similar interests and concerns. Sometimes, these unpaid jobs turn into paid positions or give you an inside track on jobs within the organization that become available. Additionally, any volunteer work can make a resume look healthier.

A TIME FOR EXPERIMENTING

This is a wonderful time to try new things. Some will be successful, while others are learning experiences. Do things and go places you always thought you might like, but never tried. Even try some things you think you would not like; you might be pleasantly surprised. One young widow took golf lessons because her girlfriend convinced her that's where all the men were. The widow never cared for golf and thought it would be a dull and boring game. To the contrary, she found it a lot of fun and even met a few men in the process, just as her girlfriend promised.

Did you ever think about learning to fly? One lady did, at the age of 50. She even took aerobatics (stunt flying) classes. By the time she was 56, she was licensed to teach not only fixed wing, but also ballooning.

How about sailing? Most communities that have a marina also have a sailing club. You rent the boats from them and they give you lessons.

Is there a hidden artistic talent lying beneath the surface? There are many stories of people who began painting or sculpting in their later years. Parks and recreation centers, continuing education, and private teachers are all available to nudge you into the world of shapes, colors, and designs.

Experiment with a new hairstyle and a new wardrobe. If you are a woman, have a make-over done at your salon or department store cosmetic counter. Hair grows out; if you don't like one style, try another.

Get a massage. Join an aerobics group. Take your dog to obedience school. Plant a garden. Buy a bicycle. This is your time to do whatever you like. Discover a new person within yourself. As you broaden your horizons, you will have so much to share with others.

Soon, with all of your new knowledge and experiences, you will be able to help someone else build a bridge from their endings to new beginnings.

Checklist

Survivor's First Year:
What to Do and When to Do It

The following checklist is a guide for knowing the tasks that you must perform to deal effectively with the practical aspects of death. A timetable will help in accomplishing a smoother transition. Your particular circumstances may warrant quicker action or slower action. These timeframes are based on the experience of many widows and not on any hard, fast rules. Use them as a guide and make notes and adjustments when necessary.

There are three types of tasks that need to be accomplished: emotional, legal, and practical. Perhaps another way of stating it is what you need to do, what you must do, and what you should do.

Disposing of your loved one's personal items falls under the category of emotional tasks. These types of jobs should be done when you are emotionally capable. Ignore well-meaning advice givers and complete emotional tasks on your own time schedule. Legal tasks, on the other hand, leave less leeway for procrastination. Wills must be filed with the courts, certain benefits must be applied for, and taxes must be completed within certain time limits.

Practical tasks, while having no set time limits, need to be accomplished as a matter of practicality. Financial planning and investing fall into this category.

As you look at the checklist, it will become apparent into which category each task falls.

IF DEATH IS IMMINENT

_____ Investigate the possibilities of hospice care. (Chapter 2)

_____ Locate Living Will and/or Durable Power of Attorney documents. (Chapter 2)

_____ Make decision and inform physician of desires concerning organ and tissue donation. (Chapter 2)

IMMEDIATELY AFTER DEATH

_____ Make decision concerning discretionary autopsy. (Chapter 2)

_____ Locate burial instructions, if any. (Chapter 3)

_____ Contact funeral director, crematory, memorial society, or medical school. (Chapter 3)

_____ Make funeral arrangements. (Chapter 3)

_____ Contact minister or person giving eulogy.

_____ Contact organist, soloist, or other musicians.

_____ Arrange for pall bearers.

_____ Order flowers.

_____ Arrange for payment of honoraria to musicians and minister.

_____ Choose clothes for deceased. (Chapter 3)

_____ Write obituary. (Chapter 3)

_____ If flowers are to be omitted, decide on appropriate memorial and include in obituary notice. (Chapter 3)

_____ Order death certificates through the funeral director or county recorder's office. (Chapter 3)

_____ Contact friends, relatives, executor of the will, and business associates. (Chapter 6)

_____ Choose cemetery plot, columbarium, or other appropriate means for final disposition. (Chapter 3)

_____ Arrange for someone to answer phone and door. (Chapter 3)

_____ Arrange hospitality for visiting relatives and friends. (Chapter 3)

_____ Purchase clothing for yourself, if necessary.

_____ Make appointment with hair stylist, if necessary.

____ Make arrangements for child care.

____ Ask someone to stay in your home during the funeral. (Chapter 3)

____ Coordinate meals until funeral is over and guests have gone.

AFTER THE FUNERAL

____ Plan for disposition of flowers. (Chapter 3)

____ Prepare a list of distant persons who need to be notified by letter or printed notice. (Chapter 6)

Second Week

____ Contact life insurance company for claim forms. (Chapters 6 and 7) Request only the funds you need to live on until you can consult with a financial advisor. (Chapter 14)

____ Visit your bank to open an account for yourself. (Chapter 6)

____ See an attorney who can explain the terms of the Will, and file the Will with the courts. (Chapters 4 and 6)

____ Begin probate proceedings, if necessary. (Chapter 5)

____ Petition the court for appointment as executor(trix). (Chapter 5)

____ Locate important documents. (Chapter 7)

Third Week

____ Begin applying for survivor benefits. (Chapter 7)

____ Send medical claims to the appropriate insurance carriers. (Chapters 5 and 9)

____ Consult with a financial advisor about how to request large sum benefits. (Chapters 4 and 14)

____ As executor(trix) (Chapter 5)

> ____ Open a bank account to facilitate money due the estate.
>
> ____ Inventory all assets.
>
> ____ Collect all monies due the estate.
>
> ____ Apply for tax identification number. (Chapter 13)

____ File Form 56, Notice Concerning Fiduciary Relationship. (Chapter 13)

____ Send thank you notes and acknowledgements.

Fourth Week

____ See an accountant for a tax projection. (Chapter 14)

____ Review all insurance with your agent to see if coverage is appropriate and adequate. (Chapters 4 and 14)

____ Change beneficiaries on insurance policies, retirement accounts, savings bonds, etc. (Chapter 14)

____ Transfer all assets into your name or into trust accounts. (Chapters 8 and 14)

____ Make a plan for paying debts and obligations. (Chapter 10)

____ Make necessary decisions concerning deceased's self-employment business. (Chapter 5)

AFTER FIRST MONTH

____ Contact credit card and charge card companies. (Chapter 6)

____ Change billing name with utility companies. (Chapter 6)

____ Change registration on vehicles by contacting the Department of Motor Vehicles. (Chapter 6)

____ Notify book clubs, record clubs, and other subscription material. (Chapter 6)

____ Contact rental and lease companies. (Chapter 6)

____ Cancel or sell health club membership. (Chapter 6)

____ Update Will. (Chapter 14)

____ Prepare a net worth statement. (Chapter 14)

____ Make a list of income and expenses. (Chapter 14)

____ Track your expenses to see where your money is being spent. (Chapter 14)

____ Seek professional counseling or grief workshop. (Chapter 16)

____ Go through old records and files, including cancelled checks for clues to any additional benefits, assets, or obligations. (Chapter 14)

____ Choose a memorial marker. (Chapter 3)

AFTER THE THIRD MONTH

___ Create a new budget. (Chapter 14)
___ Apply for credit in your own name. (Chapter 15)
___ Begin gathering information for tax returns. (Chapter 13)

AFTER THE SIXTH MONTH

___ Begin to think about investments. (Chapter 14)
___ Investigate support groups and clubs. (Chapter 16)
___ As executor(trix) (Chapter 5):
    ___ List claims against the estate.
    ___ Liquidate assets as necessary to pay bills.
    ___ Prepare tax returns and pay tax liabilities.
    ___ Pay all bills.
    ___ Disburse assets to heirs.
    ___ Prepare an accounting for the courts.
    ___ Advise beneficiaries of new tax basis for assets.

AFTER ONE YEAR

___ Close probate (Chapter 14)
___ Make decisions about your future living arrangements. (Chapter 11)
___ Make plans for your future (life and career). (Chapter 16)

Sources of Information
and
Suggested Reading

The following books are sources for more detailed information. They were chosen because they have actually been read and recommended by widows and widowers. The author thanks Rita Watson of the Widowed Persons Association of California for her help with the compilation of this list. While it is recommended that you read any and all material that gives you solace and helpful information, you are cautioned against becoming a self-help addict. There are hundreds of books written on self-esteem, relationships, getting ahead, etc. All of these can be motivational, but confusing when ideas on how-to vary.

Personal Experience Books on Widowhood

The Widow's Guide, Isabella Taves. Schocken Books, Inc. 1981.

Widow, Lynn Caine. Bantam Books, 1974.

Widow's Walk, Pamela Cuming. Crown Books, 1981.

A Grief Observed, C.S. Lewis. (widower) Seabury Press, 1961.

Beginnings, Betty Jane Wylie. Ballantine Books, 1982.

Learning to Walk Alone, Ingrid Tarbisch. Servant Books, 1985.

The Widower, Jane Burgess Kohn and Willard K. Kohn. Beacon Press. 1978.

Widower, Elin Schoen Brockman. Bantam, 1987.

Bereavement

Recovery from Bereavement, Colin Murray Parkes and Robert
S. Weiss. Basic Books, 1983.
When Bad Things Happen to Good People, Harold S. Kush-
ner. Schocken Books, 1981.
A Personal Guide to Living With Loss, Elaine Vail. John
Wiley and Sons, 1982.
How to Survive the Loss of a Love, Melba Colgrove. Leo Press,
1976.
Live With Loss, Kate Walsh Slagle. Prentice-Hall, 1982.
Don't Take My Grief Away, Doug Manning. Harper and Row,
1984.
*No Time for Goodbyes: Coping With Sorrow, Anger and Injus-
tice After a Tragic Death,* Janice Lord. Pathfinders,
1987.
The Grieving Time, Anne M. Brooks. Dial Press, 1985.
The First Year of Bereavement, Ira Glick, Robert Weiss and C.
Murray Parker. John Wiley and Sons, 1974.
The Right to Feel Bad, Lesley Hazelton. Ballantine Books,
1984.

Psychology of Grief, Death, and Dying

Questions and Answers on Death and Dying. Elisabeth
Kubler-Ross. Macmillan Publishers, 1974.
Death — The Final Stage of Growth, Elisabeth Kubler-Ross.
Prentice-Hall, 1975.
Courage to Grieve, Judy Tatlebaum. Crowell, 1980.
A Gift of Hope, Robert L. Veninga. Ballantine, 1985.

Self-Help (stress, loss, finances, career, etc.)

Living Through Personal Crisis, Ann Kaiser Stearns.
Thomas More Press, 1984.
Living Alone and Liking It, Lynn Shahan. Warner Books,
1982.
Necessary Losses, Judith Viorst. Simon and Schuster, 1986.
Widows in the Dark. (finances), Elizabeth Smith Gaton.
Warner Books, 1985.

Starting Over. (for young widows and widowers), Adele Rice Nudel. Dodd, Mead and Co., 1986.

How to Avoid Probate, Norman F. Dacey. Crown Publishers, 1983.

New Money Book for the 80's, Sylvia Porter. Doubleday, 1979.

The Survival Guide for Widows, Betty Jane Wylie. Ballantine, 1982.

Women's Networks. (1400 women's networks), Carol Kleiman. Ballantine, 1980.

Pathfinders, Gail Sheehy. Bantam.

Feel Free. (changing careers, confronting fears), David Viscott. Pocket Books, 1987.

Winning, David Viscott. Pocket Books, 1987.

Risking, David Viscott. Pocket Books, 1979.

The Widow's Guide to Life: How to Adjust/How to Grow, Ida Fisher and Byron Lane. LaneCon Press, 1985.

Having It All, Helen Gurley Brown. Pocket Books, 1982.

Any Woman Can!, David Reuben, M.D. David McKay Co., 1971.

Go For It!, Irene C. Kassorla. Dell Publishing, 1984.

Coping with Loss through Faith

Good Grief, Granger Westberg. Fortress Press, 1984.

Mourning Song, Joyce Landorf. Fleming H. Revell Co., 1974.

To Heal Again, Rusty Berkus. Redrose Press, 1986.

Getting Through the Night, Eugenia Price. Dial Press, 1982.

The Birth We Call Death, P. Sunn and R.M. Eyre

Living When a Loved One Has Died, Earl Grollman. Beacon Press, 1977.

Concerning Death. A Guide for the Living, Earl Grollman. Beacon Press, 1974.

How Can It Be All Right When Everything Is All Wrong?, Lewis B. Smedes. Pocket Books, 1986.

How to Have a Creative Crisis, H. Norman Wright. Berkeley Books, 1987.

Index

A

Accountant, 57-8, 116, 286
 Certified Public Accountant, 57; public accountant (PA), 57; tax accountant, 57; LLM, 57
Administrator, see executor
Affidavit of Survivorship, 120
Alcoholics Anonymous, 273
American Association of Retired Persons (AARP), 21, 45, 172, 173, 176, 218, 275
American Bar Association, 70
American Cancer Society, 273-4
American Council of Life Insurance, 96
American Medical Association, 23
American Society of Appraisers (ASA), 165
Andrus, Ethel Percy, 275
Annual Percentage Rate (APR), 257
Annuities, 108, 213, 226, 251, 261
Annuity contracts, 80
Answers, 239
Assets, 79-80, 142-3, 146, 151, 193, 287
Attorney, 45, 54-7, 70, 151, 201, 241, 285
 Choosing, 54-5; fees, 55-6
Automated Teller Machine (ATM), 269
Autopsy, 25-8, 284
 for medical science, 25; funeral preparations following, 27; mandatory reporting, 25-6; procedure, 27; reports, 27

B

Bailey, Linda J., 272
BankCard Holders of America, 259
Banking, banks, 62-4, 116-8, 194, 197, 201, 226, 248, 263, 264
 Accounts, 116-7, 206 (Certificates of Deposit, 118, 226, 248, 261, 264; checking and savings, 117, 194, 226, 248, 263; custodial, 118; individual accounts, 117; money market accounts, 194; passbook, 118, 194;

pay-on-death agreements, 117; tenants in common, 117; trust, 118); choosing a bank, 62-3
Bankruptcy, 156, 262
Barker, Becky, 239
Bearer bonds, 249
Bernard, Jacqueline, 275
Bertot, Cathey, 221, 222
Best's Directory of Insurance Adjusters, 65
Best's Directory of Recommended Insurance Attorneys, 65
Best's Insurance Reports, 64
Better Business Bureau, 154, 193
Board of Health, 44
Board of Behavioral Sciences, 276
Boarding house, 171
Bolles, Richard Nelson, 280
Budget, 228-9, 287
Bureau of Public Debt, 251
Burial, 29, 31, 284

C

Caretaker, 171
Caring For Your Own Dead, 30
Carlson, Lisa, 30
Caskets, 32-3, 35, 37, 43-4
Cemetery, 29, 39, 41-2, 284
 Choosing, 39-40; opening and closing of grave, 36; types of, 39
Census Bureau, 12
Certified Life Underwriter, 66
Charitable Lead Trust, 244
Chartered Property and Casualty Underwriter, 66
Cherow-O'Leary, Renee, 72
Churning, 253-4
Civil service, 109-10
 Federal, 109; state and local, 110
Clifford, Dennis, 239
Clifford Trust, 244
Clinical psychologist, 276
Clubs and organizations, 277
Collateral, 261, 264
Collectibles, 195-6, 251
Collection agency, 152
Columbarium, 29, 37, 284
Co-mingling, 115
Commissions, 107-8